The Open Economy and its Enemies

There is a vigorous debate about the merits of globalisation for developing countries. Based on numerous focus-group discussions and over 10,000 interviews, this book studies economic and cultural openness from the perspective of the public in four developing or 'transitional' countries: Vietnam, (South) Korea, the Czech Republic and Ukraine (both before and after the Orange Revolution). It finds many supporters of opening up, but also many who are discontented with its downsides and who expect states to tackle the exploitation and unfairness that accompany it. Among the most fervent enemies of openness there is support not just for peaceful public protest to tackle the problems it brings, but for violence or sabotage. The methodology provides a unique opportunity for the public in developing countries to 'speak with their own voices' about markets and openness – and highlights the subtlety, ambiguity, tensions, conflicts and emotion that statistics alone fail to capture.

Jane Duckett is Senior Lecturer in Politics at the University of Glasgow. She has worked extensively in East Asia on research projects funded by the ESRC (UK Economic and Social Research Council), the Leverhulme Trust, the British Academy, the European Commission and the British Council; and as a policy and social development consultant on projects funded by the UK government's Department for International Development. She is frequently interviewed on East Asian politics and has made appearances on the BBC and Radio 4.

William L. Miller is Edward Caird Professor of Politics at the University of Glasgow and a Fellow of the British Academy. He acted as consultant to the Independent Media Commission during the transition to democracy in South Africa and has directed major research projects for the ESRC (UK Economic and Social Research Council) and DfID (UK Department for International Development) in Bulgaria, the Czech Republic, Hungary, Korea, Poland, Russia, Slovakia, Ukraine, Vietnam, and the UK.

The Open Economy and its Enemies

Public Attitudes in East Asia and Eastern Europe

Jane Duckett and William L. Miller

CAMBRIDGE
UNIVERSITY PRESS

CAMBRIDGE UNIVERSITY PRESS
Cambridge, New York, Melbourne, Madrid, Cape Town, Singapore, São Paulo

Cambridge University Press
The Edinburgh Building, Cambridge CB2 2RU, UK

Published in the United States of America by Cambridge University Press,
New York

www.cambridge.org
Information on this title: www.cambridge.org/9780521682558

First published 2006

Printed in the United Kingdom at the University Press, Cambridge

A catalogue record for this book is available from the British Library

ISBN-13 978-0-521-86406-0 hardback
ISBN-10 0-521-86406-2 hardback
ISBN-13 978-0-521-68255-8 paperback
ISBN-10 0-521-68255-X paperback

Contents

Tables

Acknowledgements

We would like to thank the UK Economic and Social Research Council (ESRC) for generous funding under grant R000239581; David Held, Larry Elliot, Paul Whiteley and Ed Shepherd for their encouragement when we were planning the project; and the external reviewers for Cambridge University Press for their perceptive and valuable comments. While they provided insight and inspiration they bear no responsibility for our findings, interpretations or conclusions.

Our fieldwork, both focus groups and surveys, was undertaken by researchers based locally in each of our four countries. We were lucky to work in all four countries with experienced, skilled, and conscientious teams who were also generous in hosting us and providing valuable background information as we travelled with them to observe the focus group discussions. We would particularly like to thank Ladislav Koppl, David Redheffer and Klara Flemrová at Opinion Window – Research International, based in Prague, Czech Republic; Hungsoo Khang, Shin On Yang and Kyu Hyung No at Research & Research Inc based in Seoul, Republic of Korea; Irina Demchenko and Natalia Pohorila at SOCIS based in Kyiv, Ukraine; and Pham Minh Hac, Pham Thanh Nghi and Nguyen T Phuong Mai of the Institute of Human Studies, Vietnam National Centre for Social Sciences and Humanities, Hanoi, Vietnam.

We must also thank the anonymous 2,014 officials and 8,324 ordinary members of the public who generously gave up their time to answer our long list of questions, and another 130 who gave up even more time to participate in our focus group discussions. We are very grateful to them all.

We are grateful for administrative support from Avril Johnstone, Caroline Mooney, Pam McNair and Carole McKinlay at the Department of Politics, University of Glasgow. Thanks are also due to Olga Stewart, Vu Dang Hoang, Byung O Min, Elena Korosteleva-Polglase and Nato Chitiya in Glasgow for diligently double-checking the translations (provided by our local fieldwork partners) of our focus group schedules and survey questions; and particularly grateful to Heike Hermanns, our diligent and dedicated research assistant on the first two years of the project.

Finally, we must thank our families for their support, especially during the final stages of completing this manuscript.

Acronyms

ADB	Asian Development Bank
ASEAN	Association of South-East Asian Nations
CIS	Commonwealth of Independent States (successor to USSR)
EU	European Union
FDI	foreign direct investment
GDP	gross domestic product
HDI	(UNDP) Human Development Index
ILO	International Labour Organisation – an agency of the UN
IMF	International Monetary Fund
NGO	Non-Governmental Organisation
UN	United Nations
UNCTAD	United Nations Conference on Trade and Development
UNDP	United Nations Development Programme
WB	World Bank
WTO	World Trade Organisation

1   Understanding public attitudes towards the open economy

Globalisation is a contentious subject, much criticised in street protests as well as in seminar rooms. But though many of the critics claim to defend the interests of ordinary people in the developing world, the voices of those people themselves have seldom been given as much attention as those of western protestors and academics.

Globalisation – in Stiglitz's working definition: 'the closer integration of countries and peoples of the world' (2002, p. 9) – is a process usually viewed from above. Our own perspective is less Olympian. We are interested in globalisation not viewed as a world-wide process but from the perspective of the public in developing countries, who see it as an external challenge to their own country or locality. For them, the key questions are about greater economic and cultural 'openness' to an external, rapidly integrating world; about participation in multi-national or supra-national organisations; and about embracing or resisting the inward flow of foreign ideas, customs, symbols, capital, and personnel, as well as foreign technology, economic goods and services.

From a democratic perspective, grass-roots public opinion is important in itself. But even in countries that are only partially democratic, or not democratic at all, grass-roots opinion can be important. Indeed governments may be more exposed to public opinion in such countries just because they have so little 'process-legitimacy'. The climate of public opinion affects elites and elite policy in most contemporary societies. It can always influence, if not determine policy. It constitutes the background against which elites and activists must operate, and not only sets the frame for elite policy choices, but also influences the mind-set of elite opinion itself.

Development economists have argued that public opinion is important for the sustainability of economic openness and market-oriented policies. Public discontent and resistance to outside influences can affect political stability, encourage protectionism, and discourage inward investment. The United Nations Development Programme (UNDP) has argued that opening up economies has spurred economic growth in the short run, but

1

in a form that may threaten longer-term development: 'increasing the concentration of income, resources and wealth among people, corporations and countries', 'dismantling institutions of social protection', and letting 'criminals reap the benefits', which may stimulate 'social tensions that threaten political stability and community cohesion' (UNDP 1999). In turn, that instability may restrict future development since stability-seeking investors avoid areas of conflict (Alesina and Perotti 1996; Garrett 1998; Klak and Myers 1997; see also Muller 1997). In order to encourage inward investment governments need to maintain public support for markets and openness.

In a series of influential papers, Rodrik (1996; 1997; 1998) advocated greater emphasis on 'social safety nets' and measures to 'root out corruption' in order to offset the naturally perverse distributional and social consequences of globalisation that provoke public discontent and thereby threaten longer-term stability and development. Threats to the environment (Kelly 1997) or to local culture (Appadurai 1990) may also provoke public reactions that damage prospects for long-term development. A strong sense of national or cultural identity may reinforce social cohesion and assist development in the short term. But the cultural opening that goes with economic opening may provoke fears (justified or not) that national/cultural identity is threatened, stimulate public reactions against an open economy as a by-product of cultural fright, and thus threaten economic development in the longer term.

But it is *public support* for openness that is itself the key socio-political precondition for maintaining an open economy rather than the specific factors – economic, cultural or environmental – that may tend to generate that support. Perceptions of increasing inequality, for example, may lead to political instability if inequality is attributed to the policy decisions or corrupt behaviour of local political actors. They are likely to reduce public support for openness if inequality is attributed to globalisation. But they are unlikely to have much impact on the political conditions for development if inequality is attributed to chance, to misfortune, or to circumstances beyond anyone's control. Perceptions of corruption, environmental damage or cultural threat may also have different consequences depending on the way they are viewed by the public. How ordinary citizens feel about the downside of a more open economy – quite apart from their perceptions of the downside itself – may have a significant impact on its sustainability. Attitudes cannot be inferred from perceptions, still less from objective reality.

Relatively few of the ordinary public get regularly involved in political action of any kind, least of all in active protest or resistance. Nonetheless public discontent matters. Across the mass public, the consequences of individual discontent may be regarded as trivial – nothing more than demotivation, lack of commitment, slow or bad workmanship, even purely 'psychological' or attitudinal reactions, mere grumbling to friends and family. Individually, such reactions have little or no impact. But when multiplied by millions, grumbling or enthusiasm can create a climate that may significantly promote or inhibit openness and development. Moreover, as the literature on protest indicates, a general climate of public support or disapproval has a very significant impact upon whether the relatively few potential activists are encouraged into actual activity or discouraged from it: the general climate of public opinion acts as the trigger for the actual behaviour of the relatively few potential activists (Muller 1979). Counter-elites, as well as establishment elites, operate against the background of wider public opinion.

It might be argued that the public does not have sufficiently well-formed views on such abstract issues as globalisation or openness to make them worthy of serious study. There is an element of truth in that. Technicalities are boring as well as obscure. But ordinary people do have views about the availability of foreign goods, about foreign films and TV, about foreign ideas and customs, and about the influx of foreign companies, foreign employers, foreign managers, foreign immigrants and foreign 'guest' workers into their country. Indeed ordinary people have strong views about foreigners and 'foreignness' in general. They also have views, sometimes strong views, about 'who benefits most' from market-isation and opening up (often part of the same neo-liberal package), views about the 'new rich' and the 'new poor'. Whatever the factual basis or moral status of these views, they are significant for public policy, for public order, and ultimately for economic development. And they should be heard, and heard directly rather than inferred from inspired specula-tion, from fascinating anecdotes or from press reports of 'newsworthy' incidents.

We aim to complement the well-publicised views of elite western academics, activists, international organisations and pressure-groups – valuable though these are – by listening to the views of the ordinary public in selected developing countries in East Asia (Vietnam and South Korea – hereafter called simply 'Korea' for brevity), and 'transitional' countries in East Europe (Ukraine and the Czech Republic). We accept that the public's perceptions and attitudes may be right or wrong, coherent or incoherent. Nonetheless, we believe they deserve our respect and demand our attention.

This is *not* a study of globalisation, therefore, nor of the case for or against globalisation. It is a study of public attitudes in developing or transitional countries towards globalisation. We begin by reviewing the

arguments of some distinguished critics and advocates of globalisation –
but only by way of introduction to grass-roots public opinion in these
countries.

1.1   Globalisation and economic discontent

Discontent and satisfaction are two sides of the same coin. A study of
public discontent with globalisation is the same thing as a study of public
satisfaction with globalisation. It is purely an empirical matter whether
public discontent exceeds public satisfaction or vice versa. But since
much of the literature focuses on the dangers of public discontent we
shall use that term more often than its obverse, satisfaction. Whether we
find more public discontent than satisfaction, and the nature of that
discontent, will emerge in later chapters.

The critics For a time, Joseph Stiglitz's *Globalisation and its
Discontents* (2002) succeeded in almost equating economic openness
and 'globalisation' with 'discontent'. There is good reason for discontent:
an International Labour Organisation (ILO) report (2004) *A Fair
Globalisation – Creating Opportunities for All* argued that the potential of
globalisation was 'immense' but 'not realized . . . the unfairness of the key
rules of trade and finance reflect a serious democratic deficit . . . financial
and economic considerations have consistently predominated over social
ones', and 'seen through the eyes of the vast majority of men and women
around the world, globalisation has not met their simple aspiration for
decent jobs, livelihoods and a better future for their children'.

Successive UNDP reports (1999; 2002) pointed to increasing inequality exacerbated by 'dismantling the institutions of social protection'
(UNDP 1999: p. 4), the privatisation of public services (Pollock and
Price 2000) and a decline in transfer payments. Internally, marketisation
sometimes increased inequality between ethnic groups and bred 'ethnic
hatred' (Chua 2003). Even in developed countries, neo-liberalism and
globalisation increased inequality by cutting the demand for unskilled
workers (Goodman, Johnson and Webb 1997: pp. 281–2). Globalisation
led to a world divided between 'tourists and vagabonds' (Bauman
1997: p. 93).

Increasing inequality was not the result of some impartial 'invisible
hand' however. Power remained in the hands of rich countries (Hirst and
Thompson 1999: p. 2) who defined globalisation in terms of the
'Washington Consensus': US-style free-markets and democracy (Gray
1998: p. 215), or defined it simply in terms of US national interests:
George Monbiot criticised US drug firms as 'companies now demanding

intellectual property rights [though they] were built up without them' (*Guardian*, 12 March 2002). Larry Elliot argued that 'the West talks about free trade but its approach can be summed up in four words: you liberalise, we subsidise', whereas history showed that the US, Germany, Japan, Taiwan, and indeed South Korea, 'all built up industrial strength in well-protected domestic markets' (*Guardian*, 16 November 2002).

Even the central claim that opening up the economy stimulates economic growth has been disputed. A Centre for Economic and Policy Research (CEPR 2001) analysis of UNDP data, comparing the period before and after 1980, claimed that economic growth actually slowed down during the 'era of globalisation'. Saldivar (2001: p. 10) claimed that after subtracting the identifiable costs of development, although US gross domestic product (GDP) steadily increased, 'genuine progress', even in the US, peaked in the 1970s and declined steadily thereafter: 'growth does not equal progress'. Rodrik (2002: p. 9) attacked studies that 'purport to show that globalizers grow faster' as 'misleading ... the countries used as exemplars of globalizers in these studies, China, India, and Vietnam ... remain among the most protectionist in the world'.

At the same time, specific International Monetary Fund (IMF) and World Bank prescriptions for developing countries have been labelled incompetent and perverse by long-term critics such as Joseph Stiglitz and more recent critics such as Jeffrey Sachs – notably on the Soviet transition from communism and the 1997–9 East Asian crisis, where these prescriptions contributed to decline, not growth: 'The contrast between Russia's transition as engineered by the international economic institutions and that of China, designed by itself, could not be greater' (Stiglitz 2002: p. 6). During the East Asian crisis of 1997 and the subsequent crises in Argentina and Brazil, international advice was 'like the 18th century medical practice of treating feverish patients by drawing blood from them ... hastening their deaths' (Sachs, quoted in the *Guardian*, 8 May 2002). Indeed, Stiglitz (2002: p. 97) claimed that 'the perception throughout much of the developing world is that the IMF itself had [in 1997–9] become a part of the problem rather than a part of the solution', noting that in several countries 'history is dated by before and after the IMF ... the way one would say the Plague or the Great Depression'. Korea only recovered as well as it did by rejecting international advice (Stiglitz 2002: p. 117, 127).

Finally critics argued that regional organisations such as the European Union (EU) or Association of South-East Asian Nations (ASEAN), as well as global organisations such as the IMF, World Bank, or World Trade Organisation (WTO), constrained the independence of the state: 'The nation-state, economic integration, and democracy are mutually incompatible'. (Rodrik 2002: pp. 13–14); 'as your country puts on the Golden Straitjacket [of international integration] your economy grows and your politics shrinks' (Friedman 1999: p. 87).

The advocates On the other hand, the case for marketisation and opening up has been argued with equal vigour and distinction. After the collapse of communism even long-term critics of market economies now agreed 'there is no plausible alternative' (Galbraith 2000: IX; see also Haass and Liton 1998; Rodan 1996). But support for the open economy went far beyond reluctant acceptance. Philippe Legrain (*Guardian*, 12 July 2001) listed – and rejected – charges made by critics of the WTO: (i) that the WTO 'does the bidding' of the multinationals; (ii) that it 'undermines workers' rights and environmental protection by encouraging a race to the bottom between governments competing for jobs and foreign investment; (iii) that it harms the poor. Instead, Legrain argued that opening up the economy exposes national monopolies to competition and the WTO keeps the international marketplace more competitive; that the alleged 'race for the bottom' has not prevented Britain from raising taxes and imposing a minimum wage, nor Organisation for Economic Co-operation and Development (OECD) countries generally from increasing taxes; and that the poor in developing countries get better jobs with multinationals than in 'local sweatshops'. Opening up did not inhibit the maintenance of a welfare state: 'Sweden's economy is far more open than Britain's yet its welfare state is second to none' (Legrain, *Guardian*, 9 October 2002).

The Fraser Institute's 2004 report, *Economic Freedom of the World*, suggested that an open economy is good for civil liberty, for reducing corruption and for improving human development in the widest sense. Its *Economic Freedom* ranking (one measure of an open economy) not only correlated modestly with World Bank economic growth rates, it also correlated more consistently with Freedom House scales of civil liberties, with Transparency International indices of low corruption and, perhaps most importantly, with UNDP Human Development Indicators (Fraser Institute 2004: pp. 22–6).

Even globalisation-sceptic Larry Elliot accepted that 'history suggests trade can help boost the economic growth of poor countries', and very significantly that 'the *developing world* does not have much in common with the anti-globalisation movement in the West . . . it sees trade as a key ingredient in boosting growth and per capita incomes' (*Guardian*, 12 November 2001). Contrary to the impression given by the UNDP that globalisation had not helped the poor, analyses by Dollar and Kraay (2000; 2002) at the World Bank suggested that globalisation and development *had* helped the poor – though these analyses were hotly contested by critics of globalisation (Sumner 2003).

In contrast to the ILO (2004) claim that 'for the vast majority of men and women around the world, globalisation has not met their aspirations', the Pew Center's multinational survey report, *Globalization with Few Discontents?* (2003), concluded that there were *'few discontents . . .* generally, people of the world agree, albeit to different degrees that they favour an interconnected world . . . economic globalization is particularly popular'. On Pew's remarkably positive figures, the people of the four countries in our study were exceedingly enthusiastic about 'growing trade and business ties' – 98 per cent in Vietnam felt that such economic globalisation was 'good for their country', along with 93 per cent in Ukraine, 90 per cent in (South) Korea, and 84 per cent in the Czech Republic – all significantly higher than in the US, where only 78 per cent of Americans felt it was 'good for America'. Similarly the *World Economic Forum Poll* (2002) of the public in 25 countries found that a majority in 19 of the 25 countries surveyed felt *more* economic globalisation would be good for themselves and their families. Could both the ILO and the Pew/WEF findings be right?

1.2 Globalisation and cultural discontent

Public fears (justified or not) that opening up their economy to world markets will erode their distinctive culture might provoke a public reaction against an open economy. Yet it is not entirely obvious whether the public in developing countries regard cultural homogenisation as a consensual drift towards a common culture or as a craven submission to a dominant cultural imperialism. Indeed it is not obvious how the public in developing countries define culture itself. Understanding cultural discontent is a more complex task than understanding economic discontent.

Modernisation, Westernisation, Americanisation? 'Modernisation theory', now much criticised, assumed a single 'hierarchy' of development with American culture at the top (Featherstone 1995: p. 87; Rucht 2001: p. 97). Some now argue that 'it is misleading to view cultural change as Americanisation . . . [since Americans] hold much more traditional values and beliefs than do those in any other equally prosperous society'(Inglehart and Baker 2000: p. 49). Cultural globalisation now 'frightens many Americans and has brought forth a religious-fundamentalist backlash in the United States that rivals that found anywhere else' (Thurow 2000: p. 28). Yet many critics – and some advocates – of globalisation still equate contemporary cultural globalisation with 'modernisation', with 'westernisation' (Wallerstein 1990: p. 45), and even with 'American cultural imperialism' (Chang 2004: p. 1). 'The concept of globalisation has in many ways replaced that of modernisation ... [as something] inevitable ... hegemonic ... globalisation is a kind of modernisation in one stroke' (Rucht 2001: pp. 98–9).

But others have argued that contemporary globalisation has not standardised culture at all. Instead it has led to 'hybridisation' (Holton 2000) or 'indigenisation' (Apparadurai 1990: p. 295) in which imported culture 'takes on local features' (Lull 2000: p. 115). So 'simple notions of homogenisation, ideological hegemony or imperialism fail' (Held *et al* 2000, p. 374).

Two cultures Some of the confusion about cultural homogenisation arises from the failure to distinguish sufficiently between different kinds of culture. For clarity we find it useful to distinguish between what we shall call 'identity culture, 'values culture', and 'consumer culture'. These differ in several important ways, not least in their relationship to globalisation. *Identity culture* centres on religion, ethnicity and nationalism – on the deepest, most instinctive, most emotional and least rational of human feelings. *Values culture* centres on enduring social and political values – left/right ideologies, socialism, liberalism, democracy (see for example Rieu and Duprat 1995) – which are somewhat less emotional and instinctive, more rational, less deeply held, and more open to change. *Consumer culture* centres on choice, style, fashion, entertainment – and would appear to be the most transient and superficial.

The sharpest distinction is between the two extremes of 'identity culture' and 'consumer culture': culture '*as a way of life* ... shared norms, rituals, patterns of social order and probably a distinctive dialect' if not a distinct language; and culture '*as a lifestyle*', culture as clothes, food, TV programmes, decoration, consumer durables, and leisure activities (Chaney 2000: p. 83). Pasha (2000: p. 242) complains that 'global hyperliberalists equate culture with consumption'.

There is no agreement about what constitutes the most significant aspect of 'culture' however. Arguments about culture often pass each other like ships in the night without interacting or engaging. It is tempting to dismiss 'consumer culture' as froth – superficial, unimportant, not an essential part of personal identity, malleable simply because it is so superficial. In that case, changing consumer possibilities and preferences present no challenge to deeply embedded identities and will only provoke resistance among those who mistake the superficial for the fundamental: 'entertainment, branding, language, media and television ... represent a culture that overlays or co-exists with pre-existing more local cultures' (Sweeney 2005: p. 347). But Chaney (2000: p. 83) argues that 'consumer culture' may have 'more significance than ... ethnicity or religion'. Consequently 'identity culture' and 'consumer culture' may in fact conflict: 'consumer culture is generally presented as being extremely destructive for religion ... [because it emphasises] the pursuit of pleasure here and now' (Featherstone 1991: p. 113). The essential conflict may be between personal, individual and immediate 'choice' on the one hand, and 'respect' for a community that spans both territory and time on the other. The fear that community identifiers have of being submerged and lost in a rootless, cosmopolitan world that despises community (Smith 1995: p. 22) has to be set against the fear that individualists have of community: 'one man's imagined community is another man's political prison' (Appadurai 1990: p. 295).

The impact of globalisation on consumer and identity cultures Cultural globalisation is not new. What is new is its 'nature' and 'processes' (Beynon and Dunkerley 2000: p. 13): the *nature* of global culture has shifted over the centuries from world religions, through political and scientific values, to consumerism; and the *process* has shifted from colonialism to telecommunications.

Contemporary globalisation has had an immediate, direct, visible, and large impact on 'consumer culture': 'the most obvious and tangible forms of cultural globalisation are ... Coca Cola and McDonalds ... Western consumer goods' (Beynon and Dunkerley 2000: p. 13). Values have also been affected: 'economic development is associated with shifts ... towards values that are increasingly rational, tolerant, trusting and participatory', (Inglehart and Baker 2000: p. 19) and public support for the principle of democracy has spread across the globe (Klingemann 1999). But although 'economic development tends to bring pervasive cultural changes, the fact that a society was historically shaped by Protestantism or Confucianism or Islam leaves a cultural heritage with enduring effects' (Inglehart and Baker 2000: p. 49).

State-manufactured culture Although history, historical cultures and historical legacies were manufactured in the past they are refurbished and re-marketed in the present: 'what we witness with the development of a global economy is not increasing uniformity, in the form of a universalisation of Western culture, but rather the continuation of civilisational diversity through *the active reinvention* and reincorporation of non-Western civilisational patterns' (Hamilton 1994: p. 184, our emphasis). In East Europe and the former Soviet Union, the past 'exists, if it exists at all ... in the present'; the past is ransacked by current 'cultural entrepreneurs' for 'usable pasts' (Kubik 2003: pp. 319, 325).

The state has a peculiar power and authority to manage this process of selectively preserving or reinventing the national culture. There may be problems if governments go against the grain of public opinion: 'Totalitarian states, communist states and theocratic and right-wing military regimes have all attempted to implement a closed cultural policy in which foreign influences, products and ideas have been actively controlled ... this kind of policy is the most threatened by contemporary cultural globalisation' (Held *et al* 2000, p. 370); and 'states which seek to pursue rigid closed-door policies on information and culture are certainly under threat' (Held and McGrew 2002: p. 36). But an entrepreneurial state, going with the grain of public opinion, may see globalisation as an *opportunity* rather than a *threat*. It has more resources than others within the country to 'reinvent memories, traditions and practices ... with one eye on traditional [national] integration and one eye on the international tourist trade' (Featherstone 1995: p. 116) – memories, traditions and practices which are all the more effective in gaining public support if they can be presented as national tradition rather than partisan ideology.

'Identity culture' – with a little help from the state – is the most able to resist global forces, and 'consumer culture' the least. The public may welcome the globalisation of 'consumer culture', even insist upon their right to enjoy it, yet nonetheless reject the globalisation of their 'identity culture'. Those who 'wear Adidas, drink Coke and move overseas' may nonetheless commit themselves to 'local economic development, religious fundamentalism, reform movements or nation-building programmes' that challenge – and are consciously intended to challenge – the hegemony of the 'cultural empire' (Gold 2000: pp. 85–6). So while 'there has been some degree of homogenisation of mass cultural consumption, particularly among the young ... there is little sign as yet that nationalist cultural projects are in terminal decline' (Held *et al* 2000: pp. 373–4).

A globalised identity culture? In principle identity culture could be globalised if 'a new sense of global belonging and vulnerability [transcended] loyalties to the nation-state' (Held and McGrew 2002: p. 37 – citing Falk's *New Global Politics*, 1995 and Kaldor's *New and Old Wars*, 1998). But Smith (1990; 1995) argues strongly against the possibility of a common world culture: 'cultures are historically specific' (1995: p. 23); 'a global culture seems unable to offer the qualities of collective faith, dignity and hope that only a religion surrogate [like nationalism] with its promise of territorial cultural community across the generations can provide' (1995: p. 160). There is no 'global culture and cosmopolitan ideal that can truly supersede a world of nations (1990: p. 188); 'no global equivalences to the ethnic cores ... myths, legends, memories, stories, symbols, events and heros ... which give identity to a nation and its people' (Beynon and Dunkerley 2000: p. 13). World Values Survey data for the 1990s shows that only an average of 15 per cent regarded the world or even their global region (Europe, Asia, and so on) as their primary identity, and the largest number (47 per cent) identified with a territory smaller even than their state (Norris 2000: p. 161).

Instead of generating a globalised identity, globalisation has encouraged the diversification of identities within states. Jewish, Islamic, Christian and other religious actors operate more easily than ever on a global scale. Globalisation has provided greater opportunities 'for non-state actors to create alliances and linkages across borders' (Marden 1997: p. 49); and not just religious actors but others such as the 'women's movement, the peace movement and above all the environmental movement' (Held et al 2000: p. 371).

Cultural fright, reaction, resistance Appadurai (1990: p. 295) argues that 'there is always a fear of cultural absorption by polities of larger scale, especially those that are nearby' – a fear of cultural homogenisation. But globalisation, as we have just noted, may threaten local cultures by cultural heterogenisation as much as by cultural homogenisation. Cultural communities may simultaneously fear their own absorption into a wider culture and the loss of homogeneity within their own territory though immigration or the influx of new ideas. Globalisation may challenge local identity culture by increasing religious and ethnic diversity *within* territories as well as by increasing the homogeneity of consumer culture *across* territories. Although Smith (1990: p. 188) argues that globalised culture does 'not yet offer a serious challenge to the still fairly compact and frequently revived national cultures', he admits that 'immigration and cultural mixing can produce powerful ethnic reactions on the part of indigenous cultures'.

1.3   Understanding public discontent with globalisation

The academic critics of economic globalisation are balanced by equally distinguished and persuasive advocates; those who fear globalisation will destroy cherished local cultures are balanced by those who take a more relaxed view about the strength of local cultures or the advantages of a more locally diverse cultural mix. Our aim is not to weigh the arguments on one side against those on the other. It is sufficient to note that there is *no expert consensus* about valid reasons for discontent about globalisation – whether economic or cultural. There are good reasons to expect public discontent, but also good reasons to expect public support both for an open economy and for an open culture. The level of public discontent or support for opening up could not be inferred from the balance of academic argument. Instead, we are left with empirical questions about public attitudes towards markets, openness and globalisation. These include:

- *How much* discontent?
- What is the *nature* of that discontent? Discontent with too much openness or with too little? With unfairness in practice rather than the principle of openness? With cultural openness or with economic openness? Who is blamed?
- What are the *causes* of discontent? What makes some publics, or some individuals within the public, more discontent than others?
- What are the *consequences* of discontent? How do the public feel discontent should be expressed? Do they see the state as the solution? Or as the problem?

How much discontent?

The ILO claims that globalisation has not met the aspirations 'of the vast majority of men and women around the world' have to be set against Pew surveys whose headline figures suggest quite the opposite. But the public have quite complex opinions on this subject and much depends upon question-wording. Perhaps the public can be simultaneously discontented and supportive. We need to frame questions about discontent in a variety of different ways and give the public the space to reply in their own terms. Above all, we cannot infer the level of discontent from an external evaluation of the circumstances, however authoritative.

The nature of discontent

The nature of discontent with the open economy needs to be disaggregated.

Less or more Do the discontented want less globalisation or more? In contrast to critics of globalisation, Micklethwait and Woodridge (2000), Legrain (2004), Bhagwati (2002; 2004) and others suggest that the public in developing countries should be discontented with the slow pace and incompleteness of globalisation: 'globalisation is a liberating force that brings wealth and opportunity to people in the remotest parts of the globe' (Micklethwait and Woodridge 2000: p. 338); 'globalisation is part of the solution, not the problem [though] there is legitimate impatience with the speed at which globalisation will deliver on the social agendas' (Bhagwati 2002: p. 4).

Principle or practice Are the discontented opposed to the principle of an open economy or to the way it has been implemented? Stiglitz (2002: p. xv) railed at the 'hypocrisy of pretending to help developing countries by forcing them to open up their markets to the goods of the advanced industrial countries while [advanced countries were] keeping their own markets protected ... rules must be – and must be seen to be – fair and just'. Even the anti-globalisation campaigners of the 1990s have been re-branding as campaigners for 'global justice' or 'global solidarity' in order to distinguish between support for the principle and opposition to the practice. In the words of one prominent supporter of the 1990s anti-globalisation protests: 'I was wrong about trade ... our aim should not be to abolish the WTO but to transform it' (George Monbiot, *Guardian*, 24 June 2003). Global justice, not anti-globalisation resistance, is the aim of the emerging 'G20' group of developing countries led by Brazil, India and China within the WTO itself, and of more outsider groups like the European Social Forum and World Social Forum.

Both sides in the 1990s conflict, both pro- and anti-globalisation, have converged towards a global-justice agenda. The leader of the UK delegation to the 1999 WTO meeting in Seattle has echoed Monbiot's apologetic words: 'I was wrong: free market trade policies hurt the poor ... IMF and World Bank orthodoxy is increasing global poverty' (Stephen Byers, *Guardian*, 19 May 2003). UK Chancellor Gordon Brown and the World Bank President James Wolfensohn have publicly advocated a reduction in agricultural protectionism (*Guardian*, 16 February 2004), which discriminated against less developed countries, while open markets on manufactured goods and insistence on intellectual property rights discriminated in favour of advanced countries. If the old protestors of the 'anti-globalisation movement' do successfully encourage 'a new deal on the management of the world economy, the protestors may yet prove to be the true defenders of globalisation' (Green and Griffith 2002: p. 68). On the other hand, more equitable globalisation would transfer discontent about globalisation from the public of developing countries to the public of the advanced West, especially the US. There have always been some workers and businesses in economically advanced countries that feared being casualties of globalisation. As the American grip on international organisations has loosened, however, the US has increasingly switched, under growing domestic political pressure, towards exercising purely national power through unilateral action or bilateral agreements, openly and unilaterally opting-out of globalisation whenever it found it too painful. The protagonists of Seattle may have changed sides rather than merely converged.

Collateral damage Is discontent focused on marketisation and opening up or on the largely unintended collateral damage – such as the erosion of national culture, increasing crime and corruption, or increasing pollution of the environment? In the words of one Vietnamese participant in our focus groups: 'when we open the door, fortune comes in and so do the flies'.

The blame game Who are the targets of public discontent? Do the public focus on anyone who has done well out of the open economy; or on local power-holders (Hossain and Moore 2002) and criminals (UNDP 1999) who have stolen the benefits; or on foreign or international businessmen who are skilled at exploiting the underdeveloped; or on the government for failing to seize the opportunities offered by globalising markets, or for putting private gain before public interest; or on the incompetence of international organisations like the IMF, World Bank or WTO – or the self-interest of the great powers that control them?

Modelling the causes of discontent

There are many possible explanations for public discontent with economic, social, and cultural change, with the policies of marketisation and opening up which the public associate with much of that change, and with governments that have adopted these policies and managed or mismanaged these changes.

Winners and losers models Some variant on a 'winners and losers model' provides a common explanation of discontent: winners, however defined, will be enthusiastic; losers will be discontent. 'Globalisation . . . is a story about winners and losers, not a fable about economic growth' according to Stephen King, global head of research at HSBC (quoted by Larry Elliot, *Guardian*, 7 November 2005) and 'is easy to be enthusiastic about globalisation if you are a winner, less easy if you are a loser'. A winners and losers model is also the core (but unspecified and untested) assumption behind both the UNDP critique of globalisation and Legrain's advocacy of it.

But the phrase 'winners and losers' lacks specificity. So winners and losers designates a whole class of models, not a single model, depending on the criteria by which winners and losers are defined. Usually winners and losers are conceptualised in purely economic terms, though they can also be defined in terms of culture and prestige. But even in purely economic terms, the level of public services and social welfare, for example, may be as significant as take-home pay in defining winners and losers.

Too often winners and losers models are unthinkingly formulated in terms of personal or *family* gains and losses, but they can also be formulated in terms of perceptions about whether the *country* or, within some countries (Ukraine especially) the *region or ethnic group* has done well or badly. That is particularly relevant with culturally based models because culture is a collective possession, and the public may be concerned about the impact of opening up on the erosion of regional, ethnic or national culture.

Moreover, all winners and losers models can be formulated either in a 'selfish' form or, alternatively, in an 'altruistic' form based on sympathy and concern for the plight of others. In addition, all winners and losers models can be formulated in backward-looking 'retrospective' form, or forward-looking 'prospective' form, depending upon whether they are based on the public's sensitivity to recent experience, or their hopes and fears for the future. So there are numerous variants of the winners and losers model that we need to consider. Merely to conclude that some (unspecified) winners and losers model explains discontent, actually says very little about the causes of discontent.

An altruistic international version (based on concern for less-developed countries) might provide a model to explain discontent with globalisation among western activists – though a selfish concern about competition from developing countries is certainly another. In developing or transitional countries we might expect selfish models of discontent to apply more strongly than in the affluent West – though whether they might be family-based, nation-based, or regionally- and ethnically-based is not at all obvious.

Justice and injustice models Closely related to the winners and losers models, but fundamentally distinct from them, are another class of models: 'justice and injustice models' that focus on the justice or injustice of gains and losses rather than on the mere fact of gains and losses themselves. The public generally resent a politician making millions through tenure of office, but happily accept a footballer or a national lottery winner doing the same. This too is also a core part of the UNDP argument, expressed in its moralistic allegation that 'criminals reap the benefits of globalisation'. Winners who win by effort, skill or even luck, are more acceptable than those who win through insider deals or contacts with power-holders: fairness may matter. Justice models come in both *domestic* and *international* versions, depending upon whether they focus

Table 1.1. *Models of public discontent*

winners v losers models	cultural or economic
	focused on family; on nation; or on region or ethnic group
	selfish or altruistic
justice v injustice models	internal, domestic injustice; or international injustice
	selfish or altruistic
ideology models	left v right; environmentalism v growth; nationalism v cosmopolitanism
background models	socio-economic; cosmopolitan; regional; or identity background
legacy models	long-term cultural values; short-term experience; base-line comparisons
	national; global-regional; internal regional
	regimes and regime-change
governing elite models	officials as a development vanguard; or as a conspiracy against the public

on unfair distribution of gains and losses within the country, or between countries.

Ideology models A third class of explanations for discontent or enthusiasm might be based on ideology: on socialism, environmentalism, and especially on nationalism. A 'socialist v capitalist model' would depict globalisation as just a new battle-ground for left and right. An 'environmentalism v consumption model' would suggest that those who prioritise the environment over consumption would be more discontented with blind, profit-maximising, market-led development, less happy with a pure market economy, and more sceptical of the benefits that opening up to world markets would bring to developing countries. But a simple 'nationalist v cosmopolitan model' might well be the most powerful of the ideological models. Nationalists value the nation-state and they are peculiarly sensitive to anything that might threaten their national culture, national identity, or national autonomy.

Background models We might also attempt to explain attitudes towards economic openness in terms of various 'background models' – not just 'socio-economic' background, but also 'cosmopolitan' or 'identity' background. We might expect younger generations, higher earners, urban dwellers and the better educated to be more confident, more open to change, and more willing to engage with the wider world. Similarly, we might expect those with more cosmopolitan backgrounds – those who have had more contact with foreigners at home or abroad, those who can speak languages other than the state language, even perhaps those with home computers (and thus world-wide web potential) – to be more open to the world.

But while these background factors may be regarded as the primary influences in a long chain of causation, they may not have much direct or proximate impact on attitudes towards openness. Instead they may operate only through the more proximate influences of the 'winners and losers', 'justice and injustice', or 'nationalist v cosmopolitan ideology' models. For example, those with larger incomes may take a more optimistic view about economic trends and that in turn may affect their attitude towards an open economy. Similarly, ethnic identification may affect the importance that people put on national culture and that in turn may then affect attitudes towards cultural and economic openness.

Legacy models All the models discussed so far are designed to explain differences between individuals. But sometimes the differences between countries or between global regions (East Asia versus East Europe) seem more significant than the differences among individuals within countries. All the people within a country – including minorities – are exposed to the history, institutions, dominant culture, and government of that place while those who live in other parts of the world are not. Hence the concept of 'legacy models' (Ekiert and Hanson 2003). Some broad-brush models of attitudes to development have invoked the concept of socially cohesive and industrious 'Asian values'. Conversely, problems in eastern Europe have been attributed to the state-dependency fostered by decades of communism.

'Asian values' or 'communist state dependency' are examples of 'long-term cultural legacy models'. Inglehart and his associates have used the concept of 'cultural zones', typically including an 'ex-communist' and an East Asian or 'Confucian' zone (Inglehart and Baker 2000; Inglehart and Norris 2003). Martin Jacques uses the same concept when he argues that 'the claims of *western values* are mocked by the rise of Asia ... the next quarter-century will not be simply about American hyper-power but the rise of *Asian power and values*' (*Guardian*, 15 May 2004; our emphasis). But this concept of peculiarly 'Asian' values is hotly contested. Asian values were equated by advocates such as Lee Kuan Yew with East Asia, specifically including both Korea and Vietnam (Zakaria 1994: p. 2) and with the concept of an orderly family-oriented society – in contrast to both American moral decay and Soviet state-paternalism (Zakaria 1994: p. 8). Critics focused on this model as an implicit justification for authoritarian government and disrespect for human rights (Kim Dae Jung 1994; Sen 1997) arguing that 'there are no ideas more fundamental to democracy than the teachings of Confucianism, Buddhism, and Tonghak' (Kim Dae Jung 1994: p. 2).

Given the way that western Christianity has been used over the centuries to justify everything from the most extreme autocracy to the most extreme democracy it is not obvious that any religion has a consistent and unambiguous relationship to human rights. But the second – and largely neglected – strand of Lee's argument was that Asians relied on the state less and on their extended family and civil society more than in the West. Ironically that argument might not be sustainable in a contrast between Lee's Singapore and the US, but it would be more applicable to the contrast between East Asian traditions and East European traditions. World Values Survey data provide 'clear evidence of the continuing centrality of the family in Vietnam' (Dalton *et al* 2002: p. 386). Conversely, the long experience of communist rule has perhaps given East Europeans, especially those in the former Soviet area, somewhat different expectations of state and family (Baxandall 2003: pp. 279–80) than in East Asia, even communist East Asia. So these 'long-term cultural legacy models' might help to explain differences between attitudes to markets and open economies in Asia and East Europe.

A very different possibility is that 'short-term economic legacy models' might influence public attitudes. East Asia can be distinctive here and now without being distinctively Confucian. Rather than 'Asian values', Stiglitz (2002: pp. 10–11) refers to the 'Asian model' of development, promoted by the Asian Development Bank (ADB), 'in which governments, while relying on markets have taken an active role in creating, shaping and guiding markets' which was 'distinctly different from the American model pushed by the Washington-based institutions' and more readily accepted in East Europe. Gierus (2001), like Stiglitz, distinguishes between the successful 'Asian model' of globalisation characterised by a strong, self-confident and nationalist state, and the 'Eastern and Central European model' characterised by 'huge polarisation between western-oriented elites and the rest of society' coupled with a weak and inactive state that had 'lost legitimacy', incurred 'enormous debts', and was run by a bureaucracy that was ill-disciplined, badly paid, ill-trained, and distracted from economic affairs by unresolved regional, territorial, cultural and ethnic problems. We shall see whether our data prove more consistent with Gierus than with Lee.

There is a third important 'legacy model' however: the 'base-line comparison model'. Although a winners and losers model would predict greater discontent in less successful economies, cross-national variations in discontent may also reflect national self-images of the country's rightful place in the world. Public discontent may reflect attitudes based on relative rather than absolute standards. The public may judge their own experience of an open economy against a routine comparator (Ukrainians for example routinely compare Ukraine with Bulgaria, Poland, or Russia – but not with Germany, Sweden or the US). Or they may judge their own contemporary experience of an open economy against their own past – for example, against the nostalgic image that many Ukrainians now have of their own national achievements and personal lifestyle under communism (Ekiert 2003: p. 98); or against Korean memories of steady year-on-year growth until the 1997–9 IMF crisis so rudely interrupted it; or against Vietnamese memories of the pre-'Doi Moi' ('national renewal') era of poverty and privation.

Region, regimes and regime change Legacy models do not apply only to countries and global regions however. Within countries too, different regions might have significantly different histories. They may have a history of different regimes, or of being favoured or suppressed by a regime. Throughout history Vietnam has been repeatedly divided between north and south, most recently in the decades after 1945 when a market economy was encouraged in the south and discouraged in the north. After reunification, regional tensions remained and arguably increased (Evans 2004; Marr and White 1988). Southerners might be expected to have more expertise in operating a market economy and more resentment against the communist alternative and the distant government. Ukraine remains divided regionally, culturally, linguistically, and by ethnic identification, between Ukrainians and Russians – even though these different cleavages only partially coincide. Post-communist policies of Ukrainianisation may have increased discontent among Russian speakers; while the triumph (and triumphalism) of the Orange Revolution at the end of 2004 was said to have further polarised ethno-linguistic Russians and Ukrainians. We might expect regime change to have affected Ukrainian attitudes towards openness, especially openness towards western-dominated world markets. In addition, we might expect the Orange Revolution to have changed the regional, ethnic or linguistic structure of these attitudes.

Governing-elite models The position of state officials in developing and transitional countries is particularly interesting. The question of whether government officials (appointed or elected) are representative of the public in terms of their attitudes to an open economy is important – as much so in emerging democracies or even authoritarian systems as in established democracies. How much, and in what way, officials differ from the public has implications for government sensitivity and for public discontent everywhere – as well as for the quality of democracy in democracies.

Insofar as the attitudes of officials differ from those of the public, the difference may be explained by a 'development vanguard model'. Even at a junior level, officials tend to be better educated than the general public, which typically makes people more open, more cosmopolitan. Through their work and their official contacts they may also be better placed to see the advantages of an open economy (though perhaps also the disadvantages). They may have better information about the development successes of the open economy – which may foster greater commitment to a process that could benefit the country as a whole.

But there is another model of the differences between officials and the public: a 'conspiracy model'. Hossain and Moore (2002) suggest that 'national elites in developing countries are not as pro-poor as we would wish' (p. 1). Though they say 'bureaucratic elites are relatively pro-poor' compared with 'agrarian elites' their 'motivations for action against poverty are often negative, driven by fear' (pp. 17–19). But it may be much worse than that: officials may be willing and able to take greater personal advantage of new opportunities, including 'informal payments' from business entrepreneurs large and small – which may also foster their commitment to the open economy, but alienate them from the public. A simple 'conspiracy model' – in which officials support an open economy while the public opposes it, because officials grab all the benefits and the public bears all the costs, is too extreme to occur in reality. But as public allegations against officials increase, and as officials become demonstrably less representative, the 'conspiracy model' becomes a more plausible explanation and the 'development vanguard model' correspondingly less plausible.

The consequences of discontent

Public discontent with either the principle or the practice of globalisation is likely to have consequences. Discontent with economic, social or cultural change may turn the public against markets and opening up. It may increase demands for protection. It may also increase public support for direct action, or more violent direct action, against foreign companies or international organisations. It may also erode support for a government which has failed to manage globalisation to the public's advantage.

Stiglitz (2002: p. 3) claims that 'for decades people in the developing world have rioted when the austerity programs imposed on their countries proved to be too harsh, but their protests were largely unheard in the West'. Yet it takes relatively few to riot. We investigate whether the perceived downsides of globalisation increase public support for direct action, including 'disorderly or violent' protests; and decrease public support for the government as well as for openness itself. Or whether the public see the state as the solution to their globalisation discontents rather than the problem – and opt for complaining to their government (or its officials) against the foreigners. If the public see their *government as the solution* rather than the problem, they may try to enlist its help – by appealing to local officials against bad working conditions or pollution caused locally by a multinational company, for example; or by calling for an expanded role for the state within their country. In these circumstances, discontent with globalisation may encourage the public to see their state as their principal advocate and protector in a tough, competitive, globalising world of potentially predatory big powers and potentially unfair international organisations.

1.4   Researching discontent

To test these explanatory models we opted for a 'small-N' comparison, with sixteen focus groups and over ten thousand lengthy interviews spread across only four countries. That permits analysis in depth. We have not had to spread available resources too thinly. But we have had to choose our countries carefully.

Four countries

Among global regions, East Asia was the most outstanding 'winner' and the East Europe/Commonwealth of Independent States (CIS) region the most outstanding 'loser' during the 1990s (UNDP 2002). East Asia had the greatest rise in both GDP per capita and Human Development Index (HDI); and East Europe/CIS had the greatest drop in both GDP per capita and HDI – indeed it was the only global region where HDI actually declined across that decade. Within each region we have chosen one relatively rich (and rated 'high' on the UNDP's HDI rankings in 2004) and one relatively poor (and rated 'medium' on the UNDP's HDI rankings 2004): relatively rich (South) Korea and the Czech Republic; and relatively poor Vietnam and Ukraine. It is the two poorer countries that best typify the 1990s pattern of global region growth, however – Ukraine collapsing in chaos and corruption, Vietnam growing very rapidly albeit from a low economic base. Decline was less severe in the Czech Republic and, conversely, a long period of rapid growth in Korea was interrupted by the 1997–9 Asian crisis.

An analysis of only four countries does not permit statistically definitive cross-national conclusions, but it does permit statistically compelling analysis of patterns within each of the countries. This set of four is sufficiently diverse that if we find a pattern replicated across them all – between for example 'winners and losers' or between 'public and officials' for example – it is likely to apply quite widely. Conversely, if there really are sharp systematic differences between (global) regional cultures they should be evident in the contrast between our East Asian and East European countries. If there really are sharp systematic differences between richer and poorer countries they should be evident in the contrasts within each global region.

Moreover, our data are not merely statistical but 'information-rich'. That is most obvious in the focus group transcripts from which we quote extensively. It also emerges from the depth of our survey interviews which used multiple questions to elicit the nuanced, conditional and multi-faceted nature of public opinion. We do not rely on purely quantitative answers to a limited set of questions. Together the qualitative and quantitative data, the cross-checking by use of multiple questions, and the use of 'silent codes' where we suspected respondents would criticise the question rather than pick one of the proffered options, tell us a lot about the 'why', and the 'in what sense', as well as about the simple 'what'.

The four countries have much in common. All have had relatively recent experience of opening up their economies. None have large economies capable – as are the American or Chinese – of any significant degree of self-sufficiency – which makes protectionism at once especially attractive and especially deadly for them. None of them are powerful. All have recent histories of being invaded, occupied or controlled from outside their borders. Though homogeneity is less in Ukraine than in the others, all four share a strong sense of ethnic/nationalist identity and feel threatened by powerful neighbours or the last remaining superpower. Within all four, there is the potential for territorial insecurity and cultural fright, albeit to varying degrees.

All have recent or continuing experience of a communist or authoritarian regime. Inglehart and Norris (2003: pp. 165–7) categorise Vietnam as a 'non-democracy', Ukraine as a 'semi-democracy', and Korea and the Czech Republic as rather tentative 'newer democracies' – in contrast to the more mature 'older democracies' of the West. They categorise none of the four as 'post-industrial' – again in contrast to almost all the 'older democracies' of the West. After the Asian crash of 1997–9 (what Koreans in our focus groups – echoing Stiglitz – call simply 'the IMF': an event not an organisation) even the most economically developed of our four did not feel, to its own citizens, like a fully advanced country.

We give a more extended account of each country's recent economic and political background in Chapter 2.

Two methods – and two levels

Our study was based on two methods – focus group discussions and survey interviews. The survey used a two-level, elite/mass design, interviewing officials as well as ordinary members of the public. It was a closely integrated mixed-method approach that had numerous advantages over increasingly criticised purely qualitative or quantitative approaches (see for example Brady and Collier 2004). The same questionnaire was used for interviews with officials and public; that survey questionnaire was based not only on the detailed prompts used in focus groups but also on the spontaneous contributions of focus group participants to those discussions. We can therefore compare the attitudes of officials and public, and illuminate the meaning of survey responses by reference to the focus group discussions (or conversely, quantify the views expressed in focus groups by reference to the surveys).

Because the survey questionnaires were designed to cover the same ground as the preceding focus group discussions we can integrate our analysis of the two fairly closely. The large-scale representative surveys supply us with the best estimate of the *numbers* with an opinion or the statistical correlation between different variables, while the transcripts of the focus groups often provide us with the deepest insight into the *meaning* of those answers or those correlations. Indeed, because both discussions and interviews cover the same ground, and the more rigid survey questionnaire was designed after a preliminary analysis of the focus group discussions, what we have is a single integrated methodology, rather than two separate methodologies. We quote extensively from the focus group transcripts not just to illuminate survey findings but to allow the public in developing countries speak with their own voices. Usually the focus groups and survey interviews tell the same story, but in different ways. Where they do not we draw attention to the discrepancy and attempt to provide some insight into the reasons for it.

Focus groups We started at the end of 2002 with sixteen two-hour focus group discussions, involving 130 participants. In the following chapters we will use codes in brackets to identify the country and the particular participant. Where the particular participant who made a contribution could not be identified from the video tape, the code zero is used. The sixteen focus groups comprised:

- one in each of the capital cities: Prague, Seoul, Kyiv and Hanoi;
- one in another major urban area: Brno in the Czech Republic, Taejon in South Korea, Kharkiv in an ethnically Russian area of Ukraine, and Ho Chi Minh City, the former capital of South Vietnam;

- two in more rural areas: České Budějovice and Prostejov in the Czech Republic; Yechon and Yoju in South Korea; small villages in Zhytomyr Oblast and Kirovograd Oblast, Ukraine; and villages in Hoa Binh Province in north Vietnam and Tay Ninh Province in south Vietnam.

At least one member of staff from Glasgow (the authors and/or our research assistant) was present to observe every focus group with the help of simultaneous translation. The discussions were video-recorded, transcripted in the vernacular, translated into English, and analysed using NVIVO. They were guided by local professional moderators using a fifty-two-question schedule covering six topics:
  i. recent economic, social and cultural change;
  ii. the market economy, 'marketisation' or 'market mechanisms';
  iii. the pros and cons of development;
  iv. national identity, culture and foreign influences;
  v. the advantages and disadvantages of opening up the economy to world markets;
  vi. attitudes towards so-called 'anti-globalisation' protests.

Surveys These discussions were followed at the end of 2003 by nationally representative surveys with at least 1,500 members of the public and 500 elected or appointed officials in each country – making a total of 8,202 interviews in all. The interview schedule was designed to cover not only the questions we had put to the focus group participants but also the range of answers and the additional topics these participants had spontaneously raised in the relatively flexible format of a discussion. It included 117 substantive questions about the same topics as in the focus groups, plus another twenty-seven 'background' questions – including questions about religious, ethnic and territorial identities, linguistic capabilities, and contacts with foreigners, as well as the usual socio-economic background questions.

Samples were designed to be representative of the whole country, rural as well as urban, and including villages in 'remote' rural areas as well as villages closer to the towns. (In Vietnam previous surveys had often been restricted to the towns, sometimes with the addition of their rural fringe.) In our samples, 10 per cent of Koreans lived in village compared with 20 per cent of Czechs, 31 per cent of Ukrainians and 62 per cent of Vietnamese. Altogether 80 per cent of our Vietnamese sample lived in small towns or villages.

Comparison with census data indicates the samples were closely representative in terms of region, rurality, age, gender, and higher education in the Czech Republic, Korea, and Ukraine, though somewhat less so in Vietnam where the sample was somewhat more male, older, and better educated than the population. So for cross-national comparisons we have routinely weighted the Vietnam data to represent these social characteristics (though the weighting has more impact on the numbers with 'no opinion' or 'mixed opinions' than on anything else and seldom affects the results by more than two or three percentage points). In Ukraine, where ethnic background is very important for some of our findings, the numbers of self-declared ethnic Ukrainians exactly matched the census figure.

Half the officials we interviewed in the Czech Republic, Korea and Ukraine were *elected* deputies at regional or local government level, the rest *appointed* officials in economic affairs, education, social services, environmental affairs, or general administration. In Vietnam, just over one fifth were 'elected' officials, the rest divided equally between these five categories of appointed officials. In every country, our samples of officials were spread right across the country roughly in line with the general population. The fit between the regional distributions of public and officials was particularly close in Vietnam and the Czech Republic, though Ukrainian and Korean officials were proportionately more numerous in their capital cities. In Vietnam, forty per cent of the officials we interviewed lived in villages (eighteen per cent in 'remote' villages) and seventy per cent in small towns or villages.

The Orange Revolution survey Following the Orange Revolution in Ukraine at the end of 2004 we repeated our Ukraine survey in the spring of 2005 to measure the impact of regime change – for example on attitudes towards Russia and the West. This time we interviewed another 2,136 using a sample design that 'boosted' the number of interviews with Russian speakers and Russian ethnic-identifiers by over-sampling more Russian-speaking parts of Ukraine. By down-weighting interviews in the over-sampled Oblasts, it provides a fully representative sample for 2003–5 trend comparisons. It also provides more reliable estimates (than a strictly proportionate survey design) of divergent views between Russian and Ukrainian speakers, identifiers, or areas in the aftermath of the Orange Revolution.

A framework for analysis We use multiple regression to test alter-native explanations of discontent and its consequences. Multivariate modelling also allows us to decide which elements of discontent are critical and which, though real enough in themselves, are discounted by the public as a 'price worth paying' for a greater good, and thus have little or no impact on support for development, openness, or the incumbent government.

The framework for our analysis of alternative models of the causes and consequences of discontent is summarised in Table 1.2. It assumes a flow of influence from:

1. personal background;
2. personal experience of change;
3. perceptions of broader changes;
4. attitudes towards cultural openness;
5. attitudes towards economic openness;
6. attitudes towards protest, government, and the role of the state.

At each stage all elements from previous stages, but *only* from *previous* stages, are regarded as potential influences – though many prove to be redundant once account is taken of the most important key influences.

We take people's background (gender, income, education, age, employment and so on) and their personal experiences (especially whether their family income had been rising or declining) as given. They do not depend upon attitudes. But they may shape and condition perceptions of wider changes, as well as attitudes towards cultural and economic openness, the legitimacy of protests, and the role of government.

We place perceptions of change next because perceptions of economic, social and cultural change may shape attitudes towards a more market-orientated economy and opening up to world business and markets.

We place attitudes toward cultural openness before attitudes towards economic openness. The public regard the erosion of their national culture as an inevitable consequence of opening up the economy and they cite it as the main disadvantage of opening up. But although the *sequence of perceived impact* runs from an open economy to an open culture, the *sequence of attitudinal influence,* if there is any, must run in the opposite direction: that is, from fear of the cultural consequences towards rejection of economic openness itself.

Our framework then assumes that cultural and economic openness, supplemented perhaps by perceptions of change, may have some influence on public attitudes towards anti-globalisation protests, the government and its policies, and the role of the state.

While we do not intend to apply this framework rigidly, it underlies our analysis of cause and consequence. We use stepwise regression to highlight the key influences at each stage rather than clutter up our conclusions with minutiae. We calculate regressions separately for the public within each country, as well as for a pooled data-set of the public in all four countries (with 'dummies' to account for crude differences between countries or global regions), and lastly for a pooled data set that includes

Table 1.2. *A framework for analysis*

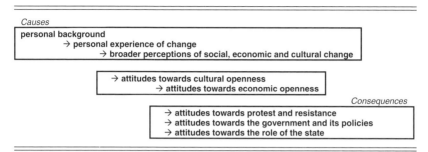

both public and officials from all four countries (with 'dummies' to account for crude differences between public and officials as well as between countries or global regions). The pooled data set of the public is slightly weighted to have (after weighting) equal numbers from each of the four countries. The pooled data set of public-plus-officials is heavily weighted to have (after weighting) equal numbers of officials and public, as well as equal numbers from each country. That allows differences between countries, or between officials and public, to emerge (if they exist) and not be suppressed by variations in sample size.

It is particularly important to double-check findings from the pooled data sets against the findings within individual countries, however. Where there is a coincidence of high values for two variables within a single country, regressions on pooled data sets may highlight relationships that do not exist *within* any country, but only *between* countries, and further consideration is necessary. The dummy variables used in the pooled data set regressions take account of different levels of opinion within different countries (or between officials and publics) on the dependent variable, but they are not a fully sufficient substitute for a within-country analysis. Often however, the pooled data analysis provides a concise summary of a pattern that does in fact exist within most or all countries.

1.5   Plan of the book

Chapter 2 looks first at the objective evidence on recent trends in our four countries, particularly the 'statistics of change' over the last decade or two. In some countries these are the statistics of development but in others they are the statistics of stagnation or even decline. It documents public perceptions of these trends and attitudes towards them: perceptions and attitudes about economic growth; trends in economic inequality; the justice or injustice of differential benefits; trends in crime, corruption and pollution; and in national autonomy and culture.

It also assesses public attitudes towards the pace of development, and the degree of public satisfaction, dissatisfaction, or discontent with the (purposefully vague) 'way things are going for my family' and 'for the country'. Finally it looks at how personal background, personal experience, and perceptions of wider change combine to affect this generalised public satisfaction or discontent with 'the way things are going'. Some complaints, some specific discontents, though real enough, have little impact on this overall satisfaction or discontent with 'the way things are going', while other particular complaints seem to matter more.

Altruistic versions of winners and losers models are admirable but ineffective. The public did recognise and lament the social and national injustices, the increasing pollution and corruption that were often associated with development. But although they expressed these concerns, they had little impact on public satisfaction with 'the way things are going' either for themselves or for their country. Selfish versions of winners and losers models proved more effective, though *not* primarily those based purely on personal gains and losses. It was discontent with the progress of the national economy rather than with rising crime, pollution or inequality – or even with personal living standards – that had by far the greatest impact on general discontent with 'the way things are going in our country today': a selfish winners and losers model, but not one that is focused on personal gains or loss.

Chapter 3 looks at public attitudes towards opening up and marketisation. The public cited the principal advantage of opening up the economy as its being 'good for shopping'; and the principal disadvantage as its being 'bad for culture'. Very few (only three per cent) insisted there were no disadvantages to opening up. But despite all of their discontents and their perceptions of the disadvantages, we found enormously strong public support for opening up (though not as high as in the Pew surveys). A majority of almost four to one said that opening up was good rather than bad for their country. Discontent did not preclude support – though support did not preclude discontent either. The public were therefore 'critical supporters' of opening up, and it would be misleading to drop either of those two words from the description.

There was less public support for the (internal) market economy, more craving for an alternative, and a notable lack of enthusiasm for working for market sector employers.

A national (but *not* a personal) version of a winners and losers model best explains why people felt the market economy made their country more prosperous and fair: those who thought their national economy had prospered were the most likely to conclude that market economies not only deliver prosperity but also that market economies are fair. A (domestic) justice model, based on perceptions that the benefits of economic change had gone to corrupt power-holders or those with contacts rather than those with greater skill, education or even luck, also had an important impact on whether the public rated the market economy as 'unfair'. But rather than any kind of winners and losers model, an (international) justice model, based on whether the public felt 'foreign companies help rather than exploit', was the best predictor of public support for opening up. Despite their very genuine concerns about the impact of opening up the economy on their culture and 'way of life' (explored futher in Chapter 4), these concerns had little or no impact on public support for opening up.

Chapter 4 looks at public perceptions and attitudes with regard to culture. It distinguishes between 'consumer culture' and 'identity culture'. The public feel that the most important elements of their national culture are language, and family or social behaviour – not films, TV, food, clothes and so on – despite the high visibility of such lifestyle or consumer culture and the consequent stress put upon it by visiting commentators. A majority say they like foreign TV, films and brands. While many feel their traditional way of life is getting lost, some do not regret the passing of traditional society, others are indifferent, others regard it as a price worth paying for economic development, and some of those that might be distressed by the erosion of their traditional culture assert that it is still strong.

There is broad public support for cultural protection, but it is based on personal respect for their national culture, even on confidence that is remains strong, rather than cultural fright or fears their culture and way of life are getting lost. What matters most is having something worth protecting and preserving, rather than panic about the decline of the national culture.

Since the majority of the public feel – perhaps wrongly, as many students of national identity such as Smith (1995) would argue – that economic openness automatically entails the erosion of their national culture and identity, the publics' commitment to their national cultures and their support for cultural protection might spill over into opposition to opening up the economy. But while cultural commitment (though not cultural fright) proves to be a major influence on support for specifically cultural protection, it had – as we found in Chapter 3 – very little culturally based influence of any kind on support for the general principle of opening up. The public recognise that opening up is something of a Faustian bargain, trading the prospect of economic gain against the erosion of their national culture. Their response, however, is not to reject economic openness but to combine economic openness with cultural protection, to offset the downsides of opening up while still reaping the benefits: to drive a harder bargain with the devil.

Even though a majority were more contented than discontented with an open economy in principle, most held attitudes that mixed general contentment with specific discontent. Chapter 5 looks at public attitudes towards the articulation of discontent. There was almost universal support for protest of some kind against international companies that caused serious local problems, or against international organisations whose policies damaged poorer countries: such circumstances justified protest. The issue for most people was not protest itself, but *acceptable methods* of protest, and *acceptable participants* in protest. Apart from in Ukraine, a majority rejected disorderly, disruptive or violent methods of protest – though we found much greater (though still minority) support for violent protest and sabotage than in some classic western studies of public attitudes towards protest methods. We also found widespread acceptance of a global dimension to protest: a majority in every country would welcome foreign participation.

A sense of national injustice, nationalism or xenophobia could not do much to inflate the already high support for protest against badly behaving foreign companies or international organisations, but they could increase public support for disorderly or even violent methods of protest. Xenophobia in particular made people both less willing to accept foreign help in their protests and more willing to support disorderly or violent methods. But it was an international justice model, based on perceptions of whether foreign companies exploited or helped the country, that had most impact on public support for disorderly or violent protest.

Chapter 6 looks at public hopes and fears with respect to four roles for the state in the context of globalisation. With an internal market and an externally open economy in a globalised world, what role is left for the state?

One approach is to look at the factors that make a government popular or unpopular. Whether self-consciously recognised or not, these factors tell us something about what the public demand of the state. Public support for the government and its policies is best explained by a combination of a national (but not personal) *winners and losers* model based on national economic trends and a *cultural perceptions* model based on perception that the national culture is becoming more or less respected. While the economic model is rather more important in some countries, the cultural model is more important in others. Cultural concerns did not erode support for opening up the economy, but they did erode support for governments. Conversely, governments could win favour by protecting and reinforcing the national culture, irrespective of economic trends. The cultural dimension was a potential *resource* for globalising governments, rather than a problem for them. Instead of focusing on cultural decline as a source of public discontent with economic openness, we should focus on the strengthening of national culture as a device for offsetting other discontents.

More explicit questions about the responsibilities of the state revealed a public demand for a state that was able to play the roles of *national entrepreneur, protector* or *physician*, and *advocate* of the national interest within a global context – encouraging but not directly controlling economic development; remedying the ills of globalisation by providing help for globalisation-losers and by protecting farmers, small businesses and the national 'way of life'; and speaking up effectively for the national interest within international organisations that could neither be ignored nor relied upon to treat developing or transitional countries fairly. East Asian publics especially saw globalisation as an arena for states that made the state more vitally necessary than ever before.

The public held the state primarily responsible for adverse economic trends in the Czech Republic, Korea and Ukraine – as well as for positive economic trends in Vietnam. Worst of all, however, the public, especially in East Europe, feared that the state had a fourth, unwanted role as a *conspiracy* against the public. They are most likely to cite 'those who already had more power' as the chief beneficiaries of recent economic change. Even when we explicitly suggested that the benefits might have gone to 'foreigners' or to 'business people', the public put 'government officials' at the top of their list of perceived beneficiaries and 'ordinary people' at the bottom. Vietnam was the only country where more than a few of the public cited 'ordinary people' as the chief beneficiaries.

Comparison of officials' perceptions and attitudes with those of the public within their own countries shows that officials in the East Asian countries, especially Vietnam, were fairly representative of their publics. But officials in the East European countries, especially Ukraine, differed much more from their publics and usually took a much harder line than their publics towards the casualties of globalisation. Taking into account the strength of public allegations that the chief beneficiaries of the open economy had been officials, power-holders or those 'with contacts', together with the extent to which officials were unrepresentative of their publics, a 'vanguard model' of officials seems to fit Vietnam best while a 'conspiracy model' of officials fits Ukraine best – and to a lesser extent, a 'vanguard model' fits East Asia and a 'conspiracy model' East Europe.

Perceptions of the state as a conspiracy against the public eroded satisfaction with 'the way things are going in our country', judgements that the market economy is 'fair', and even support for 'rapid economic development'. Most significant for governance, perceptions of the state as a conspiracy eroded public support for 'the government and its policies' and increased support for 'disorderly or violent' methods of protest, especially the use of disorderly or violent protest as a first resort rather than a last resort. In short, perceptions of the state as a conspiracy measurably eroded its legitimacy and increased the potential for political instability. The Orange Revolution in Ukraine was not entirely surprising; indeed some focus group participants back in 2002 had already called explicitly for a change of regime.

Chapter 7 looks at the legacy of regime change in Vietnam and Ukraine. In Vietnam we found evidence of a legacy of war. More than the South Vietnamese, the North Vietnamese continued to regard the US as both a territorial and a cultural threat – though the majority in both North and South did not. But we found no legacy, or perhaps an inverse legacy, of classic communism. Northerners did have a more social democratic concern for the casualties of globalisation; but although they had the least experience of an open market economy they were the most enthusiastic about marketisation and opening up. Despite their proximity to government, or perhaps because of it, northerners were more critical than southerners of government officials reaping the benefits of globalisation more than the people. Northerners were only a little more inclined than southerners to praise the 'government and its policies' and, judging by their attitudes towards markets and opening up, the policies they praised were not rooted in the communist past but rather in the market-oriented present or future.

After the Orange Revolution in Ukraine at the end of 2004, we found an explosion of euphoria that extended to a wide range of hopes and perceptions, but especially towards better economic prospects for the future. The attitudes of Russian speakers and Ukrainian speakers moved in different directions or to different degrees. On some issues that led to greater polarisation of views between them, but not always. On attitudes towards the market economy and opening up in particular, Russian and Ukrainian speakers moved in different directions – without diverging. Instead, they 'swapped places' rather than moving further apart. Russian speakers, who were by socio-economic background the natural cosmopolitans, swapped places with Ukrainian speakers, who were by background the more natural parochials. So Russian speakers who had been relatively pro-globalisation before the Orange Revolution swapped places with Ukrainian speakers who had formerly been more anti-globalisation. It was musical chairs rather than polarisation; and it left Ukrainian opinion no more divided than before.

In comparison with our other countries, overall public opinion in Ukraine remained broadly as distinctive after the Revolution as before it. In the rankings of opinion across the four countries, Ukrainian opinion generally remained in the same position or, on some issues, became even more distinctive. Although the structure of public opinion changed, as Ukrainian speakers and Russian speakers 'swapped places', even so dramatic an event as the Orange Revolution did not much affect the overall picture of Ukraine provided by our earlier findings.

Chapter 8 returns to the four key questions about public discontent with the open economy that we set out earlier in this chapter – questions about the *extent*, the *nature*, the *causes*, and the *consequences* of that public discontent – and briefly summarises our conclusions. The public in our developing or transitional countries were 'critical supporters' of opening up. They had many discontents, some of which were related to the failure to establish a 'real market' or the failure to open up sufficiently. But some were inherent in opening up itself: 'when we open the door, fortune comes in and so do the flies'. Yet some of the specific discontents did not contribute much to overall discontent. For most the remedy was not to abandon opening up, but to address its specific faults by helping the casualties of gobalisation to develop the skills necessary to compete more effectively, and to take action to protect and sustain the national culture. Nonetheless, if the state was perceived to be unable or unwilling to provide these remedies, its legitimacy could be seriously eroded. The public might not turn against opening up, but they could turn against the state.

2   Change and discontent

Over the last two decades or so, all four of our chosen countries, the Czech Republic, Korea, Ukraine and Vietnam, have experienced a great deal of economic, social, and environmental change. Much of that has been attributed quite rightly to globalisation, to the movement towards a more market-based economy internally, and towards opening up the national economy more to world markets. Other economic, social, or environmental changes that have happened at the same time might well be associated in the public mind with the process of globalisation, if only by the coincidence of timing. Public perceptions of change have thus provided a basis for public attitudes towards globalisation.

We cannot assume that economic, social, or environmental change – as described in official statistics or the reports of widely respected non-governmental organisations – would translate automatically into public perceptions, still less into public satisfaction or public discontent. Nonetheless these official or semi-official reports provide a backdrop – part explanation, part contrast – to public *perceptions* of trends in economic prosperity, inequality, pollution, crime, corruption and culture; to public satisfaction or *discontent* with 'the way things are going'; and perhaps therefore to public support for the processes of marketisation and opening up.

2.1   The statistics of change

Opening up (South) Korea adopted an export-led growth strategy in the 1960s and opened up to foreign imports and investment in the 1990s (World Bank 1993). North Vietnam, later Vietnam, remained a closed socialist economy until the late 1980s, when it adopted a more open economic policy while remaining firmly under Communist Party rule. South Vietnam, however, was only incorporated into communist Vietnam in 1976, and so experienced only one decade of classic communism. East Europe gradually opened up to international markets as the Soviet-led system crumbled, but the Czech Republic more quickly, and in more depth, than Ukraine. At the time of our survey, the Fraser Institute (2004), whose ratings unfortunately omit Vietnam, placed the Czech Republic in 15th place in terms of 'freedom to trade internationally' (well ahead of the US in 29th place) and Ukraine in 52nd place, just ahead of South Korea in 53rd place. But Ukraine slipped to 107th place on the Fraser Institute's overall measure of 'economic freedom', once the malfunctioning of its internal market, the corruption of its officials, and the reliability of its courts were taken into account.

Economic openness might be measured by exports and imports, by foreign direct investment (FDI) or by participation in international economic organisations such as the World Trade Organisation (WTO), the World Bank, or the International Monetary Fund (IMF). The small Czech Republic, located in the heart of Europe, was the most economically exposed in terms of exports and imports, which equalled 65 per cent of its gross domestic product (GDP) in 2003, compared with Vietnam's 56 per cent, Ukraine's 53 per cent, and Korea's 38 per cent (World Bank 2004). FDI varied from year to year, but over the decade 1992–2003 it averaged 26 per cent of gross fixed capital formation in Vietnam, 20 per cent in the Czech Republic, 11 per cent for Ukraine, and a mere 2 per cent for Korea (UNCTAD 2004), though Vietnam had slipped behind the Czech Republic towards the end of that decade. Only the richer Czech Republic and Korea were members of the WTO: both joined in 1995 (WTO website 2004), but all four were members of the IMF and of the various institutions that make up World Bank Group.

The status of regional organisations like the European Union (EU) and Association of South-East Asian Nations (ASEAN) is inherently more ambiguous with regard to openness. They are committed at once to encouraging trade within their region and protecting the interests of that region against the wider world. Vietnam joined ASEAN in 1995. The so-called 'ASEAN plus three', established in 1997, includes Korea alongside Japan and China. Both Korea and Vietnam were founder members of the Asian Development Bank (ADB) back in 1966, though the ADB's activities in Vietnam were later suspended and only renewed in 1993 (ADB website 2004).

Growth and decline Korea was categorised as a 'high income' country by the World Bank, Vietnam as 'low income', the Czech Republic as 'upper middle income', and Ukraine as 'lower middle income' (World Bank 2003a; 2004). But in terms of trends the United Nations Development Programme (UNDP 2002) showed East Asia as the most outstanding 'winner', and the East Europe/Commonwealth of Independent States

(CIS) region the most outstanding 'loser' over the decade of the 1990s – irrespective of whether the criterion was GDP per capita or UNDP Human Development Index (HDI).

All four countries had experienced recent economic upheavals which in some cases seem to have damaged public confidence more than they damaged the statistics of development. Korea averaged annual growth at around six per cent per annum from the 1960s to the 1980s; and almost nine per cent between 1983 and 1993 (World Bank 1993; 2004). Even between 1993 and 2003 it still averaged five per cent (World Bank 2004). But Korea was one of the hardest hit by the 1997–9 Asian financial crisis and went briefly, but sharply, into recession. Even though it recovered quickly, and more quickly than its neighbours, the psychological impact was enormous (Higgott 2000). The UNDP Report (1999) argued that 'the human impacts' of the 1997–9 crash in relatively successful East Asia were likely to persist 'long after economic recovery'.

The post-communist Czech economy had a rollercoaster ride. Following the 1991 'Velvet Revolution', Czechoslovakia liberalised the economy which then went into recession. But by the time of the 1993 'Velvet Divorce' from Slovakia, the Czech economy was moving towards positive growth which averaged two per cent per annum from 1994 to 2003 (World Bank 2004). There was another brief but sharp recession in 1997–8, however, as corruption was exposed during the privatisation of state assets, and unemployment rose sharply. Growth averaged almost three per cent per annum between 2000 and 2003 but memories of the recession, and of the corruption, lingered. As in Korea, improved statistics did not immediately boost public confidence.

Post-communist Ukraine experienced the worst economic performance. Inflation peaked at over ten thousand per cent in 1993 (Harasymiw 2002: p. 345) and the economy actually shrank by an average of over ten per cent per annum between 1991 and 1998 (Harasymiw 2002; World Bank 2004). The worst of the recession was in 1994, and the economy improved reasonably steadily after that, achieving good growth rates in the three years preceding our fieldwork. But Ukrainians still remained worse off than under communism and economic collapse was coupled with a growth in crime, especially organised crime linked to corrupt officials (Harasymiw 2002) – a combination that added insult to injury and produced extreme alienation between public and officials.

Although absolute levels of economic development were very low in Vietnam the trends were good, especially after the 'Doi Moi' ('national renewal') reform, which was initiated in 1986 and pursued more effectively after it was incorporated into the 1992 Constitution. The 1992

'Doi Moi Constitution' stressed 'expansion of economic, scientific and technical cooperation and exchange with the world market' and declared that 'the state encourages foreign organisations and individuals to invest capital and technologies ... and guarantees their lawful rights to owner-ship' (Article 25) while reasserting that 'the Communist Party ... is the force leading the State and the society' (Article 4) – albeit towards a market economy. Of our four countries, Vietnam had the highest growth of all for the period 1991–2003, averaging 7.5 per cent per annum with remarkably few disconcerting fluctuations. It suffered much less than Korea from the 1997–9 Asian crisis. Korea's average growth rate was 5.7 per cent for the same period, the Czech Republic's almost zero, and Ukraine's *minus* 4.1 per cent. Vietnamese growth slowed in the years immediately prior to our fieldwork and its FDI rates steadied or fell back slightly. But the Vietnamese experience of opening up the economy since 1986 had been the most consistently positive, in macroeconomic terms at least.

Political context None of the four countries had long-established democratic systems, but the Czech Republic and South Korea had undergone democratic transitions that appeared to be consolidating. The Czech Republic was rated as 'free' by Freedom House (2004) since 1993, and South Korea since 1988. Ukraine's transition to demo-cracy was considered incomplete and continued during our study, with the Orange Revolution at the end of 2004. Elections were marred by media harassment, biased reporting, and intimidation of candidates. Corruption was pervasive, and evidence of state violence pointed to an increasingly authoritarian presidency, particularly between 2002 and 2004. Freedom House (2004) rated it as only 'partly free'. Vietnam remained a one-party communist state. Economic reform was not matched by the same degree of political reform and the party state continued to control the judiciary, the trade unions, and the media, including the internet. Freedom to express views that differed from those of the leadership was limited (World Bank 2004). But while Vietnam cracked down hard on intellectuals promoting political reform or on hill tribes demanding religious freedoms, it permitted farmers and others to hold small-scale protests over local issues. Workers had staged 'dozens of strikes in recent years, generally against foreign and private companies' (Freedom House 2004). Spectacular economic growth con-tributed to the regime's 'performance-based legitimacy' which partially compensated for a lack of 'process-legitimacy'. Despite this, however, Vietnam was ranked by Freedom House (2004) as 'not free' and as 'one of the most tightly controlled countries of the world'.

2.2   Public perceptions of change

The public may not take the same view of their country as the World Bank, Freedom House, or the Fraser Institute (all based in north America). That does not mean they always took a more favourable view, however. Indeed they did not. Asked explicitly whether they viewed their country as 'backward, developing, or advanced', Czech focus group participants were split between describing their country as 'advanced' or 'developing'. Korean participants overwhelmingly opted only for 'developing' – inverting the rank-order assigned to these countries by international economists. Public psychology paid scant respect to economic statistics: 'nobody thinks we are an advanced country . . . we copy every technique, every process' (K2). (The codes, such as 'K2', which we use to identify participants, are explained in Chapter 1.4.)

Vietnamese participants were split between simply 'developing' and spontaneous descriptions such as 'developing but at a low level' (V18, V13) or 'developing but still backward' (V16) – all of which could be summarised as 'developing but'. Ukrainian participants simply lamented their decline, and for good reason; 'development' was not a term Ukrainians associated with Ukraine: 'decline' dominated their thoughts. The World Bank's 'lower middle income' would have seemed outrageous flattery to them.

Moreover, public perceptions of change encompassed not only national economic performance or personal living standards, but trends in crime, corruption and pollution; differential gains and losses by different sections of society; changing respect for national culture; and changing levels of national autonomy.

Public perceptions of economic trends

Overall, our surveys indicate that public perceptions of national economic trends were evenly balanced (a negligible 2 per cent net positive, i.e. per cent better minus per cent worse). Perceptions of family living standards were more positive (20 per cent net positive), however; and expectations of future trends in living standards even more so (38 per cent net positive).

Across these three indicators, both Koreans and Ukrainians were on balance pessimistic (net 9 per cent negative) though Ukrainian pessimism ran deeper than Korean: 34 per cent of Ukrainians compared with only 13 per cent of Koreans said their own family's standard of living had not merely got 'worse', but 'much worse' over the last five to ten years; and 30 per cent of Ukrainians compared with only 4 per cent of Koreans were

Table 2.1. *Economy and living standards*

	Officials %	Public %	Public within each country			
			Czech R %	Korea %	Ukraine %	Vietnam %
Over the last five to ten years ...						
... do you feel (COUNTRY'S) economy has got ...						
much better	23	22	4	2	6	77
a little better	39	27	34	23	32	19
a little worse	22	27	42	44	18	1
much worse	12	20	13	30	37	1
... has your own family's standard of living got ...						
much better	21	16	7	3	7	47
a little better	55	41	43	44	31	46
a little worse	15	24	31	38	22	4
much worse	4	13	7	13	34	0
Looking ahead to the next ten years ...						
... do you think we can expect living standards in (COUNTRY) to ...						
improve steadily	74	62	56	59	41	92
decline steadily	14	24	29	37	29	2

Note: Per cent of all respondents. Per cents giving other/mixed/'don't know' responses not shown.

so uncertain about the future that they felt unable even to hazard a guess about whether future living standards would be any better or worse.

By contrast, Czechs were on balance optimistic (net 7 per cent positive). They recognised their country's economy had declined but few felt it had declined by much. Their own living standards had improved, and they were even more confident about the future. Vietnamese perceptions of economic growth were almost off the scale. Although they differed in their perceptions of the degree of growth, an average of 95 per cent of Vietnamese felt both the economy and their own living standards had already improved and would continue to improve: 77 per cent thought the economy had not just got 'better', but 'much better'; and almost half thought their own living standards had got 'much better'.

Across the three indicators, officials were far more optimistic (net 48 per cent positive) than their publics (net 20 per cent). Significantly, the difference was most marked on perceptions of their own families' living standards (57 per cent net positive among officials, but only 20 per cent among the public).

The economic perceptions of focus group participants also varied from gloomy despair in Ukraine, through less fraught feelings of stagnation or decline in Korea, to more mixed feelings in the Czech Republic, and euphoria in Vietnam – a spectrum that matched economic *trends* better than *levels*. The euphoria of the public in the World Bank's 'low income' Vietnam contrasted with the still-shaken confidence of the public in its 'high income' Korea. Indeed, public perceptions reflected the steadiness of growth, as well as the average rate, since the average growth rate in Korea over the preceding decade was not far behind that in Vietnam. Yet Koreans remained depressed despite their growth statistics – just as the UNDP had forecast.

Only the Vietnamese were uniformly enthusiastic about economic trends. They attributed economic improvements 'to the Party, the state, the government and the people' (V2) or even to 'the government, the people, as well as the world' (V4). That may sound a little indiscriminate in distributing praise. But it was not. Indeed, quite the reverse. It was remarkably specific. Across Vietnam, the 'Party, state and government' were specifically praised, not for their communism, but for their 1990s policy reversal and reorientation towards 'market mechanisms' and an open economy. Participants stressed their enthusiasm for:

'the *new economic mechanism* and international connections' (V5); '[improvements] *since 1990*' (V18, V21); 'the *open door policy*' (V21); 'the *freer policies*' of 'the Party' (V32) or the 'state' (V9 with support from V16, V13, our emphases).

Vietnamese enthusiasm was in fact neither blind nor indiscriminate.

Czech views about the economy were no better than mixed: 'we produce more, but it's not visible' (C8); 'some movement forward, but nothing much' (C9). But Ukrainian attitudes plumbed the depths of despair despite several recent years of positive growth statistics:

'the economic situation in the country has worsened in every aspect' (U17); 'how good it used to be in our kolkhoz [collective farm during the communist era] … but now it is horrible' (U32).

Even their positive comments were ironic:

'our economy is acceptable for the time being – it has not been fully buried yet' (U9); 'in September the workers received their salaries for March – that is wonderful – the rise of the economy is right before our eyes' (U13, smiling).

There were two other significant characteristics to Ukrainian attitudes about the economy, both of which betrayed their sense of being cheated. First, like professional economists they distinguished between the national economy and typical living standards:

'our government reports that the main indicators are improving and that we expect rapid economic growth' (moderator); 'Yes, they speak about it a lot'

(U1); 'Yes, they erect more monuments' (U5); 'our government, our president, declare that the gross national product is increasing [but for] the family the situation has deteriorated sharply' (U16).

Second, they found it impossible to discuss the state of the economy without spontaneously distinguishing between the different experience of different 'strata':

'certain strata live better' (U8); '[but] the majority of people live worse' (U1, U6 agrees); '[and] the difference is very, very big' (U4).

In Korea the illusion of regular, dependable growth had collapsed. Even though the Korean economy had recovered from the crisis at the time of our fieldwork, the IMF intervention remained much in the minds of the public: 'the economy is not on the same level as pre-IMF' (K2), and the word 'unstable' kept recurring (K20, K33, K29). Koreans were aware of the statistics of the post-1999 recovery, and they expressed some hope for the future, but they had none of the Vietnamese euphoria. Korean participants were almost unanimous that they could look forward to a future of 'ups and downs' rather than steady improvement or decline.

Czechs too were uncertain about future economic trends despite the prospect of accession to the EU:

'There will be fluctuations' (C22); 'But we do not know what is ahead of us' (C21); 'I cannot imagine what this admission to the EU will bring about. I cannot really plan anything.' (C7); 'We can only guess what it will be like in the future.' (C25).

The few Koreans or Czechs who did expect a steady trend thought it would be one of improvement (K19, K1), if only a 'slow improvement' (C30, C3, C2, C8).

None of our Vietnamese participants expected a decline, and there was a general expectation of:

'a steady improvement' (V1, V5, V23); 'the speed of development will rise, the life of the people will be more improved' (V10, V11 agrees).

However, somewhat cryptically:

'This growth is good [but] we need to stabilise the politics to develop the economy' (V31); 'The policy changes can be effective but if the people do not change, it is difficult for Vietnam to develop' (V17).

There was nothing cryptic about Ukrainian participants' contributions, however: at the time (late 2002) they felt they had sunk so low they could hardly go lower, and they felt they needed a change in political leadership before the economy could improve. In the capital, Kyiv, the moderator's question about future *economic* trends produced an almost exclusively *political* response from the group:

'It may take a long time . . . before someone [worthy] . . . will get in the [Presidential] seat' (U5) . . . 'hopes are pinned on a change of leader . . . the President' (U6) . . . 'and those near to him' (U2) . . . 'so that they would deceive people less' (U4) . . . 'many people expected to have a woman President. Alas! Yulia Tymoshenko fell short of expectations' (U5) . . . 'However, as the saying goes, "hope dies last", so let us be hopeful' (U1) . . . 'A [new] leader is needed' (U3).

In Kharkiv, in the Russian-speaking east:

'God grant that it [the future economy] is at least the same as now' (U10) . . . 'the team at the top should go . . . They should have conceded their places a long time ago, not to friends, nor to relatives, but to people who are really truly competent' (U16) . . . 'They are competent, very competent' (U15, smiling ironically) . . . 'we have frittered away so much money that it would have been quite possible to buy a normal Prime Minister with a whole Cabinet in any country of the world' (U16).

In Kirovograd, central Ukraine:

'I am telling you that we will not have come to anything good [in the future economy].' (U32, angrily); 'It will be better only when none of the [parliamentary] deputies are businessmen.' (U25); 'They ought to be hard-working people.' (U31); 'There ought to be more deputies from the countryside.' (U25); 'But we will not live to see it happen.' (U26; U30 agrees); 'Maybe only if there is a change.' (U29); 'What sort of state is this if it divides people into its own children [the deputies] and stepchildren [ordinary people]? Who determines the deputy's salary?' (U30) . . . 'he who adopts the laws [i.e. the deputies]' (U28) . . . 'How can it be?' (U30, indignantly).

And in Zhytomir, western Ukraine:

'The situation will improve only when the authorities are changed completely . . . and the Constitution amended. By 80 per cent it does not work. Whether it's the Cabinet of Ministers that issue a decree or the Deputies who have passed a law, it does not work in reality. By the time that comes down from Kyiv, it is twisted hundreds of times. With these authorities and these public officials it will never improve' (U17; all agree);

'I reckon that only when the young come [to power will we get] change for the better . . . where everyone minds his own pockets there is no order . . . in a collective farm, in the city, everywhere' (U20) . . . 'the Ministries, they care only about themselves' (U24) . . . 'that is what I am talking about.' (U20) . . . 'They all need to be changed immediately and replaced with the young' (U22).

In every Ukrainian focus group – in the east, the west, or the capital – there was nothing but condemnation of the political and administrative elite for stuffing their own pockets and ruining the past performance and future prospects of the national economy. There was a lack of 'patriots' (U20) in high places, and not much hope of change for the better in the foreseeable future. Government was the problem, not the solution. Two years before the Orange Revolution they were already looking to a change of government – even of regime – as their only hope for a better future.

Public perceptions of growing inequality

On balance a majority of the public thought the rich had benefited more than the poor 'from recent economic changes in our country' (net 77 per cent), and that city dwellers had benefited more than those in villages or rural areas (net 69 per cent). To a lesser extent (net 39 per cent) the public thought the young had benefited more than the old.

But there were wide differences between countries. Ukrainians were the most likely to feel the rich had gained 'much more' (81 per cent) and Vietnamese the least (53 per cent) – though conversely, the Vietnamese were by far the most likely to feel that city-dwellers (65 per cent) or the young (53 per cent) had done 'much better' than village dwellers or the old. So while there were particularly strong perceptions of unequal beneficiaries in both countries, they focused on wealth, power and class in Ukraine but the somewhat less perverse inequalities of age and location in Vietnam.

Officials had similar perceptions to the public about the rich, urban dwellers and the young. But while the public thought their 'own family' had done *worse* (16 per cent net worse) than the 'typical family', officials thought their 'own family' had done *better* (12 per cent net better) than the typical family. Only the Vietnamese public felt that, on balance, their own family had done better than average (10 per cent net better).

There were particularly strong public perceptions of polarisation at the very extremes of wealth and poverty: 82 per cent felt the number of 'very rich' people in their country was increasing; and 64 per cent that the number of 'very poor' was increasing. Again, there were extreme differences between countries, however. Reflecting 'the IMF' and the Asian crisis, over twice as many Koreans (26 per cent) as others thought the number of 'very rich' was actually declining. Conversely, but for very different reasons, five times as many Vietnamese (86 per cent) as others thought the number of 'very poor' was declining. A simple index of extreme inequality, calculated by averaging the percentages who feel the numbers of 'very rich' and 'very poor' were both increasing, stands at 73 per cent overall, but ranges from only 50 per cent in Vietnam to 85 per cent in Ukraine (Table 2.3).

Table 2.2. *Perceived winners and losers*

	Officials %	Public %	Public within each country			
			Czech R %	Korea %	Ukraine %	Vietnam %
What kinds of people do you feel have benefited more or less than others from recent economic changes in our country?						
Rich or poor?						
rich much more	56	63	62	61	81	53
rich little more	26	22	28	35	10	15
poor little more	8	6	3	2	3	14
poor much more	2	2	0	1	1	7
Those who live in towns/cities or villages/farming areas?						
towns/cities much more	44	42	34	40	30	65
towns/cities little more	40	37	45	52	30	20
villages/farming areas little more	6	8	6	4	15	5
villages/farming areas much more	1	2	1	0	4	4
Young or old?						
young much more	26	27	16	19	24	53
young little more	36	34	38	41	34	21
old little more	18	17	20	27	12	8
old much more	4	5	6	5	4	3
Your own family – compared with the typical family in (COUNTRY)?						
own family much more	5	5	2	6	2	9
own family little more	38	24	23	17	21	31
typical family little more	27	35	35	55	27	24
typical family much more	4	10	12	8	12	6

Note: Per cent of all respondents. Per cents giving other/mixed/'don't know' responses not shown.

Greater economic inequality might be defended as an incentive. So to avoid an unthinking preference for the soft option of greater equality we reminded the public of the arguments for and against:

Some people say that having greater differences between rich and poor in a country encourages people to work harder or think up new ideas – so that the whole country gets richer. Others think that having greater differences between rich and poor is unfair and just encourages envy and crime.

Despite being confronted with the 'incentives' argument, however, the public condemned trends towards greater inequality and opted overwhelmingly for less inequality (77 per cent) rather than more (14 per cent). Only

Table 2.3. *More very rich, more very poor*

	Officials %	Public %	Public within each country			
			Czech R %	Korea %	Ukraine %	Vietnam %
Compared with five or ten years ago do you feel there are now ...						
... more very rich people in (COUNTRY)	83	82	85	70	82	89
... more very poor people in (COUNTRY)	57	64	74	83	88	10
Do you feel it would be better if there were ...						
... *greater differences* between rich and poor in (COUNTRY)	13	14	23	7	7	15
... *smaller differences* between rich and poor in (COUNTRY)	79	77	68	91	82	69

Note: Per cent of all respondents. Per cents giving other/mixed/'don't know' responses not shown.

the Czechs gave much support (23 per cent) to the incentives argument – though the Vietnamese, more surprisingly, came second (15 per cent).

Public perceptions of growing injustice

Growing inequality was certainly unpopular, but it might cause even more resentment if the benefits of development went visibly to the undeserving. A few focus group participants cited *deserving* winners, who had profited from effort, skill, initiative or at least luck:

'everybody has a chance' (C32); 'people who know how to do something and are not afraid to work have a chance to succeed' (C26); 'actors, football players' (C9); 'a lot depends on intuition, a good idea; those who set out to do business at the very beginning' (C23).

But more cited *undeserving* winners, who profited from already having more power, more resources, or at least better contacts:

'private moneylenders' (K27) ... 'the rich get richer, and the poor get poorer' (K26); 'assertive people ... those who had contacts' (C17); '[ex-communist] company managers ... so-called oligarchs ... wealthy people, they possess huge money' (U7); 'all the people here know perfectly well whom I am talking about – those who had the financial opportunities' (U28) . . . 'those who were at the helm . . . they carried everything away for themselves, bit by bit' (U31); 'many people privatized something [that they already controlled] . . . They "tunnelled" it [transl: Czech expression for asset stripping], got rich within three years' (C8).

In East Europe especially, they explicitly cited the corrupt as the main winners:

'Those who strive hard and those who swindle.' (C7); 'Those who knew how to take advantage of the immediate situation' (C25) . . . 'who know the ropes, who know how to abuse the gaps in the laws to their advantage and how to ensure that what they do will not be punishable' (C27); 'black marketeers.' (K31); 'Bribes also play a certain role' (C31; C32 agrees) . . . 'corruption, fraud' (C27).

'Do the benefits go to those who deserve them – by working harder or having better ideas and skills?' (Moderator) . . . 'These are exceptions' (all in group) . . . 'maybe not quite exceptions, but there are very few who made their way in business honestly' (U22); 'We used to have a bakery in [our village] – it was only its director who benefited from this market economy, and workers could not even get decent pensions, not a kopeck [penny]' (U2).

'The market economy works well where the living standard of the people is high, where the people are not as impoverished, as poor as we are . . . Here, profit is made primarily by people . . . who do not have outstanding professional qualities, but who have that businessman's wit' (U30) . . . 'practical [wit]' (U31 interjects) . . . 'yes, practical . . . it is only those people who are in power, who have a protector in the Verkhovna Rada [Parliament] and tax administration bodies for whom the road that lies ahead is so broad' (U30; all but one agree).

Even in Vietnam, this view could be heard, though more rarely:

'The number of corrupt people is still small. They do not exist in the market mechanism alone. They were found before. The difference is that they are so common today. If we knew ways of controlling things, we could reduce them' (V26); 'Bribery is the most burning issue nowadays' (V5) . . . 'the most problematic issue' (V1).

In survey interviews 62 per cent said the 'main reason' why some had benefited from recent changes more than others was 'more power', 'better contacts' or simple 'corruption' – rather than 'education, skill, ability' (25 per cent) or even 'luck' (6 per cent). Only the Vietnamese felt winners owed their success more to skill (51 per cent) than to 'power', 'contacts' or 'corruption' (29 per cent). At the other extreme, only 11 per cent of Ukrainians felt winners owed their success more to skill while 77 per cent attributed success to 'power', 'contacts' or 'corruption'. Czechs took a very similar view to Ukrainians, though with more emphasis on 'contacts' than actual 'power'. Koreans fell in between, though closer to the critical Czechs and Ukrainians than to the Vietnamese (Table 2.4).

Table 2.4. *Undeserving winners*

	Officials %	Public %	Public within each country			
			Czech R %	Korea %	Ukraine %	Vietnam %
In general what is the main reason why some have benefited more than others? Because they ...						
... have more education, skill or ability	34	25	14	25	11	51
... just had more luck	5	6	6	8	6	4
... already had more power	32	31	34	31	43	17
... have better contacts	14	19	33	15	20	7
... are corrupt	7	12	11	17	14	5

Note: Per cent of all respondents. Per cents giving other/mixed/'don't know' responses not shown.

Only a very few focus group participants, mainly in East Asia, cited ordinary people as the main beneficiaries of change:

'everybody in the market economy can get benefits' (K2; K7 agrees); 'everybody' (V27); 'different kinds of people' (V21); 'in general, Vietnamese people benefit more' (V12); 'both sides benefit – the foreigners have their revenue, we have jobs' (V13).

Others added qualifications:

'at present, the workers benefit as much as enterprise owners – though some private enterprises avoid paying social insurance, taking the benefit of the workers away' (V4).

More often, ordinary people denied that they got much benefit at all:

'not us ordinary people' (C28); 'not us' (U24); 'the people do not benefit' (U20); 'ordinary people have less access to opportunities than businessmen and government officials' (K8); 'ordinary people benefit because they can buy products of higher quality at lower price – of course, they may lose their jobs ... [in the IMF affair] ordinary people lost' (K22, supported by others); 'it is the ordinary people who suffer losses' (V15); 'those who participate in actual production suffer the biggest losses' (K15).

Still more often, participants focused their attention on winners rather than losers. Many cited local business as the chief beneficiary:

'the privileged' (K32); 'the propertied' (K22, K26, K33); 'larger enterprises' (K33); 'conglomerates' (K3; K20); 'major companies' (K5; K10); 'only major companies are competitive in the market' (K19); 'brokers rather than major companies ... merchants' (K15); 'middle merchants ... wholesalers' (K23) ... 'exploit and the producers get fewer benefits' (V12); '[merchants] get much more than farmers' (K21); 'businessmen benefit most' (V21; V26); 'enterprise owners are the ones to benefit the most ... they are dynamic and take control of their fate' (V4).

Others cited foreign businesses:

'foreigners' (K3; K23; C26; V5; V1); 'foreigners ... exploit our people and resources' (V32); '[local] opportunists – and foreigners too' (V21); 'we are cheap labour' (C11).

Especially in Ukraine they cited political or administrative elites. One Ukrainian put in a good word for a local politician:

'he entered parliament wearing torn trousers and he went away no better off' (U12).

But that was exceptional. Most Ukrainian participants felt the winnings went to power-holders:

'top-ranking officials' (U5); 'only high-placed people' (U2) ... 'those in power ... taking into account the corrupt nature of the system of government, they have certain advantages, unfortunately' (U8); 'those 300 millionaires in Parliament' (U28); 'business people' (U20) ... 'public officials' (U19, interrupting) ... 'yes, public officials. They lived well before, when they had the power. And now they are even better off. Those who had sat on Party Committees have now opened businesses because they had the money to do this' (U20; U22 agrees) ... 'those who rule, they benefit!' (U24, getting agitated).

Worse, Ukrainians alleged that officials acted as toll-collectors or gate-keepers, actually depressing the national economy in order to reap personal advantage. Who benefited most from letting foreign companies into Ukraine?:

'Those who authorize this all' (U17); 'those who let them in here ... government officials ... from the Ministry of Foreign Affairs or the Ministry of Foreign Economic Relations ... [selected foreign firms] are allowed to come in – this one is backed by a [local] acquaintance, that one by Ivan Ivanovych [transl: meaning a high official]' (U28); 'the chief executive [of the local plant] will sell the plant to that person to whom he has been told to sell it ... in each oblast [administrative region] there are 20 to 30 people who keep the whole oblast under their control' (U12); 'opening up the economy to the West is in principle of benefit to the ordinary people ... if it all really happens in an honest, open, and fair way ... But to government officials that is of no benefit ... that is why everything is done to discourage anyone [except friends of officials] from coming here' (U16) ... 'how could a big [local oblast] boss purchase several distilleries and several McDonald's restaurants, the price for the whole lot coming to three kopecks [almost nothing] if normal western capital were available?' (U12).

In terms of developing the local market economy:

'take our village council, the chairman benefits personally from having bars, shops, co-operatives opened … because he takes a bag – I know what I am talking about – and goes raiding those bars, shops, one by one' (U17) … 'a racket!' (U22).

Though such views were expressed most often and most forcefully in Ukraine, they were echoed elsewhere, even occasionally in Vietnam. The benefits went mainly to:

'politicians' (K33, K10); 'officials' (K16); 'those with power' (K10, K15); 'politicians' (C21); 'those in leading positions' (C11); 'politicians are the biggest thieves' (C3); 'officials' (V17) … 'officials get the most benefit. People who have new ideas do gain benefits, but not much' (V18); 'businessmen benefit most, then governmental officials' (V18); 'ordinary people benefit least, then come businessmen … those who benefit most are government officials' (V3); 'government officials are those who benefit most, then enterprise owners, farmers benefit least' (V16).

In survey interviews the public cited 'high-ranking government officials' (30 per cent) as the top beneficiaries, followed by local businessmen (23 per cent) and foreigners (21 per cent). By contrast, officials themselves put (local) businessmen top (28 per cent), followed by foreigners (22 per cent), with 'high-ranking government officials' only in third place (at 17 per cent).

Only the Vietnamese put 'ordinary people' anywhere near the top (17 per cent, compared with no more than 7 per cent elsewhere). Indeed, the Vietnamese actually cited 'ordinary people' 2 per cent more often than 'high-ranking government officials' (15 per cent) – while Czechs and Ukrainians were over six times as likely to cite 'high-ranking government officials' (39 per cent) as 'ordinary people' (6 per cent). The Vietnamese put local businessmen top (19 per cent), just ahead of 'ordinary people' (17 per cent) though an unusually large number of Vietnamese (23 per cent) cited a mixture of beneficiaries.

In terms of countries, both the public and officials cited 'richer and more powerful countries' as the chief beneficiary – by margins of 34 per cent among officials and 44 per cent among the public. Czechs and Ukrainians were close to that overall average. But the Vietnamese were about equally likely to cite Vietnam as to cite 'richer and more powerful countries'. At the other extreme, Koreans overwhelmingly cited 'richer and more powerful countries' (89 per cent) rather than Korea (a mere 8 per cent). And Koreans were especially likely to volunteer 'the US'

Table 2.5. *Foreigners and high officials benefit most*

	Officials %	Public %	Public within each country			
			Czech R %	Korea %	Ukraine %	Vietnam %
Which of these do you feel benefit most from opening up our economy to the world-wide market?						
high-ranking government officials	17	30	38	27	39	15
local officials	1	3	2	2	3	5
businessmen – I mean (COUNTRY) businessmen	28	23	17	29	25	19
foreigners	22	21	29	30	14	12
ordinary people	13	9	5	7	7	17
(VOL) the US	7	9	5	20	6	4
richer and more powerful countries (incl. volunteered 'US')	58	64	67	89	63	33
(COUNTRY) ie the respondent's own country	24	20	19	8	19	32

Note: Per cent of all respondents. Per cents giving other/mixed/'don't know' responses not shown. VOL indicates that a particular answer was not offered by the interviewer, but was spontaneously volunteered by some respondents.

(20 per cent) rather than merely opt for the phrase 'richer and more powerful countries' used by our interviewers. In economic terms, the Korean public harboured far deeper suspicion and greater resentment towards their long-term ally than did the Vietnamese towards their erstwhile enemy. So in public perspectives on foreign countries as beneficiaries, in contrast to public perspectives on their own governments, the great divide in popular opinion was (very unusually) within Asia rather than between East Asia and East Europe.

While the public generally felt richer and more powerful countries had been the chief beneficiaries of their own country's exposure to global markets that, in itself, did not imply malicious intent. To distinguish perceptions of accidentally differential benefit from malicious intent we asked explicitly about: (i) exploitation by foreign companies; (ii) powerful countries like the US or blocs like the EU 'fixing the rules' of trade in their own favour; and (iii) whether international organisations like the WTO, IMF or World Bank could be expected to work in the interests of poor countries and, in particular, to treat the respondent's country fairly. Focus group participants were critical of all three, though much less critical of companies than of countries or international organisations. Despite recognising that companies were driven by profit maximisation the public could see tangible benefits from foreign companies.

Foreign companies Did foreign companies merely exploit local people and resources or make a valuable contribution to development?

'both' (U16, V25); 'they both exploit and contribute – though their target is profit' (V21); 'they seek their own interests, but we also gain' (K30); 'those [companies] that came here in the first wave [after the collapse of communism] only sought short-term profits [but] those that came in the second wave were a benefit' (C18); '[foreign companies act] exclusively for their own benefit, but ... in McDonald's, undergraduate girls earn more than the lecturers in their institute' (U12).

Some voiced unqualified criticism:

'foreign investors come to Korea because they judge that it is profitable ... then they withdraw the bulk of their money when things change' (K16); 'they are not pure-minded' (K13); 'they exploit our people and resources' (V32); 'just as we give basic tasks to Malaysians and Filipinos, high-tech foreign companies do not reveal their know-how or technologies [to us]' (K33); 'our people are absolutely unprotected [against foreign companies]' (U20, U22 and U24 agree); 'we are cheap labour. Their workers [in their own countries] must be paid – ours do not have to be ... they exploit us' (U23; U19 nods agreement).

But such criticism was outweighed by praise for better wages for workers or better service for consumers:

'they are a plus' (C7); 'good for the country's budget' (C1); 'they create jobs' (C30); 'they employ our people' (C21); 'our people ... will work for anyone who pays' (U19, U18 agrees); 'a benefit ... absolutely' (C5); 'they make a contribution' (V9, V16); 'a contribution to the development of our economy' (V1); 'they help' (U20, U22, U19); 'they come in and create more jobs for us [and] pay rather high salaries' (V5).

'Tesco: that is a benefit' (C0); 'I used to live in a small town and there was only one supermarket there and it was expensive. It makes you angry, if you don't have a Tesco, that there is no competition' (C6); 'remember our [former communist-era] self-service shops!' (C4).

Even those who complained of exploitation, usually welcomed it:

'they get more benefit, but they make a contribution to creating new jobs' (V18); 'they contribute more than exploit' (V23, K6 similar); 'we are exploited but get good pay' (U3); 'at least foreign companies pay much more' (U5); 'they exploit but ... this exploitation is still to the better because if there were no exploitation, it is not clear whether these people would have employment at all' (U8); '[workers]

Table 2.6. *Foreign companies exploit us*

	Officials %	Public %	Public within each country			
			Czech R %	Korea %	Ukraine %	Vietnam %
On balance, foreign companies ...						
help a lot	15	14	5	12	10	28
help a little	47	38	33	50	34	34
exploit a little	26	29	44	31	28	10
exploit a lot	5	9	10	3	19	6

Note: Per cent of all respondents. Per cents giving other/mixed/'don't know' responses not shown.

would have been exploited just the same by the State and would have received less' (U7, U8 agrees).

So even recognised exploitation did not necessarily cause resentment if there was no better alternative. There was an element of 'please come and exploit me' or 'better to be exploited by foreign companies than by state enterprises' in some of these comments.

To quantify these perceptions we asked survey respondents whether foreign companies were 'good because they bring new technology and investment and help our economy grow or bad because they exploit our low-paid people and cheap resources'. There was a clear divide between public perceptions in East Asia where by a margin of 37 per cent on average the public felt foreign companies 'help', and East Europe where more felt foreign companies 'exploit' rather than 'help'. Within East Asia, the Vietnamese were much more positive about foreign companies even than Koreans. More significantly, however, within East Europe, Czechs were even more negative about foreign companies than Ukrainians. That contrasts with generally more negative perceptions in Ukraine than in the Czech Republic. But Ukrainians blamed their own government more than foreign companies for their troubles.

Foreign countries Focus group participants were almost unanimous in their condemnation of the unfair and unjust behaviour of powerful countries or blocs, such as the US or EU. If any participants held contrary views, they very seldom chose to voice them with much conviction:

'they treat us rather kindly' (V12); 'they want to fix the rules within our country [but] I think that they are suitable. We only protest against those doing harm to our independence or interests' (V4).

Some critics expressed understanding of the problems of foreign power-holders. Did Czechs feel that the EU treated them fairly?

'I do not think so. The EU is pressed by [member] governments' (C8); 'there are many lobbying groups there who always want to protect their interests. The EU tries to play fair, but the reality is different' (C2); 'they dictate conditions that we should observe. We are sort of poor relations' (C25); 'but when we become an EU member, we will also start to dictate, we will also be pushy' (C30).

Far more typically, however, they alleged, without qualification or excuse, that powerful countries and blocs simply 'fixed the rules':

'it is inevitable that they seek their own national interests – but they seem to go too far' (K19); 'they fix the rules to favour themselves' (V5, V31); 'always fix the rules' (V18, V21 agrees); 'for example, on agricultural products' (K32); 'we pay huge amounts of money to a foreign company . . . as a royalty . . . [but] the USA hampers our exports' (K27); 'the EU is a result of regionalism, seeking their regional interests' (K23); 'they treat everybody like this, the Americans' (C24); 'they do not have any culture' (C20); 'they will not come here with open arms' (C21); 'there was a conflict about [Ukrainian manufactured] CDs . . . Ukraine had to agree' (U19); 'who ever wants another state to get richer?' (U17).

What is most striking are the discussions of rule-fixing that we cannot report – because there were none: in several Korean or Ukrainian groups participants were so unanimous that powerful countries 'fixed the rules' that there was little more than a general chorus, 'of course', in answer to the moderator's question.

International organisations Participants were also unanimous about the unfair and unjust behaviour of international organisations 'like the WTO, IMF and World Bank'.

'they never act fairly' (V18); 'they favour big countries like USA because it can contribute more money' (V4, V25 similar); 'they defend the interests of the USA' (C2); 'small countries always get disadvantages' (V21); 'the World Bank reprimands us for our [state] deficit and yet ours is lower than that of the USA' (C11); '[treatment] is based on the size of our country' (C22); 'on our economic significance' (C18); 'they rob us smiling and in a decent way' (C21); 'but that is what everybody does' (C18).

In Korea, attitudes towards the unfairness of international organisations were so unanimously and so strongly negative that the moderator always moved the discussion on by asking whether Korea should therefore *withdraw* from these organisations. Paradoxically, Korean participants always combined strong and unanimous criticism with a firm and unanimous view that Korea should remain a member. Withdrawal would be:

'too much' (K32); 'because we would lose more' (K33:); 'we need to reform them' (K1); 'stay in reluctantly . . . at some time we may benefit from them' (K32);

'if we become more powerful later?' (moderator); 'exactly!' (K32); 'we need to grow our power' (K19); 'to have an iron hand in the velvet glove' (K26); 'because we will be powerful sometime in the future' (K14).

Like others, Ukrainians criticised the bias and unfairness of international organisations:

'they serve the interests of big and powerful countries' (U7, all nod agreement); 'they influence us, and that influence is strong' (U32); 'they dictate to us' (U25, U26 agrees); 'dictate . . . there were the cases of our CDs . . . our metallurgy, and of the [chicken] legs from Bush . . . He who pays the money orders the tune' (U28); 'they are . . . under American control . . . they advance . . . the interests of its businessmen' (U12); 'Ukraine was turned into a market for selling junk' (U32); 'our poverty brought us down to our knees' (U30).

But, unlike others, Ukrainians blamed their *own government* for their problems with international organisations – often *defending* the international organisations themselves. International credits had been misused or siphoned-off by Ukrainian power-holders:

'somehow we do not feel the impact of the investment of those credits' (U28); 'just take a look at the way people live!' (U30); 'unfortunately, that is high politics' (U28); 'many of us heard about those tranches – $250 million . . . Have we felt that money? Ten years have passed. Where are they, those tranches?' (U17); 'it has never come down to [our] level' (U19);
   'suppose our state received a credit, one million for example. A year passed by . . . Was there any improvement in the life of U31, a pensioner, or U27, a young man? Did it change at least by one rouble for the better? If there was no benefit then it simply makes no sense to feed people like Lazarenko, Tymoshenko, or Vitrenko [prominent politicians]. All of that [credit] was deposited in Swiss banks' (U30);
   'if we borrow money from them [the IMF, the World Bank] then we must . . . explain what we spent all that money on. But to borrow that money and give it to the [parliamentary] deputies?' (U25); '[international organisations] have no incentive to develop countries which, after taking a credit, use it to the wrong purposes. The money vanishes, and nothing comes out it' (U2); 'our grand-children will have to return these credits. International trade organisations will squeeze such credits back anyway' (U4);
   'I think that [the IMF] is unjustifiably criticised . . . the government failed to use [its aid] properly. [Other countries] managed to do so, repaid the debts and forgot about them, continue to live excellently. Spain has already completely forgotten what those loans are [because Spain] coped with that issue. But if you do not know how to borrow properly then, I am sorry . . .' (U16); 'our government is unable to distribute [loans] properly, to invest in something' (U14).

Although the public everywhere except Vietnam expected international organisations to work mainly in the interests of rich countries, they none-theless expected to get fair treatment more often from 'international

Table 2.7. *International organisations are unfair, but less unfair than foreign countries*

	Officials %	Public %	Public within each country			
			Czech R %	Korea %	Ukraine %	Vietnam %
How often would you expect big and powerful countries to act fairly towards countries like ours?						
usually	11	10	12	7	8	11
sometimes	36	33	36	43	28	22
rarely	35	36	36	41	37	28
never	10	12	7	7	16	18
How often would you expect international organisations like the WTO, IMF and World Bank to act fairly towards countries like ours?						
usually	22	18	19	11	11	27
sometimes	41	35	34	49	31	23
rarely	22	26	28	31	32	17
never	5	7	5	7	11	4
Do you feel that international organisations like the WTO, IMF and World Bank work mainly in the interests of . . .						
poor countries	17	17	10	11	9	33
rich countries	56	56	61	74	64	26
(VOL) the US	5	8	9	13	6	3

Note: Per cent of all respondents. Per cents giving other/mixed/'don't know' responses not shown. VOL indicates that a particular answer was not offered by the interviewer, but was spontaneously volunteered by some respondents.

organisations like the WTO, IMF and World Bank' than from 'powerful countries like the USA'. Only 18 per cent of the public (27 per cent in Vietnam, but only 11 per cent in Korea or the Czech Republic) expected they would 'usually' get fair treatment from *international organisations* – but that was almost twice as many as expected they would 'usually' get fair treatment from *powerful countries*. Their expectations were never very high, but much higher with respect to the international community than with respect to powerful states driven by national interest. To a very limited but nonetheless valuable extent, international organisations provided some protection (See Table 2.7).

Yet public perceptions of *international organisations* driven by the national interests of powerful countries within them still seem less positive than public perceptions of foreign or *international companies* driven by profit-seeking. Koreans in particular, still bitter about the IMF's role in the Asian crisis, were at once more positive (28 per cent net positive) than the average (14 per cent net) about foreign companies, and yet more negative (76 per cent net negative) than average (47 per cent net) about international organisations acting in the interests of 'rich' countries – a category in which the Korean public, unlike the World Bank, did not place Korea.

Public perceptions of trends in crime, corruption and pollution

Though they admitted their perceptions were based mainly on the media or on hearsay rather than on direct experience, focus group participants in every country thought crime and corruption were increasing.

There was wide agreement that lack of order, lack of strict laws, and the loose morals of the young were to blame for increasing crime and corruption. But the public did not cite development as the cause of increasing crime and corruption: it was rising inequality rather than development itself that they blamed for crime and corruption. Especially in Vietnam, rising crime and corruption was blamed on *economic growth*. But in others, they were linked in the public mind to *economic decline*: either increasing crime and corruption was blamed on economic decline; or, especially in Ukraine, economic decline was itself blamed on corruption.

Rising inequality, crime and corruption caused most anger in Ukraine and least in Vietnam. In Vietnam, they were all linked by focus group participants to globalisation and development – but as part of the necessary price of progress. They were reluctant to blame officials. Indeed they quoted their leaders' warnings:

'the late president Nguyen Van Linh said that "when we open the door, fortune comes in and so do the flies" – as the economy grows, social evils, prostitution, motor racing [presumably speeding on public roads, not the sport] and drugs for example, also increase rapidly – opening brings social evils' (V4).

Vietnamese participants viewed social evils as inextricably linked not only to greater openness but to economic growth itself – linked to the end as well as to the means:

'as the economy grows, people's lives get better and so do the temptations' (V13); 'in every society, criminals increase as the economy increases' (V25); 'the market economy has both positive and negative aspects' (V27).

Uniquely, Vietnamese perceptions of growing inequality were also framed in terms of countries rather than individuals within Vietnam – so perceptions of growing inequality, in its international dimension, served to unite the Vietnamese rather than divide them. They attributed this adverse trend to impersonal forces, to their own inadequacy, and to incomplete or unenthusiastic globalisation:

'Vietnam has not fully integrated into the [ASEAN] region and the world' (V21); 'the life of people in many countries is improved through globalisation – but the difference between the rich and the poor countries is increasing because the education and trade knowledge between them are unequal – and because some [poor] countries support development while others resist' (V12); '[because] rich countries have more scientific knowledge' (V1); '[because] poor countries have low technology and education' (V27); '[because they lack] initial investment capital [and because] the mechanism of rich countries is freer, making business and development easier – in Vietnam, the incomplete [market] mechanism results in bigger hindrances' (V5).

Ironically, of course, Vietnam itself was not only growing fast in absolute terms, but actually closing the gap with developed countries such as Japan or Europe (with faster growth rates in both GDP and UNDP-HDI) and not falling further behind.

In complete contrast, at the other extreme, Ukrainians detected not just an increase but an *explosion* of crime, corruption and inequality; and they viewed their own politicians, officials and power-holders as the problem not the solution. They detailed – at great length – the explosive growth of crime and corruption which, in turn, exacerbated the problem of interpersonal inequality not only by increasing it, but by doing so without any mitigating moral or functional justification. There was alleg-edly a vicious circle: those at the top chose corruption to get richer and thereby forced those at the bottom into crime merely to survive. For Ukrainians increasing crime and corruption were *not consequences of devel-opment* as in Vietnam, but *causes of decline*.

Crime and corruption was also 'a major issue' (C24) in the Czech Republic. But, unlike Ukraine, allegations focused mainly on the very top elite, they were vague and unspecific, derived from media-coverage not from the more immediate experience cited by Ukrainians, and they lacked the depth of anger found in Ukrainian comments:

'in our country, corruption is the highest' (C1, C0 agrees); 'stealing is quite widespread in our economy' (C2); 'I think it goes up steeply' (C27); 'same as everywhere – lots of bribery, fraud, going around the laws' (C14);
   'I have not done it [bribery] myself yet but I know this happens' (C6); 'it exists here but it is lower than in Prague' (C12); 'only based on what you read in the papers, one can't find out about it in any other way' (C4); 'the place where I live is relatively all right, but what I have seen on TV, that is really horrible' (C17); 'we hear it on TV all the time that it is like this, but TV prefers to show bad news' (C21);
   'politicians are the biggest thieves' (C3); 'we can see it on TV: politicians just rake in money' (C4); 'I think that lots of people who are in Parliament abuse their positions to arrange deals for someone, state contracts and things like that' (C2);

'everybody lies … when [a politician] wants to be a President, he says completely contradictory things and he is not at all ashamed of what he is doing' (C7); 'state administration, that is a trough beyond price. That is where corruption exists. That is where I would come in to a lot of money. That is where one does not need any salary' (C3).

The overwhelming majority of Korean participants also felt crime and corruption were increasing. But in addition to complaints about 'morality having lost its hold' especially on 'young people' (K13), about the 'credit card culture' (K29, K28, K4) which encouraged debt, and about a lack of discipline especially in 'traffic' (K25) or in 'public washrooms' (K25), they had two peculiarly Korean explanations for it: 'the IMF' and 'local autonomy'. They attributed growing crime and corruption to:

'close relationships between business and political circles during the IMF period' (K4); 'businesses felt quite insecure going through the IMF only two to three years ago – through those years they gradually turned to shortcuts' (K3); 'both politics and business are not transparent' (K32); 'Presidents often give special pardons to the corrupt' (K25);

and to 'local autonomy':

'the problems of factions, school relations [a source of lifelong loyalties in Korea] and regionalism are serious – corruption is a natural result' (K10); 'the corruption of officials is getting more serious – local autonomy turned out to be not so much good as bad' (K16).

Overall, our surveys indicate that the public sensed increasing crime and corruption (58 per cent net increase) and pollution (35 per cent net increase). But in Ukraine, 64 per cent felt crime and corruption were increasing 'a lot', compared with a mere 5 per cent in Vietnam. Indeed Vietnam was the only country where more of the public claimed crime and corruption were decreasing rather than increasing.

Perceptions of rising pollution also varied sharply. In Ukraine, 67 per cent felt pollution and environmental damage were getting 'much worse', compared with only 9 per cent in the Czech Republic – the only country where more of the public said pollution was decreasing (64 per cent) rather than increasing (30 per cent). So Ukrainians were the most pessimistic on both counts while the Vietnamese were the most optimistic about crime and corruption, and Czechs the most optimistic about pollution. Overall, a majority attributed trends in crime and corruption, and in pollution, to local rather than foreign influences.

Officials took a significantly more optimistic view than their publics, both about crime and corruption (45 per cent net increasing, compared with 58 per cent net among the public) and pollution (22 per cent net increasing, compared with 35 per cent net among the public).

Table 2.8. *Perceived trends in crime, corruption and pollution*

	Officials %	Public %	Public within each country			
			Czech R %	Korea %	Ukraine %	Vietnam %
Do you feel crime and corruption in (COUNTRY) are ...						
increasing a lot	30	39	49	36	64	7
increasing a little	38	35	43	52	20	23
decreasing a little	17	11	6	10	8	21
decreasing a lot	6	5	0	1	2	21
Do you feel that pollution and environmental damage in (COUNTRY) are getting ...						
much worse	30	37	9	31	67	41
a little worse	30	29	21	50	21	24
a little better	31	25	51	18	7	22
much better	7	6	13	2	2	9
Has this trend in crime and corruption been caused ...						
more by the changing attitudes of our people and officials	50	51	52	75	59	20
more by foreign influences	27	29	40	18	24	33
Has this trend in pollution been caused ...						
more by the changing attitudes of our people and officials	66	68	62	80	66	63
more by foreign influences	15	17	26	12	15	13

Note: Per cent of all respondents. Per cents giving other/mixed/'don't know' responses not shown.

In Vietnam and Korea focus group participants saw pollution as the price of economic development while in Ukraine it was seen as the consequence of economic decay. But Czech participants, like survey respondents, actually thought their environment was improving – despite the impact of more cars, and recent floods that had exposed the problems of riverside factories:

'the air is better, cars now have to be equipped with catalytic converters' (C14, C9); 'river waters have improved, they are clean now' (C14); 'fish are returning to our rivers' (C24, C19); 'waste is now being recycled' (C14, C32).

Everyone in Vietnam agreed pollution was a consequence of development. One suggested people 'do not dare to fight [i.e. protest against pollution] because of fear of involvement' (V33). But for most Vietnamese, it was an *avoidable* consequence – caused as much by the 'low educational level of the people' (V21), 'people's [lack of] awareness' (V17, V5, V9, V12 similar) or the lack of 'environment-cleansing technology' (V4) as by development itself. 'We just care about solving current problems and do not take into account their long-term consequences' (V18).

After the 'IMF' shock, Korean participants explicitly prioritised growth above the environment:

'as the economy grows, consumption increases and problems such as disruption of the ecosystem are inevitable – nevertheless the economy should grow' (K8); 'we must lure factories in spite of air pollution – it will bring back young people and development' (K16).

On the bright side, the IMF event – never far from Koreans' thoughts – was for once presented as a solution rather than a problem:

'there are many bankrupt companies since the period of IMF – for that reason, industrial waste has decreased' (K29); '[despite] problems when the buildings and materials of bankrupt companies are not properly disposed of' (K28).

Only one Ukrainian saw anything positive being done to reduce pollution. Most pointed to pollution remaining the same or getting worse: forests were being polluted by 'garbage' and destroyed by 'felling' (U16). Agricultural pollution was blamed on:

'the 1986 Chernobyl accident ... the 1970s and 1980s chemicalisation of our agriculture, and the collapse of agriculture in 1991' (U28, supported by all in group).

Urban pollution was blamed on poverty and corruption rather than growth:

'streets are packed with automobiles and the volume of exhaust is just awful' (U7); 'the water and air in Kyiv are polluted, and the health of children is worsening with every year' (U3); 'foreign car manufacturers like Volvo often install special filters to purify the exhaust but Ukrainians cannot afford them' (U5); '[and] oil traders [blocked a switch to LPG engines because they] would lose much money' (U2).

As in Korea, Ukrainians pointed grimly to:

'the good side of bad luck – the air has become cleaner only because the giant plants have been at a standstill' (U13, supported by everyone in the group); 'the environment has improved a bit, automatically so to speak, as factories have been shut – so the river got cleaner' (U17, U19 agrees); 'fewer tractors on the collective farm, so the air got cleaner, too – but only weeds grow in our fields' (U20); 'cornflowers instead of wheat' (U22); 'everything ruined – what a farm it was, such a collective farm' (U24).

Overall therefore, the public perceptions of increasing crime and corruption, pollution and environmental damage contributed to public discontent in our four countries. It was especially severe in Ukraine. But there were some bright spots. Czechs felt their problems of pollution and environmental damage were decreasing and cited evidence for that. Vietnamese survey respondents claimed that crime and corruption were actually decreasing. Vietnamese focus group participants did not make that claim, but in contrast to East Europeans they blamed it not on their government and officials, nor even on foreigners as such, but on the increasing temptations that flowed from successful economic development itself.

Public perceptions of national autonomy and cultural change

Overall, the public felt their country's 'most important policies' were determined more by 'world markets and powerful international organisations' (58 per cent) than by what their own citizens wanted (25 per cent). Perceptions of this lack of national autonomy were most widespread in the Czech Republic (79 per cent) and least in Vietnam (16 per cent). The Czechs lived of course in a very small country, surrounded by larger states, and were on the brink of joining the EU.

The Vietnamese were also the most likely to feel their 'traditional way of life remained strong' rather than 'getting lost': over twice as many Vietnamese (46 per cent) as Czechs (20 per cent) or Koreans (19 per cent) thought it 'remained strong'. Ukrainians were less pessimistic about their traditional way of life than Czechs or Koreans but not as optimistic as the Vietnamese: 28 per cent thought their culture 'remained strong'. By majorities of 29 and 38 per cent respectively, both the Czechs and the Koreans felt their 'language, culture and traditions' were *less respected* than in the past. By contrast the Vietnamese, by a margin of 69 per cent felt their 'language, culture and traditions' were *more respected* than in the past. In Ukraine we asked separately about Ukrainian and Russian 'language, culture and traditions'. By a margin of 55 per cent, respondents in Ukraine thought 'the Ukrainian language, culture and traditions' was *more* respected than in the past, though by a margin of 16 per cent they also felt the Russian 'language, culture and traditions' was *less* respected.

Overall, a majority attributed these trends to local rather than foreign influences, though Czechs were evenly divided while Koreans, Vietnamese to a greater degree, and Ukrainians to an overwhelming degree, cited local influences.

In focus groups, too, both Czechs and Koreans felt their language, culture and traditions were under threat from globalisation. In reality

Table 2.9. *National autonomy and culture*

	Officials %	Public %	Public within each country			
			Czech R %	Korea %	Ukraine %	Vietnam %
In today's world, do you feel (COUNTRY)'s policies on most important matters are determined more by ...						
world markets and powerful international organisations	59	58	79	65	65	16
more by what (COUNTRY) people want	25	25	8	29	16	49
Which comes closer to your view? Our traditional way of life ...						
... is getting lost	64	62	68	80	59	39
... remains strong	27	28	20	19	28	46
Compared with 10 or 20 years ago do you feel that (COUNTRY'S) language, culture and traditions these days are ...						
... much more respected than 10 or 20 years ago	31	28	5	8	38 (10)	65
... a little more respected than 10 or 20 years ago	27	25	26	23	35 (24)	18
... a little less respected than 10 or 20 years ago	26	28	37	48	11 (30)	12
... much less respected than 10 or 20 years ago	12	13	23	21	7 (20)	2
Do you feel these changes in respect have been caused ...						
more by the changing attitudes of our people and officials	60	58	44	57	70	62
more by foreign influences	29	31	45	36	14	25

Note: Per cent of all respondents. Per cents giving other/mixed/'don't know' responses not shown. Figures in brackets show Ukrainian responses to a similar question about respect for the 'Russian' language, culture and traditions.

Korean culture was perhaps no more under threat than Czech – and perhaps less so. But Koreans cared more about their unique culture and about differentiating themselves from other cultures. Vietnamese participants felt able to at least preserve their culture and Ukrainian focus group participants were the most confident of all – about Ukrainian culture if not about Russian culture. Ukrainian participants felt there was increasing respect for Ukrainian culture, traditions, and above all language – even if many Russian-speaking Ukrainians had difficulty speaking

Ukrainian well. In the relatively Russian-speaking capital, Kyiv, specifically 'Ukrainian' culture, traditions and language:

'seem to be more respected in general' (U5, U7, U6); 'first-graders and pre-schoolers are increasingly beginning to speak Ukrainian' (U5, U6 agrees); 'partly this attitude is cultivated in school, but self-confidence has also risen' (U5); 'when I went to school, I thought of Ukrainian as something unnecessary – we began to study it in fourth grade as a foreign language' (U7);

though a sceptical Ukrainian-speaking teacher claimed that:

'parents send their children to schools with instruction in Ukrainian only because they want them to know the "state language" which may be useful later in applying to a university or to Kyiv Mohyla Academy – however, I know that these children speak Russian at home . . . I do not say that they study Ukrainian under compulsion but . . .' (U3, U6 agrees).

There was no feeling among participants that specifically Ukrainian culture was under threat. Indeed Ukrainian complaints about Ukrainian culture focused on its resurgence rather than its decline. Participants in the ethnically-Russian and Russian-speaking city of Kharkiv in eastern Ukraine almost equated Russian with English, complaining that Russian-speaking Ukrainians:

'should not be obliged to know Ukrainian at any cost – or to know English at any cost' (U14); '[but] it is necessary now to know Ukrainian' (U9); '[and] for us, that is very hard' (U16).

At the opposite extreme, the vast majority of Korean participants felt their language, culture and traditions were less respected than in the past. There were some consolations, however. Even if English was spreading, 'words from the Japanese occupation are disappearing' (K1). One participant saw 'more efforts than ever before to preserve' (K5) Korean language, culture and traditions. Korean identity and culture were more widely recognised internationally – in part as a result of Korea's highly successful staging of the 2002 World Cup football contest:

'Korean people are proud of their nationality after the World Cup' (K30); 'there is a tendency to replace our traditional culture with new culture, but it is good for foreign countries to know more about us – and we held the World Cup games' (K29).

But Korea was one of the most wired-up societies on the planet: internet penetration was 67 per cent in Korea (www.internetworldstats.com), about the same as Japan and the US. So the internet as well as foreign films and TV, was a threat:

'because of internet chatting, our language has changed and been badly affected' (K18); 'college students in their early twenties are so poor at grammar, most of them write without final consonants' (K8); 'listen to the speech of children – there are big differences from five or ten years ago – they use foreign words too much – and slang also' (K27); 'English, Chinese, and Japanese languages are regarded as more important than Korean owing to globalisation' (K12); 'when you look for a job, English is the first requirement' (K11).

Korean traditions placed great emphasis on respect for the old. One or two participants felt such traditions were being maintained. But most felt they were now:

'disregarded' (K25); 'in the past, the young left seats for the old in a bus but nowadays they pretend to sleep' (K24); 'when I was young, I was not able to smoke in public – but these days, the young ask the old for a light for cigarettes' (K23).

Younger participants confirmed the generation gap:

'the young are not interested in traditions – to be honest, I am not interested in traditional culture '(K12, supported by K11).

Czechs also thought their culture – in terms of music, human relations and especially cuisine – was being eroded by tourism, development, and lack of interest among the young:

'older people perhaps preserve it, but young ones do not have time for it' (C11); 'music has declined' (C26); 'people are forgetting about history' (C20, C18 agrees); 'there is less culture – we have hamburgers' (C7).

Economic growth had made personal relations:

'worse than before, when people had less' (C27); 'families stick together until there is an inheritance' (C25); 'if you want to punish your children, give them a house to share' (C32).

Vietnamese participants, like Czechs and Koreans, sensed that young people were drifting away from their national culture. Many, as in the survey, claimed they were able to at least preserve their national culture – but qualifications and doubts kept bubbling up in the focus group discussions, in a way that was impossible in a more formal survey interview. Some were overtly complacent and balanced increasing international respect against declining local interest:

'although we are integrating, we preserve our traditions well – and our traditional arts are welcomed abroad' (V4); 'in the integration for economic development, both rich and poor countries have to accept the rules of the game – we have to understand each other – they have to understand us – they generally respect us' (V31).

But others admitted there were 'exceptions':

'our traditions and morals are preserved – except for some young people' (V33).

Or that traditions were preserved only by political will:

'we can preserve our traditions because of the resolution of the Communist Party. Observing that our traditions and culture tend to disappear, the Party has made resolutions, which have won the support of the people' (V4).

This is an altogether less confident perspective on national culture than in Ukraine, where people *complained* about the strength of their national culture. Other Vietnamese participants doubted the effectiveness of such artificial political action:

'as the Party resolution states, we are trying to preserve the national culture but, actually, we have not succeeded – for example, our language is affected, everyday life is influenced by foreign tastes, and we do not respect our identity – we just do it to show outsiders' (V8).

This view puts a different and rather negative interpretation on increasing international respect for Vietnamese culture, and one that was reinforced by other sympathetic but negative comments:

'it is difficult for older people, who have experienced two wars against the French and Americans, to lose their spirit of national independence, unity and national identity – but the young are exposed to various cultures, which easily affect Vietnamese tradition' (V16); 'if this situation continues, our national culture will disappear' (V18).

With the striking exception of Vietnam, therefore, the public felt on balance that their country's most important policies were determined by world markets and international organisations and their traditional way of life was getting lost. On balance, the Czech, Korean, and, within Ukraine, the Russian 'language, traditions and culture' were seen as losing respect. But the Vietnamese 'language, traditions and culture', together with the specifically 'Ukrainian language, traditions and culture' in Ukraine, were seen as gaining respect.

Public perceptions of rapid development

Taking the perspective of the UNDP (1999), we reminded survey respondents of the problems cited by the UNDP as well as the benefits of rapid economic development, and asked whether they felt 'the *benefits* such as improved opportunities and living standards' outweighed 'the *problems* such as increased crime, corruption and environmental pollution'.

Overall, the public felt 'rapid development' was good rather than bad – though only by a margin of 20 per cent. Officials were much more enthusiastic (36 per cent net positive). But there were huge differences

Table 2.10. *Public perspectives on the pace of development*

| | Officials % | Public % | Public within each country | | | |
			Czech R %	Korea %	Ukraine %	Vietnam %
On balance, do you feel rapid economic development is ...						
good – because the						
benefits are greater	61	51	39	42	52	68
bad – because the						
problems are greater	25	31	41	51	21	8
Do you feel the pace of economic development in (COUNTRY) is ...						
too fast	23	28	15	49	7	42
too slow	55	53	62	44	77	23

Note: Per cent of all respondents. Per cents giving other/mixed/'don't know' responses not shown.

between countries. In highly developed Korea, the public on balance had a negative view of rapid development (9 per cent net negative) while in relatively under-developed Vietnam they had a very positive view (60 per cent net positive). Similarly they were almost evenly divided in the more prosperous Czech Republic but strongly positive in poverty-stricken Ukraine (31 per cent net positive).

Overall, by a margin of 25 per cent, the public judged the pace of development in their country to be 'too slow' rather than 'too fast'. Again, there was considerable cross-national variation, but not the same cross-national pattern as before. Net criticism of development for being 'too slow' reached 47 per cent in the Czech Republic and 70 per cent in Ukraine. Conversely, in fast developing East Asia, the pace of development was described as 'too fast' rather than 'too slow' – by a margin of only 5 per cent in Korea but 19 per cent in Vietnam.

Instead of (East Asian) high rates of development reflecting a public 'thirst for development', it seems that it is (East European) stagnation and decline that generate an unsatisfied public 'thirst for development'.

2.3   Public discontents and public discontent

The public had much to be contented with, and much to be discontented about. Some trends were positive but others negative. The key question is how the many particular discontents sum up to produce overall discontent. Some complaints, though real enough, may have no impact on overall discontent. But others may largely determine overall discontent. Some complaints may really matter more than others; some not at all.

Before asking about the many particular things about which they might be discontent, we had asked:

'overall, are you satisfied or dissatisfied with the way things are going in our country today? And overall, are you satisfied or dissatisfied with the way things are going for your family?'

Overall, the public were *dissatisfied* with 'the way things are going in our country today' (20 per cent net negative) yet *satisfied* with 'the way things are going for my family' (13 per cent net positive) – on balance content with their own lives, but discontent with their country's progress. Officials were much more satisfied than the public on both counts, but especially with the way things were going for their own families (44 per cent net positive compared with 13 per cent among the public).

Vietnam was the only country where a majority – and it was a very large majority – expressed satisfaction with the way things were going both for their country and for their families: around 88 per cent were content with both. Conversely, over three-quarters of Ukrainians were discontent with how things were going – both for their family and for their country. In Korea, discontent with the country's progress was greater than anywhere else (85 per cent), yet combined with twice as much satisfaction (63 per cent) as discontent (32 per cent) with the way things were going for the family.

Table 2.11. *Discontent*

| | Officials % | Public % | Public within each country | | | |
			Czech R %	Korea %	Ukraine %	Vietnam %
Overall, are you satisfied or dissatisfied with the way things are going ...						
... in our country today						
satisfied	45	36	28	12	16	87
dissatisfied	44	56	56	85	78	1
... for your family						
satisfied	68	53	41	63	21	89
dissatisfied	24	40	45	32	75	5

Note: Per cent of all respondents. Per cents giving other/mixed/'don't know' responses not shown.

We use correlation and regression to provide an overview of the impact of personal background and experience on public perceptions of change, and the impact of all these on public discontent. We use ten indicators of 'socio-economic background' covering age, gender, education, rurality, income level, relative income, employment, unemployment, pensioner status, and public versus private sector employment. We also use twelve indicators of 'cosmopolitan background' covering access to TV, home computers, personal transport, contact with foreigners at home or abroad, and the ability to speak a variety of foreign languages; five indicators of 'identity background' covering religion and religiosity, supra-national identities, and, in Ukraine only, the language used at home; and two indicators of ideological background covering preferences for greater or lesser equality and the prioritisation of growth over the environment. In addition we use an indicator of whether the person was an official or ordinary member of the public; and six indicators of historical legacies: whether they were in East Asia or East Europe; whether they were in a richer or poorer country; and which particular country they lived in.

To that we add two indicators of personal experience of change: whether their family income had got better or worse, and whether they had done better or worse than the 'typical' family in their country. We also add twenty-one indicators of perceptions of wider changes – covering perceptions of past and future trends in the national economy; of trends in crime, corruption and pollution; of increasing inequality between rich and poor, young and old, towns and villages; of exploitation by local power-holders or foreign companies and of unfair treatment by powerful countries or international organisations; and perceptions of trends in national autonomy, the strength of local culture, and the respect accorded to local culture.

Insofar as any aspect of personal background and experience had an impact on perceptions of change, it was predominantly trends in personal or family income that did so. Changes in personal income correlated strongly with perceptions of recent trends in the national economy, and with expectations of future trends. But no aspect of personal background or experience correlated well with perceptions that the young, the rich, or urban areas had benefited more from recent trends; nor with perceptions of growing pollution; nor with perceptions that national traditions remained strong or that the country remained autonomous in important decision-making. These perceptions were not greatly influenced by personal background.

Our main aim, however, was to see how background factors of all kinds, personal experience, and perceptions of change combined to affect overall public discontent with 'the way things were going' for either the family or the country. Each of our indicators of background, experience or perceptions can be associated with one of the models of discontent that we set out in Chapter 1. So our regressions help us to assess the significance of different *models of discontent* rather than merely discriminating between a mass of different indicators. We use stepwise regression terminated after any 'beta' coefficients fall below 0.10 in order to highlight the key influences on public discontent rather than clutter up our conclusions with minutiae. All our indicators of personal background, experience, and perceptions of development are used as potential influences in the regressions, but few prove to have a major direct and independent impact on public discontent.

Discontent with 'the way things are going' for the family is highly predictable (RSQ = 0.46). It reflects a cross-national pattern of East European gloom versus Asian optimism (beta = 0.33), the level of family income (beta = 0.23) and even more important, recent trends in family income (beta = 0.34). This pattern also applies within every country. Measured by betas, the impact on personal discontent of being a personal winner or loser in terms of family income trends ranges from 0.15 in Vietnam, through 0.22 in Korea, to 0.34 in Ukraine and 0.39 in the Czech Republic. In addition, the levels of family income – as well as the trends – also have a strong impact in three of the four countries, with the better-off being less discontented. The exception is Vietnam where those with below average incomes are actually more contented, perhaps because they are convinced that Vietnamese development – unlike that elsewhere – really is providing some help to the poorest.

So a regional Asia/Europe legacy model, combined with a family version of the winners and losers model, and (to a lesser degree) with an income-based background model, provide the best explanation of personal or family discontent. We can illustrate this regression finding with a simple cross-tabulation of discontent 'with the way things are going for my family' by global region and family income trends. Within every country, personal experience of being a winner or loser has a large impact on this kind of discontent; but among both winners and losers, East Europeans are more discontent than their family experience would suggest (Table 2.13).

Discontent with 'the way things are going' for the country is even more predictable (RSQ = 0.54). But the basis of this discontent is significantly different. This discontent does *not* divide East Europe and East Asia, nor does it depend primarily upon family experience. Instead, it reflects

Table 2.12. *Explaining discontent with the way things are going for the family*

	All four countries		Public within each country			
	Public and officials	Public only	Czech R	Korea	Ukraine	Vietnam
RSQ =	42	46	44	17	30	6
MODEL (see text) INDICATOR	beta.100	beta.100	beta.100	beta.100	beta.100	beta.100
W&L (egocentric) family income got worse	28	34	39	22	34	15
BKD (social) income good	-23	-23	-24	-15	-29	
BKD (social) income below average	11			13		-10
W&L (national) expect economy will decline			14			
W&L (sociotropic) think there are less very rich now				12		14
BKD (identity) have supra national identity					11	
Justice (domestic) think winners are those with skill and luck			-12			
LEGACY East European	31	33				

Note: All betas shown are statistically significant at the one per cent level.

Table 2.13. *Per cent of public dissatisfied with 'the with way things are going for my family'*

	E Asian countries		E European countries
	KOR	CZ	
(family are) winners	17		24
losers	49		88
	VIET	UKR	
winners	5		56
losers	31		94

Notes: Percentages exclude 'don't know', mixed other responses.
Losers: family living standard got worse; Winners: got better.

perceptions about national economic trends (beta = 0.26 overall, rising to 0.37 in the Czech Republic) plus extreme euphoria in Vietnam – which does not extend to Korea, however. Perceived trends in family income also have an independent impact on feelings about how things are going for the country (beta = 0.18) but that is not the most important factor, either in our overall analysis or within any of the individual countries.

So a national version of the winners and losers model predominates. Supplemented by a weaker additional impact from a family version, the national winners and losers model provides the best general explanation of national discontent – though Vietnamese discontent is much lower than can be explained by this general model.

Within each country, perceptions of the country's economy winning or losing have a significant impact on discontent with 'the way things are going for our country', and especially so in East Europe. But discontent is extremely low in Vietnam, even among the very few Vietnamese who think – against all the statistical evidence – that their economy is in decline. We might reasonably speculate that if the economic record in Vietnam were more ambiguous, and larger numbers could plausibly believe their economy was declining, they would not only be more numerous but more discontent. The pattern within Vietnam is not inconsistent with our general model.

Again, a simple tabulation illustrates the main regression finding: discontent is outstandingly low in Vietnam but, within every country, those who think the national economy has got worse are more likely to be discontent. The impact is greatest in East Europe, especially in the Czech Republic (52 per cent) but also in Ukraine (24 per cent).

In terms of our 'framework for analysis', we can go back along the causal chain and ask what made people think their national economy was

Table 2.14. *Explaining discontent with the way things are going for the country*

	All four countries		Public within each country			
	Public and officials	Public only	Czech R	Korea	Ukraine	Vietnam
RSQ =	50	54	38	10	19	2
	beta.100	beta.100	beta.100	beta.100	beta.100	beta.100
W&L (national) economy got worse	29	26	37	13	19	11
W&L (egocentric) family income got worse	16	18	15	12	18	
BKD (social) income good	−11		−13		−13	
Justice (international) rich countries benefit more			12	11		
Justice (domestic) think winners are those with skill and luck			−11			
BKD (social) income below average				11		
W&L (national) expect economy will decline				10		
World ideology prioritise growth over environment						10
W&L (national) pollution got better					−10	
Justice (international) intl organisations favour rich countries					10	
Legacy Vietnam	−38	−42				
Legacy Czech Republic		−12				
Legacy East Asia	11					

Note: All betas shown are statistically significant at the one per cent level.

Table 2.15. *Per cent of public dissatisfied with 'the way things are going for our country'*

		E Asian countries	E European countries
		KOR	CZ
If think country's economy has got...			
	better	77	36
	worse	91	88
		VIET	UKR
	better	6	69
	worse	(15)	93

Notes: Percentages exclude other, mixed, 'don't know' responses.
Percentages in brackets are based on fewer than fifty respondents.

getting better or worse. Of all the many indicators of background and experience, regression analysis shows that the best predictors of public perceptions of trends in the national economy were trends in personal or family living standards (beta = 0.31 overall; and between 0.22 and 0.39 in each country). Those who felt their own living standards were getting better were the most likely to feel the national economy was improving. But two other factors were also important. First, Vietnamese perceptions of national economic growth were simply much greater (beta = 0.35) than elsewhere, irrespective of the changes in their personal circumstances. The impact of improving personal circumstances had less impact on perceptions of national economic growth in Vietnam (beta = 0.22) than anywhere else. Even those who were not doing particularly well in Vietnam had to admit that the national economy was improving. Conversely, Czech evaluations of national economic trends were particularly sensitive (beta = 0.39) to changing personal circumstances. Second, in East Europe, though not in East Asia, public ratings of current national economic trends were quite strongly influenced by expectations – by hopes and fears about future national economic trends (beta = 0.22 on average in East Europe). For East Europeans, perceptions of how well the economy was performing had an unusually strong element of hope and fear rather than strict attention to the present.

But we can push even further back along the causal chain and ask what made people report that their own personal or family income was getting better or worse. Our regressions point to four key factors. Those who reported low incomes (beta = 0.28) or below average incomes (beta = 0.25) were the most likely to report declining living standards and the least likely to report improving living standards. (The beta rises to around 0.41 if only one of these income measures is used.) There may be some element of reverse causation in that: perhaps their income was low because it had declined. But it is more likely that the public consciously felt at a very personal level what focus group participants alleged – and statisticians confirmed: the poor were getting poorer and the rich were getting richer. In terms of conscious public perceptions of trends in their own personal living standards, this pattern was significantly stronger in East Europe than in East Asia. But irrespective of these internal variations, the Vietnamese were outstandingly (beta = 0.32) likely to report improving living standards. Once again, though more surprisingly this time, East European, though not East Asian, reports of trends in personal income appeared to be influenced by their expectations of future living standards (beta = 0.20).

So we can trace a chain of causation that runs from (i) originally low income, through (ii) a failure to reap the benefits of economic change, to (iii) relatively pessimistic perceptions about national economic trends to (iv) discontent with 'the way things are going in our country'. It is a national winners and losers model that best predicts discontent with national progress, though a personal winners and losers model has a strong (but not determining) influence on the public's perception of whether the national economy is improving, and it was those who were already better-off who were more likely to become personal winners.

2.4   Conclusion: egocentric not altruistic

The key influences on public discontents are those associated with *legacy models* (mainly regional or growth-based; but also prosperity-based) or *winners and losers* models of various kinds. Perceptions associated with *justice models* (international or domestic) have a much smaller and less consistent impact. Amongst *personal background* characteristics only family income has a sizeable impact – and then only on discontent with the way things are going *for the family*.

Winners and losers models of several kinds – but not all kinds – have a key impact. But only self-interested *egocentric models* operating at the family or national level (as appropriate) have a major impact. Altruistic models based on a concern for others (growing inequalities between rich and poor, young and old, rural and urban) have little or no impact. External *international justice models* (foreign companies exploit us; international organisations treat us unfairly) have only a small impact and internal domestic justice models (whether domestic winners merit their gains) have less. The public express concern about these trends but their

Table 2.16. *Per cent of public dissatisfied with 'the with way things are going for our country today' (extended analysis)*

| | per cent dissatisfied with 'the way things are going for our country today' | |
	... if prefer more inequality to provide incentives	... if prefer less inequality to provide more solidarity
Public (all four countries merged)		
... if think country's economy has got better	28	35
... if think country's economy has got worse	84	91
Czech public		
... if think country's economy has got better	30	38
... if think country's economy has got worse	84	89
Korea public		
... if think country's economy has got better	86	75
... if think country's economy has got worse	92	91
Ukraine public		
... if think country's economy has got better	69	69
... if think country's economy has got worse	82	94
Vietnam public		
... if think country's economy has got *much* better	1	5
... if think country's economy has got *a little* better	6	10

Notes: Percentages exclude other, mixed, 'don't know' responses.
Very few in Vietnam thought the economy had got worse.

concern does not affect their level of discontent with 'the way things are going'. Indeed, both the international justice questions that do help in any way to explain public discontent are about injustice towards the respondent's country – so they might be considered an international version of an egocentric winners and losers model.

What matters most is always *being* a winner or loser rather than being motivated by a concern for losers. Whatever the level it is always *egocentric/selfish* rather than altruistic: always based on *my* family's rising or falling prosperity, *my* country's rising or falling prosperity, or injustice towards countries like *mine*. A simple tabulation of public discontent against a combination of national economic perceptions and a preference for a more equal society provides one easy way (among many) to illustrate the dominance of selfish rather than altruistic models. Within the merged four-country data set, a preference for greater equality increases discontent by about seven per cent, but its impact is dwarfed by that of economic perceptions which is eight times as powerful. Within countries, the impact of attitudes to inequality is always small (and in Korea it runs in the opposite direction to its impact elsewhere).

The impact of economic perceptions is particularly visible in the East European countries, but also in Korea. Within Vietnam, economic perceptions are almost universally positive and discontent with 'the way things are going' is extremely low. By itself the Vietnamese data cannot prove the dominance of economic perceptions. But the Vietnamese data are at least entirely consistent with a general model which would predict: (i) that discontent would be low where perceptions of economic progress were high; and (ii) that public attitudes towards inequality would only have a small impact on overall discontent.

Finally, we have found differences between officials and their publics on backgrounds, perceptions and discontent. Officials were more favourable than the public towards rapid development and more satisfied with the way the country was going. But significantly, they differed from the public most of all in terms of their satisfaction with the way things were going *for themselves or their families* – reflecting their better incomes, and better income trends. So despite the raw differences on discontent between publics and officials, the regression findings suggest that these differences are largely 'explained' by the differing economic experiences of officials and their publics. Officials were more likely than their publics to be personal winners, and therefore less likely than their publics to be discontented – for largely personal reasons. That may explain the different levels of discontent among the public and officials but it does not 'explain away' the difference in anything more than a purely statistical sense. Politically it raises a more serious question than it answers – a point to which we shall return in later chapters.

3   Public support for economic openness

This chapter looks at public attitudes towards an 'open economy' – where producers and consumers are exposed to freely operating world markets externally, and to a freely operating domestic market internally. In principle it might be possible to have one without the other. Communist regimes did engage in external trade with each other and with a wider world market though they attempted (not entirely successfully) to suppress domestic markets. Conversely, it would be possible to conceive a regime with an entirely free market internally, yet sealed off from the world economy – some remote Himalayan kingdom, an idealised Chinese or British Empire founded upon 'imperial preference', or a more inward-looking European Union. Some of our Czech focus group participants looked to European Union (EU) accession as a means of insulating themselves from the world market as much as integrating into a pan-European market. But the much debated 'Washington Consensus' (Teunissen and Akkerman 2004) was based on the ideal of a seamless market, independent of political boundaries. Thus the Fraser Institute's (2004) *Economic Freedom of the World* rankings, for example, are based on indicators of both an *external* and an *internal* market. Though a country may score higher on one than the other, *both* are regarded as essential components of a truly 'free market'.

Like outside observers, most of the public in our countries could distinguish between the internal and external components of an open market economy, however. Although on balance they supported both, they were somewhat more favourable towards opening up to world markets than they were to a fully market-based economy at home. In addition, the basis of their support for opening up to world markets was different from the basis of their support for an internal market economy – quite different factors affected public support for these two components of an open market economy.

Yet, as our focus groups made clear, and our later survey confirmed, attitudes towards an open economy were even more complex than that, especially in East Europe where the public insisted on drawing another very sharp distinction: a distinction between theory and practice. East European publics supported the concept of an open market economy but asserted that their 'actually existing' economy did not merit that description – just as they recalled that 'actually existing' communism never matched its ideals. Perhaps just because of their long exposure to a theory that did not correspond to practice, ordinary members of the public in East Europe were particularly sensitive to the discrepancy between the theory and practice of the market. So they criticised the post-communist regime from a market economy perspective as well as from a social welfare perspective. At best they saw post-communist reality as a transition process that was making slow, chaotic and painful progress towards a better future. At worst they saw it as the worst of all possible options, with neither the dynamic virtues of an open economy nor the paternal virtues of a socialist economy.

3.1   Public support for an open market economy

Opening-up Despite their discontent with recent changes, public attitudes towards 'opening up the economy to international and world markets' were strongly positive. Respondents were reminded that 'most people say there are both advantages and disadvantages to opening up our country's economy to foreign companies and the international markets' and asked whether such 'opening up' brought 'more, or more important, advantages' or 'more, or more important, *dis*advantages'. Over twice as many took a positive than a negative view. They were even more positive when subsequently asked whether 'opening up our economy to international and world markets' was simply 'good or bad for our country'. Overall 66 per cent of the public (and 75 per cent of officials) said it was 'good': just over half of the public in both East European countries, two-thirds in Korea and 88 per cent in Vietnam. Only 17 per cent said it was 'bad'.

In focus groups, some (mainly Vietnamese) were positive without reservation, though more often individual participants combined generally positive views with reservations:

'the advantages outweigh the disadvantages – if we can take control of the situation' (V31); 'this is a long-term affair from which perhaps the younger ones will benefit' (C20); 'a short-term disadvantage and then positive' (C18, all agree); 'it is advantageous for us now, but it may be only for now' (U5); 'it is good – but in consequence of corruption ... [foreigners] just will not come here' (U13); 'the USA and Japan raise tariffs and even commit dumping. Under these circumstances, it is not appropriate for us to open our economy. A big country like the USA restricts imports [but it] exports as much as possible' (K2); 'reciprocity matters' (K7).

Table 3.1. *Public support for opening up*

	Officials %	Public %	Public within each country			
			Czech R %	Korea %	Ukraine %	Vietnam %
Most people say there are both advantages and disadvantages to opening up (COUNTRY)'s economy to foreign companies and the international markets. Do you feel there are ...						
more, or more important, advantages	65	55	46	51	46	76
more, or more important, disadvantages	19	25	28	40	28	5
So overall, do you feel that opening up our economy to international and world markets is ...						
good for (COUNTRY)	75	66	55	65	53	88
bad for (COUNTRY)	12	17	19	27	18	1

Note: Per cent of all respondents. Per cents giving other/mixed/'don't know' responses not shown.

Marketisation Public attitudes to the other part of the 'Washington Consensus', an internal market economy, were also positive, though less so. By an overall margin of 25 per cent (rising to 42 per cent among officials), the public felt a market economy made their country 'more prosperous'. But by an overall margin of 30 per cent they also felt it made their country 'less fair'. There were huge differences between countries, however. The Vietnamese were extremely positive about the internal market on both counts. Only a third or less in Ukraine and the Czech Republic said it made their country more prosperous, compared with over half of the Koreans and 87 per cent of the Vietnamese. While over half the Vietnamese rated the market economy as 'fair', only around 18 per cent in Korea and the Czech Republic, and a miserable 4 per cent in Ukraine agreed.

When Ukrainians discussed whether an internal market economy was 'on the whole, good or bad' they spontaneously focused on its unfairness and on the negative role of the post-communist state:

'I hope [a market economy] is good' (U2); 'it seems to be good since it exists around the world' (U3); 'it is 50/50' (U20); 'hard to tell – it can be good [but] it is bad for our village' (U19); 'with a chairman of the collective farm like ours, we shall achieve nothing even in 100 years [though] there are heads of collective farms who get loans, get support from the state, and have no problems' (U22); 'the best thing we had under socialism was trust in tomorrow ... a man was sure

Table 3.2. *The market economy: prosperous but unfair*

	Officials %	Public %	Public within each country			
			Czech R %	Korea %	Ukraine %	Vietnam %
Do you feel the market economy makes (COUNTRY) ...						
more prosperous	58	51	29	55	34	87
less prosperous	16	26	37	38	25	4
Do you feel the market economy in (COUNTRY) is ...						
fair	23	23	17	19	4	53
unfair	46	53	48	75	66	24

Note: Per cent of all respondents. Per cents giving other/mixed/'don't know' responses not shown.

that tomorrow he would not be left hungry, would get support, we had savings, some kopecks [pennies]. And now you do not know' (U17); 'there are people who have no money to buy themselves a piece of bread' (U24).

At the other extreme, Vietnamese participants focused on increasing prosperity and the positive role of the Doi Moi state in encouraging a market economy or the 'market mechanism':

'our market mechanism . . . is basically good, making life better'(V4, V1 agrees); 'it is obvious that market mechanisms are both good and bad [but] *if we want to go forward to socialism, it is essential to have market mechanisms.* Market mechanisms create more jobs, encourage the development of goods' (V27, our emphasis); '[the market] can mobilise the creativeness and strength of each individual. In the past, if some people had an idea, they would not have been helped by the state to realise it' (V16).

This was a vision of the market in which the state now provided *more* support for individuals than before the Doi Moi reforms, not less.

Czech and Korean participants presented the mix of good and bad in more neutral terms:

'the market economy is the right way, but in reality it is hard to say that it turned out to be successful' (K7); 'I do not mean that the market economy is absolutely bad. I have been in Hong Kong, where the state regulates the market economy . . . we can decrease the gap between rich and poor if the state regulates the market well' (K29); 'the problem is not the market economy as such, but the incompletion of market economy in Korea. Government has to lessen regulations' (K19); 'was the introduction of market economy in the Czech Republic a plus or a minus?' (moderator); 'a plus, definitely a plus – if a person looked at it globally' (C3); 'a plus – if we do not think about it too much' (C7); 'a plus after fifty years perhaps – but ten years is a short time, it only lets us see the mistakes' (C2); 'a plus, we could not do anything else – but laws were not adapted to it' (C0); 'we were not ready for it' (C28); 'we all hope that things will be better – there is already a basis for that' (C11); 'I am an optimist, it is good, but some rules should be introduced. The problem does not rest with the market economy, but in something else. For instance, farming: that will be liquidated from abroad' (C10).

So the market was 'good, but'. This was faint praise, and the divisions of opinion lay as much within individual people's minds as between different individuals.

3.2 Advantages and disadvantages of opening up

When asked to cite the *advantages* of opening up the economy to the world, focus group participants cited shopping:

'Better choice ... [and] it pushes prices down' (C2); 'the [communist era] Pobeda factory made such wretched toys ... how could anyone educate a child with such toys?' (U3); 'in the past ... frocks all looking the same ... now, if you go to the marketplace, oh my God, you are dazzled ... But "your finances sing romances" [Russian proverb]. So, those who have money wear nice clothes and look real nice' (U30);

and better jobs:

'higher earnings [though a] higher workload' (C2); 'better working conditions ... five-day week ... minimum wage raised' (K18);

or at least the *prospect* of getting better jobs with:

'new customs, some holidays' (U19); '[and] the same amount of earnings that is earned abroad' (U14);

plus access to:

'capital' (K4); 'new technology' (K3); 'advanced technologies' (K24); 'from advanced countries' (K28); '[which] may enhance our living standards' (K26); '[and] make our economy more competitive' (K23);

and more opportunities to trade:

'to trade good products with foreign countries ... develop our beautiful scenery into tourist products' (K14); 'our domestic market is comparatively limited, so that we need to expand our market' (K13).

To quantify these perceptions more precisely, we asked survey respondents whether the *most important advantage* to opening up the economy to foreign companies and world markets was its benefit to:

> *shopping* – 'more choice, better quality or lower prices of products in our shops';
> *workers* – 'more jobs, better wages and conditions for workers';

our businesses – 'they can learn more advanced technologies and better business methods';
trade – 'more markets for our products';
our culture – 'we get good ideas from foreign cultures and foreign ways of living'.

The short explanatory phrases were designed to echo focus group comments and remind survey respondents of the potential advantages of opening up – including cultural advantages, which had not been cited by participants in focus group discussions. Overall, between 19 and 23 per cent opted for each of 'shopping', 'workers', 'business', and 'trade'. Czechs focused more than others on shopping, Koreans on trade and especially on business methods, and the public in the two poorer countries on jobs, pay and conditions. Only 3 per cent cited cultural benefits as the most important advantage – despite our efforts to remind them that foreign culture might be beneficial.

By disaggregating perceptions of pay and conditions, it becomes clear that even Czechs recognised that opening up their economy had

Table 3.3. *Perceived advantages of opening up*

			Public within each country			
	Officials %	Public %	Czech R %	Korea %	Ukraine %	Vietnam %
The most important *advantage* of opening-up? It is good for ...						
our businesses – technology and business methods	30	23	21	31	22	16
workers – jobs, wages and conditions	21	22	13	17	25	30
trade – markets for (COUNTRY) products	22	20	21	28	17	11
shopping – choice, quality, prices	14	19	30	16	14	14
our culture – good ideas from foreign cultures and ways of living	3	3	3	6	2	3
(VOL) there is no advantage	1	3	4	1	7	0

Note: Per cent of all respondents. Per cents giving other/mixed/'don't know' responses not shown. Entries ranked by importance assigned by public. VOL indicates that a particular answer was not offered by the interviewer, but was spontaneously volunteered by some respondents.

Table 3.4. *Jobs and conditions*

	Officials %	Public %	Public within each country			
			Czech R %	Korea %	Ukraine %	Vietnam %
Do you feel that opening up our economy more to world markets has had a good effect or a bad effect on ...						
... the availability of good-paying jobs?						
good effect	77	69	63	61	67	81
bad effect	11	17	21	32	11	4
... the working conditions of ordinary workers?						
good effect	65	57	39	59	61	69
bad effect	22	27	46	32	15	11

Note: Per cent of all respondents. Per cents giving other/mixed/'don't know' responses not shown.

increased the 'availability of good-paying jobs' though they regretted that working conditions had got worse. By an overall margin of 52 per cent, the public across all four countries felt 'opening up our economy more to world markets' had had a 'good effect on the availability of good-paying jobs'. But while the Vietnamese by a margin of 58 per cent felt 'working conditions' had also improved, the Czechs by a margin of 7 per cent felt they had deteriorated.

When it came to the *disadvantages* of opening up the economy, focus group participants cited greater economic pressure:

'greater pressure on people' (C2); 'you may lose your job anytime' (C3); 'in foreign companies people are mere numbers' (C7); '[foreigners locate] environmentally dangerous production at our enterprises ... and our people are forced to work there because of the absence of other work' (U6); 'if prices decline, there is no way we can get back production costs such as labour, agricultural chemicals' (K15); 'global conglomerates will overwhelm our market ... ordinary people like us will go into poverty' (K10); 'we must protect our companies, and farmers' (C8);

though they also voiced cultural fears:

'of course we may learn something, but I am ... concerned about losing our culture' (K28); 'I worry that there will be the second generation of foreigners in our country – I am not comfortable with that' (K23); 'our culture is much affected' (V19); 'we have to accept it, although no one likes it' (V4).

Some thought they could take the economic advantages without accepting the cultural disadvantages:

'considering our national consciousness, I think it is possible for us to think of culture and economy separately. Although our people are familiar with foreign culture, commercials, commodities, movies, we are immune to them. Our culture is stable' (K27); 'economic development and culture are different' (K8, supported by K4, K5 and K7); 'because culture has intrinsic characteristics' (K4).

Or at least they might confine cultural change to what might be called 'consumer culture':

'about *clothes*, we cannot deny that our culture is westernised' (K22); 'we are affected *in living style* ... for example, young Vietnamese imitate Korean girls and apply blue lipstick' (V9); '[but] Vietnamese are still Vietnamese' (V31); 'as the economy develops and culture is westernised, our culture changes to some extent. You know we do not wear our traditional clothes now. But our cultural foundation should be maintained ... Even when *lifestyle* changes, people do not lose their [national] *spirit*. That is obvious' (K18, our emphases throughout).

We asked survey respondents whether the *most important disadvantage* to opening up the economy was its impact on:

> *shopping* – 'higher prices in our shops';
> *workers* – 'more insecurity, harder work, dangerous working conditions';
> *our businesses* – 'our businesses cannot compete against foreign businesses';
> *trade* – 'foreign countries dump their products in our country but will not open up their markets to our products';
> *our culture* – 'too many foreigners and foreign ideas are flooding into our country'.

Again, the short explanatory phrases were designed to echo focus group comments and remind survey respondents of potential disadvantages. Overall, if only by the narrowest of margins, culture was the most frequently cited disadvantage – especially in East Asia (26 per cent in Vietnam, 32 per cent in Korea), though much less in Ukraine (16 per cent) and the Czech Republic (9 per cent). So the public viewed cultural change not only as by far the least advantageous consequence of opening up but also as the single most disadvantageous.

Across the four countries, the public were evenly divided on whether opening up the economy had had a good effect on 'the gap between rich and poor' or 'the ability of people to provide for themselves in their old age', but by a margin of 12 per cent they felt it had been bad for 'the spread of diseases'. (Officials were more optimistic than their

Table 3.5. *Perceived* dis*advantages of opening up*

	Officials %	Public %	Public within each country			
			Czech R %	Korea %	Ukraine %	Vietnam %
The most important *disadvantage?* It is bad for ...						
our culture – too many incomers and foreign ideas	22	21	9	32	16	26
our businesses – cannot compete internationally	21	19	21	21	13	14
trade – foreign countries dump their products in (COUNTRY) but will not open up their markets to our products	21	19	22	19	23	13
workers – insecurity, harder work, dangerous conditions	15	18	29	18	16	6
shopping – higher prices	4	6	4	6	10	7
(VOL) there is no *dis*advantage	5	3	4	0	5	2

Note: Per cent of all respondents. Per cents giving other/mixed/'don't know' responses not shown. Entries ranked by importance assigned by public. VOL indicates that a particular answer was not offered by the interviewer, but was spontaneously volunteered by some respondents.

Table 3.6. *Perceived social impacts of opening up*

	Officials %	Public %	Public within each country			
			Czech R %	Korea %	Ukraine %	Vietnam %
Do you feel that opening up our economy more to world markets has had a good effect or a bad effect on ...						
... the ability of people to provide for themselves in their old age?						
good effect	43	38	27	46	51	26
bad effect	32	36	48	41	18	36
... the gap between rich and poor?						
good effect	45	37	26	44	37	36
bad effect	36	41	56	44	26	36
... the spread of diseases?						
good effect	32	33	25	48	36	24
bad effect	48	45	54	41	33	50

Note: Per cent of all respondents. Per cents giving other/mixed/'don't know' responses not shown.

publics about the impact of opening up on everything except 'the spread of diseases'.)

3.3   Better alternatives?

A large majority of the public felt that opening up their economy had been good for the availability of well-paid jobs, and a smaller majority that it had improved the working conditions of ordinary workers; they were divided on whether it has been good or bad for the ability of people to provide for themselves in their old age; but by narrow majorities they felt it had been bad for the gap between rich and poor and for the spread of disease; and they also felt it posed some threat to their national culture. A large majority felt the market economy had made their country more prosperous but, at the same time, less fair. In focus group discussions individual participants voiced a mixture of support and criticism.

Because there was such widespread recognition that the impact of opening up the economy was a mixed bag of advantages and disadvantages, to say that the balance was good, or that the advantages outweighed the disadvantages, did not preclude the perception that there might be some alternative, perhaps difficult for ordinary people to specify, that might be *even better* or have *even more advantages*. The open economy, at least as it had been implemented, could be good, but still 'second best'.

Claims that 'there is no third way' between the market and socialism 'that would work' (C2, C4 similar), that 'market mechanisms are the only way to go' (V19), 'an irresistible trend' (K27), or that opening up is 'the current of the time' (K14), 'unavoidable' (K27), or necessary 'to survive' (K30), are barely distinguishable from straightforward support for an open market economy with all its acknowledged downsides:

'before 1985, life was tough because we did not open up. Although in the market mechanism, the gap between the rich and poor is bigger, the life of the people is improved. In spiritual and cultural life, people feel more comfortable, more free, less worried. So we should continue opening up' (V25).

Conversely, some Ukrainian critics of the market economy expressed nostalgia for the old regime with its fixed prices and rigid planning:

'businessmen ... fix the prices on their own ... previously the price was the same in all shops ... prices must be controlled by the state' (U25); 'the state should regulate prices' (U21; U20, U18, U19 agree).

But many participants could see a viable alternative to the contemporary market economy that was also different from the past. Many argued in favour of 'a mixed economy' (K12) with 'a greater role' (C0; C11, C15, C12 similar) for the state, provided that it intervened within 'certain limits' (C11) and 'did not throw away money on useless things' (C14; C9 similar):

'the state should manage [the market economy] but not get directly involved in business activities. The state should be the watchdog to limit bad activities' (V18); '*market-mechanisms [combined] with state regulation is the way to go* in order to develop the economy. However, it is necessary to reconsider the role of the state. The state should create conditions for enterprises, not interfere . . . create favourable conditions for the enterprises to decide their own ways of functioning' (V3, our emphasis).

We asked survey respondents whether 'opening up our economy to international and world markets' and a 'commitment to a market economy' was 'the only way to go' or whether 'there must be a better alternative' of some (deliberately) unspecified kind.

Economists have often pointed out that, historically, economies like those in Europe and more recently in East Asia have developed successfully by establishing an effective domestic market economy first before opening up to the world market. But among our publics, opening up to the world was more popular than an internal market economy. Judged by vague feelings that there must be some unspecified 'better alternative', the overall balance of public opinion was 16 per cent more favourable to opening up than to the internal market. Indeed, public opinion clearly rejected any alternative to opening up but were very marginally favourable towards the idea of an alternative to the domestic market economy.

By a margin of around 43 per cent the Vietnamese public felt that both an internationally open economy and a domestic market economy were 'the only way to go'. Elsewhere, more felt there must be 'a better alternative'. Czechs still backed opening up to world markets as 'the only way', but by a narrower margin (17 per cent); and Koreans and Ukrainians were fairly evenly divided. On a domestic market economy, Czechs were evenly divided while Ukrainians opted for 'a better alternative' by a margin of 21 per cent and Koreans, remarkably, by a margin of 38 per cent.

A recurrent response by focus group participants in East Europe (not echoed in East Asia, however) to questions about the market economy in their countries was to deny its existence. Paradoxically, for them a 'real'

Table 3.7. *A better way?*

	Officials %	Public %	Public within each country			
			Czech R %	Korea %	Ukraine %	Vietnam %
For (COUNTRY), is opening up our economy to international and world markets ...						
... the only way to go	55	49	51	47	35	59
there must be a better						
alternative	31	35	34	45	41	18
For (COUNTRY), is a commitment to a market-economy ...						
... the only way to go	50	42	43	29	29	64
there must be a better						
alternative	40	44	40	67	50	19

Note: Per cent of all respondents. Per cents giving other/mixed/'don't know' responses not shown.

market economy would be that 'better alternative' to the only market economy they had actually experienced:

'the market economy is correct but it is not very good here. They did not take it up properly' (C8); 'did not observe the rules' (C2); 'a good idea, but the implementation [was bad]' (C12); 'during the process of privatisation our companies were bought by foreigners' (C14);

'the market economy is fair in itself, but what does that have to do with Ukraine? We should have made a transition to a normal [market] economy some nine years ago ... we have no market economy ... what we have is not a market but a bazaar instead. The bazaar economy and the market economy are different things' (U16); 'at present, I do not see any market economy' (U11); 'we have a state of chaos' (U14); 'the state must put things in order ... [market reform] should have been implemented right to the end, or not at all' (U28).

'Is the market economy a fair system?' (moderator); [long pause while all reflect on their answers] 'do you mean our Ukrainian economy or the market economy in general?' (U28) ... 'in general' (moderator) ... 'this question is hard to answer ... [heaves deep sigh] ... yet it can be so ... under a normal legislative basis, if the state really does exist ... if it starts taking care of its people' (U28) ... 'protecting its people' (U30) ... 'it can be so, it can' (U26) ... 'the market system can be fair' (U29) ... 'a lot depends on who implements [market reform] and in what form it is done, whether it is planned or unplanned, chaotic, like the one we have here ... Where is our state regulation?' (U28; U32, U31 nod assent) ... 'I believe that there must be market economy. But in our country it can only emerge in ten years' time. It will not emerge in our country any sooner than that' (U25);

'internationally the market economy has apparently proved itself ... it is just that we cannot pick up the pace, and there is too much gangsterism ... dishonesty' (U3); 'in principle there is seemingly no alternative to the market economy at the moment ... [but] the main drawback of our society is that many people do not have a habit of working and acting honestly. Therefore, *our* market economy becomes twisted, corrupted and tailored to [the interests of] certain individuals and forces – so much so that one involuntarily begins to think that the market economy is an evil for Ukraine. Whether this situation can be corrected, is another question' [everybody laughs]' (U8).

'Is the market economy a fair system?' (moderator) ... 'it can be' (U19) ... 'it can be ... [but] the way it is done here? Today they pass a law, tomorrow it must be in effect. Today there is still no market economy, tomorrow it should exist. Hey, let's do the market! ... [they] sold and plundered everything – and they want a market economy?' (U17).

Ukrainian participants especially argued that the implementation of a market economy was not so much incompetent as a conspiracy by existing power-holders against the public, a transition from communism to crony capitalism rather than to a real market economy. They defined the state as the problem, not the solution:

'the market economy has not reached its normal level – or some do not want it to reach this level' (U4; U3, U7 agree); 'it is clear to all that the economy has got to be of the market type, and all of us here agree with that, I believe. But there is no order, nor will there be any. What we call the state is in fact concrete people: the President, the Verkhovna Rada [Parliament] and the provincial hierarchy: those representatives, governors and all the rest. They are *the state which keeps robbing us*, and there is no way to correct them; it will all go on the same way' (U13, our emphasis).

To create a functioning market:

'it is necessary first to establish order within the state' (U9) ... 'a clear legislative basis ... an enhancement of the market, an enhancement of transparency' (U14); 'Yes indeed, there must be an enhancement of the market, but at the same time the state should assume the function of taking care of its citizens. Strictly speaking, that is the main purpose of the state ... to serve them. But here, unfortunately, everything happens the other way round [i.e. the people serve the state!] ... it has not created a market for us here, and the state has not developed into something good. On the contrary, I think that it is simply the role of the state that has been enhanced' (U16); 'I would also like the people to be able to see where the tax proceeds go ... [taxes are collected but] nothing is done at all ... We do not need this state. It keeps robbing us' (U10).

This 'concrete' state intervened to help its 'friends' not to create a free and fair market:

'prices are out of control' (U1) ... 'But shouldn't a market mechanism, competition, work towards lowering prices? Why doesn't it function this way in Ukraine?'

(moderator) ... 'Because we do not have a full-fledged market economy' (U8; U6, U7 nod agreement) ... 'The market economy is viewed negatively in this country because what we have is not a normal market ... and the state intervenes at the wrong points. As U1 said, some intervention is needed, but [in practice] it largely takes the form of writing off the debts of certain state-owned enterprises ... The state protects the interests of certain businesses ... actions of the anti-monopoly committee are very selective ... maybe it is simple corruption, maybe indulgences are made for certain friends at the state level. I repeat, the state favours the businesses of certain people and circles at the expense of other businesses and ultimately, of the population' (U8); 'for some [the state] offers indulgences, for others it makes unbearable conditions' (U2);

'it does not matter [whether we] incline towards the market or towards state control – those are absolutely useless debates. As long as the group of those Vasyas [disdainful nickname] keeps sitting by that bowl of sour cream in the form of Ukraine, all conversations on the subject of what we need and which road we should take are absolutely useless. As long as a group of people is literally *plundering the state*, no one can do anything' (U12, our emphasis).

We return to this vision of the state-as-conspiracy against the public in Chapter 6. But the claim that Ukraine did not have a real market economy was so prevalent and so vehement in our focus groups that we included a 'silent code' in our survey questions about whether the market economy made the country prosperous and fair. Interviewers were instructed *not* to read out the option of 'there is not a real market economy here'; but they were required to record such replies if spontaneously volunteered.

Table 3.8. *No real market economy here*

		.... within each country			
		Czech R %	Korea %	Ukraine %	Vietnam %
Do you feel the market economy makes (COUNTRY) more prosperous or less prosperous?					
(VOL) there is not a real	**Public**	14	23	4	27 (25)	1
market economy here	**Officials**	19	24	6	45	3
Do you feel the market economy in (COUNTRY) is fair or unfair?					
(VOL) there is not a real	**Public**	12	22	2	19 (23)	2
market economy here	**Officials**	17	21	5	40	4

Notes: Per cent of all respondents. Per cents giving other/mixed/'don't know' responses not shown.

Figures in brackets are from our post-Orange Revolution survey in 2005. VOL indicates that a particular answer was not offered by the interviewer, but was spontaneously volunteered by some respondents.

Very few in Korea or Vietnam volunteered that response. But without any encouragement or prompting, around 23 per cent of the public in the Czech Republic as well as Ukraine spontaneously denied that they actually had a market economy in their country; as did 23 per cent of Czech officials and a remarkable 43 per cent of Ukrainian officials. Outsiders agreed: the EU did not formally grant Ukraine 'market economy status', which was essential for World Trade Organisation (WTO) membership, until a year after the Orange Revolution (see 'EU sees Ukraine as market economy', www.bbc.co.uk, 1 December 2005). Perhaps the EU was too hasty: when we repeated our survey in Ukraine after the Orange Revolution, the number of Ukrainians who spontaneously insisted they had 'no real market economy here' was almost unchanged, indeed slightly higher at around 24 per cent.

3.4   Personal employment preferences

In every country except the Czech Republic, a majority of the public thought a market economy made the country more prosperous, even if at the expense of some unfairness. But remarkably few in any country would choose to work for a private-sector employer – overall just 20 per cent of the public. Among this small number who opted for a private-sector employer, twice as many would prefer a foreign employer (13 per cent) as a domestic one (7 per cent). At least as many would prefer to work in their own family business (21 per cent) as for any private-sector employer, foreign or domestic. More than half would prefer to work for the state, either in state administration or in state-owned enterprises. Only in the Czech Republic was there a clear majority who would prefer to work outside the state sector – and that reflected not an unusual preference for private-sector employers, but an unusual preference for working in a family business.

Attitudes towards opening up, or even towards the internal market economy, did not divide neatly between those who wished to work in the public and private sectors. Those who worked (or would prefer to work) in state enterprises or 'cooperative' farms expressed a little less than average support for the internal or external market, while those who worked for themselves or for foreign companies (but not for local private sector companies) expressed above average support. Others who worked for the state in health-care expressed about average support for the market, and those working for the state in education or in state administration expressed *above average* support for both the internal and external market (as indeed did our special samples of officials).

Table 3.9. *Support the market but prefer to work for the state themselves*

| | Officials % | Public % | Public within each country | | | |
			Czech R %	Korea %	Ukraine %	Vietnam %
If you had a choice, where would you yourself like to work?						
government office/state administration	49	31	25	33	19	52
state-owned company	14	23	13	29	30	19
Total: public-sector	63	54	38	62	49	71
foreign company in (COUNTRY)	8	13	16	15	13	7
private (COUNTRY) company	6	7	8	9	9	2
Total: private sector	14	20	24	24	22	10
your own family business	21	21	32	12	23	13

Note: Per cent of all respondents. Per cents giving other/mixed/'don't know' responses not shown.

Why so much personal preference for employment in the public sector when the market was applauded for bringing prosperity? Among the public, high wages were valued – but not as much as stability and job security. Overall, 53 per cent cited job security or pensions as their criterion for employment preferences, compared with only 25 per cent who cited high wages, and 17 per cent who cited personal development.

In every country except Ukraine job security came top. Job security or pensions were cited by 47 per cent in the Czech Republic, 62 per cent in Korea and 69 per cent in Vietnam. But Ukraine was a striking exception: 52 per cent cited high wages and only 18 per cent job security – though Ukrainians had too much experience of secure jobs and guaranteed pensions which paid a pittance, offered 'payment in kind, not cash', or for months on end paid nothing at all. In post-communist Ukraine, security of employment had become divorced from security of income.

Among the public in the two richer countries, Korea and the Czech Republic – and even more so among officials – 'personal or career development' rather than high wages came second to job security as a criterion for employment choice. It was cited by a fifth of Koreans, by a quarter of Czechs and by over a third of officials.

There was a complex three-way correlation between the sector-of-choice and the criterion-for-choice: public sector employment was equated primarily with security; foreign companies primarily with high wages.

Table 3.10. *What the public want to get from employment*

	Officials %	Public %	Public within each country			
			Czech R %	Korea %	Ukraine %	Vietnam %
Which of these would be the most important reason for your choosing to work there (in preferred employment)?						
job security/stability	46	42	39	50	18	60
pension/social security	8	11	8	12	15	9
Total: job security & pension	*54*	*53*	*47*	*62*	*33*	*69*
high wages	15	25	23	16	52	12
personal development/						
career development	35	17	24	21	8	11

Note: Per cent of all respondents. Per cents giving other/mixed/'don't know' responses not shown.

No single factor dominated the attractions of working for local companies or family businesses in that way. But the main attraction of local companies was a mix of personal development and high wages, while the main attraction of a family business was a mix of personal development and security. Between 75 and 88 per cent cited security as the attraction of public sector employment in every country except Ukraine (where a remarkable 42 per cent cited high wages). Between 61 and 76 per cent cited high wages as the attraction of foreign companies in every country except Korea where personal development (34 per cent) was almost as important as high wages (39 per cent). Personal development was the most frequently cited reason for preferring a family business in every country except Ukraine (where, once again, high wages was the dominant reason cited). Ukrainians found it very difficult to focus on anything beyond income.

Focus group participants also linked the public sector to security:

'state administration means security' (C28); 'you get your pay on the tenth of each month and that is a certainty' (C29); 'a state-owned company is a good place to work . . . better plans for retirement and welfare . . . and no worry of layoffs' (K27); 'although state enterprises pay a low salary, there is a lot of free time and stability' (V31; V28 similar); 'in state agencies [workers] are less worried' (V26); 'we prefer stable jobs, so we want our children to work for stated-owned enterprises' (V17).

But some Ukrainian participants were not so sure that state employment actually guaranteed stability:

'I want to have a normal wage' (U30); 'It makes no difference to me if it is a state or a private company' (U23); 'I spent my whole life working at a state enterprise with half-year arrears of salaries' (U13; U16 agrees); 'I would work for a foreign company … No arrears there … A foreign company is a guarantee that each month you are sure to receive your money' (U15).

High wages were a great attraction, and for many outside Ukraine they were the *only* attraction of a foreign company:

'people who want to earn much money choose foreign companies' (V4).

But foreign companies:

'manage workers only for the purpose of increasing productivity. You cannot make friends there' (K22); 'a Korean company will treat us better … have better understanding of our way of thinking' (K13); 'working for foreign companies, we just have the immediate benefits' (V13); 'if two enterprises pay the same salary with the same working conditions, we will choose the Vietnamese one' (V26); 'working for Vietnam companies, we have a lot of free time but the salary is low. Working for foreign companies, we are managed closely but the salary is high. In general, it is better to work for foreign companies' (V14); 'not every foreign company pays high salaries. Some Taiwanese textile and assembling companies pay low salaries though some people are unemployed and have no choice but to work for them. Most people want to work for Vietnamese companies, except for those foreign companies that pay high salaries. In general, Vietnamese are the best' (V5).

But Korean focus group participants (like Korean survey respondents) were more inclined than others to cite *personal development* as an attraction of foreign employers. Foreign companies were more technically advanced:

'a foreign company is advanced and different. They are equipped with various different systems. We need to learn from them' (K20); 'foreign companies are advanced in most cases' (K30); 'I prefer foreign companies especially from advanced countries. My relative works for a foreign company from Italy … [as well as] good welfare … they also provide many opportunities for employees to develop their capabilities, for example sending them abroad for studying' (K29).

They rewarded merit rather than personal 'connections':

'foreign companies encourage individual creativity. Personal connections, which is the main element of promotion in a Korean company, is not the basis for promotion in a foreign company' (K10); 'foreign companies do not consider school background or personal networks' (K19).

They respected and encouraged junior employees:

'there is no reciprocal respect between low and high positions in a Korean company, whereas they discuss freely and respect each other in a foreign company' (K16); 'you can show your ability in a private company' (K11); 'a private company gives an opportunity to people to maximise their capabilities' (K26).

Table 3.11. *Why the public choose different employers*

	Officials %	Public %	Public within each country			
			Czech R %	Korea %	Ukraine %	Vietnam %
Which of these would be the most important reason for your choosing to work in ...						
PUBLIC SECTOR						
... government office/state administration						
job security/stability/ pensions	74	79	75	86	50	88
high wages	8	14	23	6	42	3
personal development/ career development	15	5	1	7	5	5
... state-owned company						
job security/stability/ pensions	68	71	81	76	50	85
high wages	15	21	16	13	43	5
personal development/ career development	15	6	3	10	3	6
PRIVATE SECTOR						
... foreign company in (COUNTRY)						
high wages	43	59	61	39	70	76
personal development/ career development	35	23	26	34	14	10
job security/stability/ pensions	20	15	12	26	10	14
... private (COUNTRY) company						
high wages	29	39	28	25	65	39
personal development/ career development	47	32	34	51	9	36
job security/stability/ pensions	21	26	36	23	23	18
FAMILY						
... your own family business						
personal development/ career development	49	39	50	50	12	46
job security/stability/ pensions	26	33	38	37	18	43
high wages	18	23	8	13	63	5

Notes: Per cent of all respondents. Per cents giving other/mixed/'don't know' responses not shown.
Entries ranked by public criteria for choosing each employer.

They treated women better:

'foreign companies provide female workers with higher benefits' (K18).

In the survey, Czechs cited personal development slightly more than Koreans. But within every category of employment preference, Koreans put at least as much emphasis (and usually considerably more) than the Czechs on personal development. The explanation of this statistical quirk is that Czechs were more likely than Koreans to opt for employment sectors like family businesses where both Czechs and Koreans emphasised personal development. As employees, however, it was Koreans rather than Czechs who looked for more encouragement to develop personal skills.

3.5   Explaining public support for economic openness

In Chapter 1 we suggested that attitudes towards economic openness might be influenced by personal background and experience and by perceptions of or attitudes towards recent economic and cultural change. So to explain support for economic openness, we calculate regressions predicting attitudes towards the internal market economy and towards opening up to the world. As predictors we began by assessing all the indicators of background and experience, perceptions of and satisfaction with change that we used in Chapter 2, along with a wide range of indicators of aspects of attitudes towards national culture and xenophobia.

These wide-ranging analyses provided quite powerful explanations of public support for the internal market economy *as an engine of national prosperity* (RSQ = 32 per cent). Two key elements of a national winners and losers model best explained why people felt the market economy generated prosperity: those who thought their national economy had prospered over the last decade and/or that it would prosper over the next decade were the most likely to conclude that the market economy produced prosperity. A personal winners and losers model, based on whether family living standards had got better or worse, was much less important; and perceptions of domestic or of international injustice even less so.

The basis for public criticism of the market economy *for being unfair* was different, though equally predictable (RSQ = 33 per cent). Overall, the most powerful predictor was simply general discontent with the way things were going in the country. Perceptions that international organisations were unfair had a weaker but consistent impact, though the direction of causation between internal and external unfairness may be somewhat ambiguous. Beyond all individual-level influences, however, the regressions on the merged data sets indicated that Ukrainians had particularly strong feelings that the market economy was unfair, while the Vietnamese had particularly strong feelings that it was not.

Public criticism of opening up to the world economy was only slightly less predictable (RSQ = 30 per cent). An international justice model and a national winners and losers model rivalled each other as explanations of support for opening up. But the justice model predominated and was reinforced by some simple xenophobia – dislike of foreigners in general, and of international businessmen in particular, made opening up unpopular. While fears for future national living standards were important, the most powerful predictor was the feeling that foreign companies exploited local people and resources (beta = 0.23 overall, but higher in East Europe). Surprisingly perhaps, no aspect of cultural perceptions or even cultural attitudes proved to have much impact on support for the principle of opening up (or establishing an internal market economy) – despite the threat to culture being cited as one of the main disadvantages of opening up.

A simplified analysis

These comprehensive regression analyses looked at a very wide range of potential influences upon attitudes towards internal and external markets – so wide indeed that a strictly numerical comparison is impeded by focusing upon whichever aspects of public opinion in different places most affected particular aspects of support. The regressions themselves require a lot of study before clear themes emerge. So to simplify our findings we turn to a more restricted, disciplined approach using a very short, standardised set of variables representing the core elements of different explanatory models:

> Trends in family income – the key element of a *personal winners and losers model*;
>
> Perceived national economic trends – the key element of a *national winners and losers model*;
>
> Perceptions that foreign companies exploit local people and resources – a key element in an *international injustice model*;
>
> Perceptions that the local winners have been those with more skill, ability or luck rather than those with more power, contacts and corruption – a key element of a *domestic justice model*;
>
> Perceptions of trends in respect for the national culture – a key element in a *cultural model*;
>
> ASIAN – An East Asian/East European contrast – the basis of a (global) *regional model*;
>
> OFFICIALS – A contrast between officials and the public – a key element in an *elite model*.

Most of these emerged as important in our more wide-ranging regressions. The exceptions are the indicators of the *domestic justice* and *elite models* which we include for their theoretical rather than empirical importance. We include all seven indicators in all regressions, though we omit from our tables any entries that fail to meet the five per cent criterion of statistical significance (numerically the omitted coefficients are very small anyway and merely distracting).

Explaining public support for the market economy A national winners and losers model best explains attitudes towards the internal market economy – either in terms of creating prosperity (beta = 0.22) or fairness (beta = 0.25). That is followed by a personal or family-based winners and losers model (beta = 0.14); and then by weaker impacts from the other factors. The domestic justice model, represented by our measure of whether the public felt the benefits of recent changes had gone to the deserving, has very little impact on attitudes to the market as an engine of prosperity (beta = 0.06), but rises to third place in explanations of whether the public felt the market economy was fair (beta = 0.11). In the combined data set of public and officials, this domestic justice model rises to second place (beta = 0.16).

Explaining public support for opening up The basis of public support for opening up is very different from the basis of public support for the market economy. The impact of a national winners and losers model on public support for opening up is much weaker (beta = 0.17) and the impact of a personal or family winners and losers model even less (beta = 0.12). The most powerful factor is the international justice model (beta = 0.26). Public perceptions that foreign companies help rather than exploit is the predominant influence upon support for opening up, though improvements in the national economy and family income also have some additional impact.

Similarly, the national winners and losers model, based on perceptions of the economy's recent performance, is by far the most powerful influence (beta = 0.25) upon public feelings that there is no viable alternative to the market economy. It has twice the impact of anything else. The international justice model, based on perceptions of the behaviour of foreign companies, is by far the most powerful influence (beta = 0.23) upon public feelings that there is no viable alternative to opening up – half as much again as the impact of anything else.

Perceptions of whether the national culture was gaining or losing respect had very little impact on public support for opening up. Neither, in our wider regressions, did any other aspect of cultural perceptions or

Table 3.12. *Explaining public support for the market economy*

		All four countries		Public within each country			
		Public and officials	Public only	Czech R	Korea	Ukraine	Vietnam
Market economy brings prosperity	**RSQ =**	22	24	24	3	18	3
MODEL	INDICATOR	Beta	Beta	Beta	Beta	Beta	Beta
Winners and losers – national	economy got better	21	22	23		23	16
Winners and losers – family	family income got better	9	14	19	13	15	
Culture	national culture gaining respect	11	10				
International justice	foreign companies help	11	9	17		19	
Domestic justice	winners are those with skill and luck	6	6	7	7	8	
Legacy	Asian	12	11				
Elite	Officials	7					
Market economy is fair	**RSQ =**	24	28	25	8	6	5
MODEL	INDICATOR	Beta	Beta	Beta	Beta	Beta	Beta
Winners and losers – national	economy got better	25	25	22	16		
Winners and losers – family	family income got better	11	14	12	10	11	7
Domestic justice	winners are those with skill and luck	16	11	15	7	6	
International justice	foreign companies help	11	10	18	10	12	10
Culture	national culture gaining respect	6	9	9		10	8
Legacy	Asian	4	8				12
Elite	Officials	-4					

Note: All betas shown are statistically significant at the five per cent level.

Table 3.13. *Explaining public support for opening up*

Opening up more advantages than disadvantages

		All four countries		Public within each country			
		Public and officials	Public only	Czech R	Korea	Ukraine	Vietnam
RSQ =		22	21	33	3	20	1
		Beta	Beta	Beta	Beta	Beta	Beta
Model	**Q and descriptor**						
International justice	foreign companies help	26	26	41	12	39	10
Winners and losers – national	economy got better	20	17	16		6	
Winners and losers – family	family income got better	11	12	14	8	11	
Culture	national culture gaining respect	9	7	2			
Domestic justice	winners are those with skill and luck				6		
Legacy	Asian	2	5				
Elite	Officials	−9	−6				

Note: All betas shown are statistically significant at the five per cent level.

attitudes. In particular, perceptions that 'our way of life is getting lost' – another, perhaps more direct indicator of cultural fright – contributed nothing towards explaining public opposition to opening up. In regressions using just three predictors – whether foreign companies exploit, whether the national economy had got worse, and whether 'our way of life is getting lost' or 'remains strong' – the coefficients of the first two are very close to those shown in Table 3.13. However the coefficients of this indicator of 'cultural fright' are a statistically insignificant 0.02 on the merged data set of the public in all four countries; they average just 0.04 in the East European countries; and in the East Asian countries they average 0.07 but have the 'wrong sign' – suggesting that, if anything, those who feel their national culture 'remains strong' are (if only very slightly) more opposed to opening up. There is no reason to doubt that the public have genuine concerns that opening up the economy is likely to erode their national culture. (We explore those concerns in greater detail in Chapter 4.) These concerns, though genuine, have a minimal impact on public support for opening up the economy. That support is driven by economic perceptions, and is largely unaffected by cultural perceptions.

3.6   Conclusions

Despite all of their specific discontents and their more general discontent with 'the way things are going for our country today', despite acute awareness of the disadvantages of opening up, and despite some vague longing for a better alternative, there was enormously strong public support for opening up. Only three per cent insisted there were no disadvantages to opening up. But by a majority of more than two to one the public said there were 'more, or more important' advantages than disadvantages; and by a majority of almost four to one they said opening up was good rather than bad for their country. Discontent and support co-exist. Discontent did not preclude support, but conversely, support did not preclude discontent. The public were in general 'critical supporters' of opening up.

Public support for the (internal) market economy was less clear, however. By majorities of two to one, the public characterised the market economy as making their country more prosperous but also less fair. There was more craving for an alternative to the market economy than for an alternative to opening up. In East Europe the market economy was criticised from a free market perspective as well as from a social democratic solidarity perspective: around a quarter of the public insisted that they 'had no real market economy here'.

Moreover, the public were not enthusiastic about working for private companies – especially local private companies. Foreign companies paid more, but self-employment was good for personal development, and working for the state – the most popular choice – was good for security of employment and guaranteed pensions, the public's top priority. Ukraine provided an exception to all of this. In Ukraine the top priority was cash in hand – high wages now. That was their principal motivation for choosing to work for themselves or a local private company as well as for a foreign company. Indeed, high wages rivalled hopes of long-term security as Ukrainians' motivation for taking state employment. For good reason, they did not trust the long-term.

A national (but *not* a personal) version of a winners and losers model best explains why people feel the market economy makes their country more prosperous: those who thought their national economy had prospered over the last decade and/or that it would prosper over the next decade were the most likely to conclude that market economies deliver prosperity. The public extrapolated from perceptions of national economic success or failure to economic principle, even though a significant number of people in the worst-performing economies denied that they did in fact have a 'real market economy'.

A (domestic) justice model, based on perceptions that the benefits of economic change had gone to corrupt power-holders or those with contacts rather than those with greater skill, education or even luck, also had an important impact on whether the public rated the market economy as 'unfair', though only a very marginal impact on how they rated it as an engine of prosperity.

But rather than any kind of winners and losers model, an (international) justice model, based on whether the public felt 'foreign companies exploit rather than help', was the best predictor of opposition to opening up to the world economy. That was, of course, a selfish rather than altruistic version of a justice model.

4 Public support for cultural protection

In Chapter 1 we outlined some good reasons why the public might wish to change their traditional culture or preserve it; why they might welcome or resist cultural globalisation. Our aim in this chapter is to see how the public themselves define and value their culture. Do they fear that their culture, however defined, is threatened by opening up the economy? Insofar as opening up might erode their culture, are they willing to strike a Faustian bargain and trade culture and identity for material gain?

4.1 A Faustian bargain?

By instinct, the public were not very modest about their 'culture', whatever they meant by that. (We explore their meanings later.) Two-thirds agreed their 'culture' was 'superior to others' and wanted more emphasis on their own country's distinctive 'culture and traditions' (see Table 4.1).

At the same time, two-thirds felt that opening up the economy would inevitably bring cultural homogenisation and that their 'traditional way of life' was already 'getting lost'. Significantly, it was in Ukraine and Vietnam, where the public felt their culture was strongest and homogenisation was less likely, that they were most keen to emphasise it more. Cross-nationally, public support for emphasising national culture therefore reflected cultural security rather than cultural fright. Nonetheless, even in Ukraine and Vietnam around 60 per cent felt opening up the economy would inevitably erode their cultural distinctiveness, and only around 24 per cent disagreed.

In Chapter 3 we found that cultural change was by far the least cited advantage of opening up the economy and, by a narrow margin, the single most often cited disadvantage. Yet we also found overwhelming public support in all countries for opening up the economy. So the public everywhere recognised that opening up the economy could involve a 'Faustian bargain': trading the erosion of traditional national culture and identity for economic development. The best they could do would be to drive a hard bargain: minimising the cultural loss and maximising the economic gain.

Table 4.1. *Cultural pride*

	Officials %	Public %	Public within each country			
			Czech R %	Korea %	Ukraine %	Vietnam %
Our people are not perfect but our culture is superior to others						
completely agree	23	26	18	29	26	36
mostly agree	44	43	47	61	31	30
mostly disagree	20	18	22	8	26	13
completely disagree	4	5	5	1	10	7
Prefer (COUNTRY) to ...						
... emphasise culture and traditions a lot more	29	28	21	12	33	41
... emphasise culture and traditions a little more	43	37	47	51	32	15
... become a little more like other countries	18	22	20	30	21	20
... become a lot more like other countries	7	8	8	7	10	10

Note: Per cent of all respondents. Per cents giving other/mixed/'don't know' responses not shown.

Table 4.2. *Opening up will homogenise culture*

	Officials %	Public %	Public within each country			
			Czech R %	Korea %	Ukraine %	Vietnam %
Is it inevitable that our culture and way of life will become more and more like other countries if we open up our economy more to foreign companies?						
yes	67	66	72	74	62	58
no	26	23	19	23	22	26
Our traditional way of life ...						
... is getting lost	64	62	68	80	59	39
... remains strong	27	28	20	19	28	46

Note: Per cent of all respondents. Per cents giving other/mixed/'don't know' responses not shown.

4.2   Lessons from abroad

In classic accounts, 'modernisation' meant learning lessons from abroad –
especially from the US (see Chapter 1). We found the public were
particularly wary of the US. More generally, they were eager to learn
lessons from abroad – though lessons on business rather than culture.

Minds were not closed to lessons from abroad. There was broad support for accepting 'international standards' on matters like pollution.
Indeed a large majority felt their country had at least '*something* to learn'
from other countries on 'business', 'politics' and even on 'social affairs
and family life'. But only 27 per cent felt they had '*a lot*' to learn from
other countries about 'social and family' matters, compared with 40 per
cent on 'political affairs', and 46 per cent on 'business affairs'. The
contrast was particularly sharp in Vietnam where twice as many felt
their country had 'a lot to learn' about business (61 per cent) as social
affairs (31 per cent).

Table 4.3. *Lessons from abroad*

	Officials %	Public %	Public within each country			
			Czech R %	Korea %	Ukraine %	Vietnam %
On problems of pollution and environmental damage it is better …						
for [COUNTRY] to take its own decisions	37	38	34	44	40	33
to accept international standards	50	48	42	52	46	48
(VOL) we have no choice – we have to accept international standards	8	7	19	2	5	2
In economic and business affairs … … lot to learn	52	46	35	36	50	61
In political affairs … … lot to learn	43	40	38	50	39	34
In social affairs and family life … … lot to learn	29	27	24	22	34	31

Notes: Per cent of all respondents. Per cents giving other/mixed/'don't know' responses not
shown. VOL indicates that a particular answer was not offered by the interviewer, but was
spontaneously volunteered by some respondents.

Lessons on business and politics Some focus-group participants rejected lessons from abroad even on economic or political affairs:

'we ourselves should correct our problems, not foreign people' (K5); 'it is not good to follow others blindly' (K20); 'Shevchenko said learn foreign ideas but do not abandon your own ... it is no problem to learn things, but there must be no blind imitating' (U28); 'let us learn, but stay ourselves' (C26); 'it is not necessary to go abroad' (U17); 'it is useless for us to borrow some model from anyone ... we need to be different' (U12); 'in the Soviet Union we knew how to do everything' (U25) ... '[now] practically everything has been privatised ... even the oblast power companies are being sold' (U28) ... '[we will] turn into some sort of colony if that foreign capitalism comes rushing in here ... leaving us entirely ripped off' (U30).

But more expressed their willingness to learn business methods and better technologies from abroad:

'scientific achievements, new technology' (U30); 'engineering ... ours is no good' (U22); 'we care about immediate economic effects only ... in Australia, a company considers the environment first in planning and managing a factory' (K10).

One Ukrainian hinted at the significance of consumer culture – or rather the hunger for it – in undermining communism. Fashion might not be of deep fundamental importance, but freedom of choice was. In that context post-communist business had to learn consumer responsiveness rather than the efficient production of unwanted goods:

'there are things to learn ... when the [communist] system was in place, public catering establishments were all alike throughout Kyiv, even the prices were the same ... now every restaurant, every café is different and the quality is good ... people do not have to accept whatever is offered, they can choose ... take clothes, a person can buy what they like rather than domestically produced, out of fashion items' (U5).

There was some emphasis on learning business probity as much as efficiency or even consumer responsiveness, good corporate governance as much as advanced technology:

'in a foreign country, ability is the first criterion in employing men' (K11); 'not self-centered thinking that a business wholly belongs to an owner only' (K5); '[better] working attitudes' (U21); '[respect for] obligations' (U19); 'more discipline in ... paying taxes on time and in full ... moreover, state tax policy should be more transparent and prevent a situation where certain businessmen are taxed in full, while others enjoy tax holidays for unknown reasons, their debts written off ... more order in this sphere' (U8); 'more transparent opportunities for foreign investors' (U14); 'what is going on here is what America used to have in the nineteenth century ... plain brigandage ... people thieve and send their children to study abroad – [though perhaps] those children will learn something abroad and come back, and then their children or maybe even grandchildren will run the economy here in a civilised way' (U13); 'we can learn from China and Singapore ... how to apply law strictly, reducing corruption' (V26).

On politics, too, the emphasis was on learning integrity more than anything else:

'high-ranking officials are apt to ... stay in their positions even though nobody wants them any more ... they should know when to leave' (K8); 'our politics is too much focused on party interest and disregards the genuine national interest ... they should put nation and state before political parties' (K23); 'both politics and economy in our country are not transparent' (K32); 'foreign politicians are fairly clean ... Korean politicians not at all' (K9); 'there are some exceptions, but corruption of officials is getting more serious' (K16); 'yes [we should learn business lessons from abroad], and in politics too ... frauds exist everywhere, but if there were not so much here, things would be better' (C11).

This was not the case in Vietnam. Although the Vietnamese focus group moderator meticulously asked: 'do we have a lot to learn from other countries in running our economic *and political* affairs?' there was a deafening silence about learning political ideas from abroad. Focus group participants were reluctant to spell out their views about political lessons – though we know from the survey that over a third of the Vietnam public felt they had 'a lot' to learn from abroad about political affairs. Instead Vietnamese participants focused exclusively on economic lessons:

'in adopting the open economy ... we should learn economic management from foreign partners' (V3); 'financial management' (V18); '[foreign] ways of doing business' (V21); 'industrial style which is more dynamic' (V23); 'industrial manner' (V17); 'working style ... sound management' (V16); 'technology' (V12); 'new technology and economic management in the market mechanism' (V31).

There are several possible explanations for this: either Vietnamese participants were simply unwilling to articulate criticisms of officials – though they did so in other parts of our focus group discussions; or they simply judged that the outside world had far more to teach them about business and technology than about politics and administration; or perhaps learning market methods from abroad was itself 'political' in Vietnam.

Lessons on social and family affairs In the survey, Koreans were the most willing to learn political lessons from abroad, but the least willing to take lessons on social affairs. Similarly, in focus groups many Koreans simply dismissed without comment the very notion of taking lessons on social affairs. Participants in other countries also rejected such lessons:

'we live in a cosmopolitan society ... there is no space for overdone patriotism ... but people should respect their country, have their traditions, though not overdo it ... we do not want to adopt other cultures' (C2); 'there are things we should *not* learn ... the relationship between girls and boys' (V16); 'let them learn from us ... we have things like family values, goodwill, generosity inherent in Ukrainians' (U21) ... 'more hearty relations in families, goodwill ... foreigners are ... rather dry, pedantic, rigid ... I do not think their values are good to us' (U17); 'we have friendlier relations ... when I dug potatoes today neighbours came saying we shall help you ... today they help one, tomorrow another, the day after someone else ... in a village like ours there is kindness, respect for the old ... there is nothing like this abroad' (U20); 'the best social basis was in the Soviet Union ... if you fell ill you would be paid, you would be employed; when your maternity leave was over you would still have the same job' (U16).

It is irrelevant to contest the accuracy of this idyllic view of social life in communist Ukraine – nor the suggestion that neighbours in other countries are any less helpful. What these claims make clear is the fact that these participants had no desire to take any lessons from abroad on social or family affairs.

Some Czech participants lamented the displacement of 'Ježíšek' (the Christ Baby who brings presents to Czech children on Christmas Eve) by Santa Claus:

'the young ones see Santa everywhere ... I can tell my son about Ježíšek at home but when he goes to school and thirty other children say Santa, he will say Santa too' (C6); '[we should] return to our traditions' (C22).

Those who did welcome social lessons from abroad stressed freedom and independence *within the family* though some had reservations about the erosion of family ties:

'we have a lot to learn ... our society was organised on the principle of eastern feudalism ... when we make contact with western cultures ... however, the structure of our family gets weaker' (V21).

Some younger Koreans preferred more independence:

'the tradition to live together with old parents is lasting, not like foreign countries where they live separately ... we should carry on this tradition in our country' (K5) ... 'I oppose that ... you stand on your own legs at the age of eighteen in foreign countries ... that does not mean the breakup of the family ... we should learn that ... when three or four generations lived together we were too poor to have separate houses' (K1).

The same view was expressed in Europe:

'the family is different [in England]' (C24) ... 'it is freer there, maybe too much' (C21); 'people [in the West] feel themselves free, while here ...' (U5) ... 'every-thing is very austere' (U6, interrupting) ... 'having traditional views, parents are tempted to rule their children with a rod of iron; so one day the youth decide that they have had enough of it and girls of fifteen or sixteen go and get themselves married, boys do the same or move to other places' (U5).

Participants were impressed particularly by the personal independence of even quite young western children:

'our education is based on learning-by-heart and that is bad ... [English and American kids] have less knowledge, but they are self-confident, they are the ones who will succeed' (C31); 'Korean mothers raise their kids to lose independent spirit ... in that respect foreign kids look so strong ... we should learn such things' (K5); 'we take care of our children with the notion of protection ... in America they emphasise the spirit of independence instead of giving protection, so they are able to perform social life well ... we raise weak people' (K22); 'in the West, a child begins to feel himself an individual while still very young ... treated like a grown-up ... unlike our children ... he is very sure of himself ... radiating self-confidence' (U4; U3 agrees).

Modernisation not Americanisation Confident kids apart, the acceptable face of cultural modernisation was *not* American – not in any of our countries. We asked whether there was any particular country whose culture 'we should welcome and try to learn from'; and whose culture 'we should try really hard to keep out'. On average, four times as many cited some European country (24 per cent) rather than the US (6 per cent), as the country whose culture should be welcomed. Taken together a West European trio came top in every country except Ukraine – where there was even more sympathy for Russian culture (23 per cent compared with 19 per cent for the West European).

Conversely, the US topped the list of countries whose culture should be 'kept out' (19 per cent). That was true in every country except Korea – where although US culture was resented more than in any other country (21 per cent), Japanese culture was resented even more (34 per cent). If only to defend themselves against American and Japanese culture, per-haps, Koreans were twice as likely as people anywhere else to welcome European culture (46 per cent). Openness towards foreign cultures was therefore more likely to mean openness to European culture than to American – despite the ubiquity and visibility of US brands.

Generally the public focused their likes and dislikes on the culture of near-neighbours or of superpowers. There was one rather odd exception: in both our East European countries, about ten per cent prioritised

Table 4.4. *Welcoming European culture, rejecting American*

	Officials %	Public %	Public within each country			
			Czech R %	Korea %	Ukraine %	Vietnam %
One country whose culture we should try to welcome in (COUNTRY) and try to learn from						
No	26	24	32	3	25	34
France + Germany + Britain	23	24	24	46	19	5
Russia	6	7	1	1	23	5
Japan	7	7	5	14	3	5
America	5	6	5	12	3	3
China	4	4	1	8	0	8
North Korea	0	1	0	3	0	0
Other Asian countries	1	1	1	1	0	2
Other non-Asian countries	2	2	4	2	2	1
One country whose culture we should try really hard to keep out of (COUNTRY)						
No	35	29	30	5	42	39
America	14	19	17	21	19	15
Japan	9	8	0	34	0	0
Russia	3	4	8	4	2	1
North Korea	4	4	4	11	1	0
China	2	3	4	4	2	1
France + Germany + Britain	2	2	3	4	0	1
Other Asian countries	6	6	9	3	10	1
Other non-Asian countries	2	2	3	3	2	1

Note: Per cent of all respondents. Per cents giving other/mixed/'don't know' responses not shown.

excluding Asian culture. The focus group discussions reveal why (see section 4.5 below).

4.3   Culture: 'most obvious' and 'most important'

Most obvious 'The western media' and brands such as 'Coca Cola and McDonald's' have been cited as among the 'most obvious and tangible forms of cultural globalisation' (Beynon and Dunkerley 2000; p. 13). They are the epitome of globalised 'consumer culture'.

Table 4.5. *Foreign brands, films and TV*

	Officials %	Public %	Public within each country			
			Czech R %	Korea %	Ukraine %	Vietnam %
Feelings about the presence of foreign brands like Coca Cola and McDonalds in (COUNTRY)						
like a lot	4	7	7	3	8	10
like a little	33	37	37	41	34	38
dislike a little	37	28	34	42	18	17
dislike a lot	13	15	12	14	26	10
Feelings about foreign films or TV in (COUNTRY)						
like a lot	5	9	7	7	7	18
like a little	43	44	37	56	37	45
dislike a little	32	26	35	31	22	13
dislike a lot	10	13	12	6	29	7

Note: Per cent of all respondents. Per cents giving other/mixed/'don't know' responses not shown.

Public attitudes towards 'the presence of foreign brands such as Coca Cola and McDonald's in our country' were almost exactly balanced numerically between positive and negative, though those who disliked them had more intense feelings, especially in Ukraine. Numerically however, Koreans were the most negative and the Vietnamese, despite their history, the most positive about such US brands. Attitudes towards 'foreign films or TV' were more positive, but there was a clear Europe/Asia divide. In Korea and above all in Vietnam, large majorities liked them. But in the Czech Republic and Ukraine public opinion was on balance negative. In Ukraine the *intensity* (though not the extent) of antagonism was outstanding: 29 per cent not only disliked 'foreign films and TV' but disliked them 'a lot'.

In focus groups, criticism of foreign films and TV was more striking than criticism of foreign brands, however. There were mixed views about *adverts* for foreign brands. Some were positive:

'advertising at least gives people an idea about what they can buy' (U7); 'they are very interesting' (V26); 'I just watch them comfortably without any thought' (K5); 'our eyes felt uneasy at the first sight of them, but as time went by we have got used to them' (K7);

– and some negative:

'there are too many foreign advertisements … [there] should not be more than ten per cent' (K26); 'we cannot deny that our culture is westernised, affected by

TV or ads ... once foreign culture prevails, we cannot help being dependent' (K22); 'in the past, I had admired them but recently I feel a sort of objection, considering many incidents in the US ... they wield power too much' (K20).

Several Vietnamese participants criticised their own authorities for exercising too little control. They called explicitly for tighter censorship:

'because state management is bad, foreigners can do whatever they want ... it is annoying but we have to accept it and get accustomed to it but it is not good for us' (V4; V3 similar); 'some advertisements have a bad impact on our morality and culture but people seem not to care about this, they care more about making money from selling broadcasting time to advertisers ... in Vietnam, advertisements are culturally very poor' (V18); 'the state should allow advertisements [but] with controls to avoid bad images that have bad influences on Vietnamese' (V12) ... 'they can affect the young ... pervert humans' (V13); 'advertisements should be censored before being launched' (V16).

Yet focus group participants – including the Vietnamese – were generally favourable towards foreign products and brands *in themselves* as distinct from adverts for them. A few even contested the 'foreignness' of Coca Cola or Marlboro:

'I know Coca Cola is from abroad, but ... I think of it as ours' (K2); 'Korean people would think of Coca Cola not as a foreign product, but as a Korean drink' (K9); 'Marlboro cigarettes are already produced in Ukraine' (U5) ... 'in Kharkiv' (U7).

Others just rated foreign manufactured products as better:

'preferring foreign products has become a habit' (V18); 'foreign brands are good, local products not as good' (V25); 'imported goods offer more variety' (C30); 'nicer packaging' (C29); 'better quality' (C0).

They were more critical of foreign films and TV. Some liked their toughness and brutality:

'I prefer foreign films' (K33); 'ours are too sentimental' (K3); 'in action movies, foreign actors are more realistic than ours ... they act more realistically when they are shot by a bullet' (K28).

Others criticised foreign films for this same realistic brutality:

'I am not against all of them but probably against some eighty per cent ... I have a fifteen-year-old brother, he is not interested in our own films, he would rather watch films with Jackie Chan and learn some martial art' (U7); 'I do not like American movies due to violence ... most American movies are violent' (K5); 'violence promoted primarily by films worsens the crime situation, many want to emulate these crimes' (U8; U7 nods in approval).

In East Europe, TV – and especially American TV – was criticised for its violence, its pornography, and its ready accessibility to children:

'formerly we had more Russian films and now there are more American ones . . . trash, but the ratings are high . . . sometimes I just stare open-mouthed . . . how far have these American films gone' (C8); 'Russian films could not have this influence, every child laughed at them, but American films attract them' (C7); 'there should be more Czech films' (C8); 'now I have been watching those Russian videos, Russian films with greater pleasure than English or American ones . . . we have eaten a bit too much of that stuff' (U16).

'TV programs are rather brutal' (C24); 'violence, terrible . . . children are now more aggressive, they play at war . . . fairy tales used to be so nice in the past' (C0); 'our children always ask for Nova [a commercial TV station] . . . they show vulgar cartoons . . . there are fairy tales on ĖT [Czech public TV] but our children want Nova, and they grow up with this' (C0); 'it cannot be regulated . . . if they show it on TV, children switch it on . . . it harms children . . . I have a younger brother and he only wants weapons, weapons all the time' (C11); 'it affects children' (C14); 'there are many pornographic films' (U1); 'TV is all murders or sex . . . everyone shoots and kills and strangles . . . how did kids play earlier? . . . now they have to kill, strangle, put a plastic bag on the head' (U20); 'I would exclude horror films from the air altogether because children watch them . . . I have an aversion to such films myself' (U4).

Most important As Beynon and Dunkerley (2000) argued, the 'consumer culture' of foreign brands and media is indeed the 'most obvious form of globalisation' – but it is *not* the aspect of culture that the public say is most important to them. Most say that their country's 'culture and traditions' are of some importance 'to me personally'; and about half say it is '*very*' important – though that varies from only 26 per cent of Czechs, though 34 per cent of Koreans and 47 per cent of Ukrainians, to 80 per cent of Vietnamese.

What do they mean by their 'culture and traditions'? In focus groups, both support for – and criticism of – culture and traditions focused on language and social relationships, on what we label 'identity culture' rather than 'consumer culture'. Echoing the relatively low importance they placed on their national culture, Czech participants in focus groups were self-consciously adaptable:

'France sticks to its culture and its language' (C8) . . . '[with] a law that clearly bans all kinds of foreign influence' (C2) . . . '[but] we are a country that adapts' (C0) . . . 'we lack the sovereignty to hold our own and not give in to anyone' (C1).

While most Korean participants routinely asserted the importance of their traditional culture, once they got into detail, they began to express more criticism of it than praise. On the positive side:

'our traditional culture is for me represented by national holidays . . . I think this culture should be maintained' (K19).

Table 4.6. *The public rate national culture and traditions as 'very' important to them personally*

	Officials %	Public %	Public within each country			
			Czech R %	Korea %	Ukraine %	Vietnam %
How important are (COUNTRY) culture and traditions to you personally?						
very	58	47	26	34	47	80
somewhat	38	42	55	59	40	15
not very	4	8	15	6	9	2
not at all	0	1	2	1	3	1

Notes: Per cent of all respondents. Per cents giving other/mixed/'don't know' responses not shown.

In Ukraine the question read '*Ukrainian* culture and traditions' even for Russian-speaking areas and respondents.

A separate question in Ukraine found that 23 per cent of the public and 29 per cent of officials said '*Russian* culture and traditions' were 'very important' to them personally – compared with 47 per cent of the public and 70 per cent of officials who said '*Ukrainian* culture and traditions' were 'very important' to them personally.

More often Korean culture was defined – and criticised – in terms of family traditions and obligations; 'respect for parents' (K32), 'Confucian ideas' (K26), and 'memorial services':

'we cannot abolish memorial services just because there are no such customs in America' (K2); 'I am the eldest grandson of the head family ... so we keep graves ... while cutting weeds around the graves, you can talk about your grandfathers with your kids' (K16).

Yet while:

'respecting old people is good, it is unfair that women only cook [for the service], not participating in the memorial service itself ... we should reform what should be reformed' (K11); 'I feel unhappy to be the eldest grandson of the head family in the thirteenth generation ... we have thirteen memorial services a year' (K1);

'In foreign countries people do not take care of parents. Since my husband is the oldest son, we took care of father when he was sick, spending considerable costs ... the younger brother did not do anything ... when father died, there was no insurance and we are left with hospital bills ... I wish I were in a foreign country' (K31).

More broadly, others criticised:

'Confucian ideas, which emphasise hierarchical ranks ... if I respond to what older people say, it is accepted in foreign countries, but it is taken as resistance in our country' (K32); 'The Confucian idea of the predominance of men over women?' (Moderator) . . . 'should be rooted out!' (K30).

Some younger Korean participants declared a complete lack of interest:

'if our traditional culture mattered to me, I would have to live my life according to its norms and rules' (K18); 'to be honest, I am not interested in traditional culture . . . but when foreign cultures flow in . . . they clash with traditional ones . . . bad effects take place in the transition period' (K12; K11 agrees);

– though:

'I thought like that when I was younger . . . but as I got older . . . traditional culture . . . has become very important to me' (K20).

Just as Koreans complained about the *persistence* of their culture, many Ukrainians, especially Russian speakers, complained about its *resurgence*. It was too much of a good thing:

'our culture has begun to rise' (U25); 'Ukraine should be Ukraine' (U21); 'let our things remain ours' (U22); 'our traditions, our national symbols . . . you see our country so rich' (U20 with ironic laughter from U18); 'there are beautiful old traditions . . . but too many of them' (U19) . . . 'a bit too much' (U17); 'we are going from one extreme to another' (U20); 'stupid pressure . . . to save national traditions . . . irritates children . . . they need discos, rock, rap . . . traditions are not that important to them' (U17).

Russian speakers complained about the practical difficulties:

'At school . . . we studied and studied and then bang! Speak in Ukrainian! And I cannot' (U10); 'if you know the Ukrainian language, that is perfectly all right . . . [but] people must not be re-educated . . . they must not be obliged to know Ukrainian at any cost' (U14) . . . '[but now] you *must* know it' (U16); 'it is necessary' (U9); 'Ukrainian speech can already be heard in the streets [of Kharkiv] . . . it did not happen in the past' (U13) . . . 'and thank God for that' (U16).

Our surveys confirm that, to the public personally, social behaviour and family relationships were by far the most important aspects of their culture and traditions – cited as such by 42 per cent. Language was cited by a significantly smaller but still large number: 28 per cent. Nothing else came close: films and TV, food and cuisine, clothes, dress style, make-up – all these highly visible, highly globalised aspects of the consumer culture, the 'most obvious and tangible forms of cultural globalisation' to outsiders, were rejected by the local public as relatively unimportant to them personally. However much the public enjoyed consumer culture and indulged in it, they did not themselves regard it as culturally important.

Table 4.7. *What the public mean by national culture and traditions*

	Officials %	Public %	Czech R %	Korea %	Ukraine %	Vietnam %
			Public within each country			
Which aspects of (COUNTRY) culture and traditions are most important to you personally?						
... our social behaviour/ traditional family relationships	50	42	32	51	41	43
... our (COUNTRY) language	32	28	40	22	21	24
... our TV/films	5	9	9	10	11	8
... our food/cuisine	4	8	10	9	10	3
... our clothes/way of dressing/use of make-up	3	4	1	6	2	9
(VOL) our culture and traditions are *not* important to me personally	1	2	3	0	5	2

Notes: Per cent of all respondents. Per cents giving other/mixed/'don't know' responses not shown. VOL indicates that a particular answer was not offered by the interviewer, but was spontaneously volunteered by some respondents.
In Ukraine, two per cent of the public and four per cent of officials cited the Russian language as the most important part of their culture.

4.4   Culture: 'most threatened' and 'most important'

Overall, the public cited social relationships (33 per cent), the national media (27 per cent), and the national language (15 per cent) as most under threat from foreign influences. Beyond that, there were especially strong public perceptions of foreign threats to 'social behaviour and family relationships' in Korea (49 per cent); to the media in Ukraine (47 per cent); to the national language in the Czech Republic (28 per cent); and to neat and respectful dress codes in Vietnam (22 per cent).

One complacent Korean focus group participant saw no threat to their national culture:

'we go around relatives to salute them at the start of the lunar calendar ... I am in my 50s, and my children are in their 20s. My kids will take [their own children] to visit our ancestors' grave' (K26);

Table 4.8. *National culture under threat from foreign influences*

	Officials %	Public %	Public within each country			
			Czech R %	Korea %	Ukraine %	Vietnam %
Which if any do you feel is most threatened by foreign influences?						
... our social behaviour/ traditional family relationships	38	33	25	49	21	33
... our TV/films	28	27	25	17	47	18
... our (COUNTRY) language	16	15	28	16	11	5
... our clothes/way of dressing/use of make-up	7	9	3	7	4	22
... our food/cuisine	3	5	8	9	2	2
(VOL) our culture and traditions *not* threatened by foreign influences	3	4	5	0	5	5

Notes: Per cent of all respondents. Per cents giving other/mixed/'don't know' responses not shown. VOL indicates that a particular answer was not offered by the interviewer, but was spontaneously volunteered by some respondents.

Only three per cent of the public and two per cent of officials in Ukraine cited the Russian language as most under threat from foreign influences. Such as it was, the threat to Russian was from domestic influences, not foreign.

– and others took a positive view of external influences:

'culture flows from the more developed to the less ... we had washrooms outside in the past' (K19); 'positive foreign culture is good for us' (V26); 'we need to be receptive to tolerably good cultures' (K16).

Some Czechs saw no intentional external threat:

'the EU presses us in other matters but they will not meddle in our traditions' (C8); 'nobody wants us to give up our customs' (C0); 'nobody exerts any great [cultural] pressure on us' (C0).

Others did. Some Ukrainians felt international organisations were insensitive to the subsidies that had become embedded in the culture of communism:

'take the issue of payments for utilities and apartments ... we are advised to pay 100 per cent out of our pockets, without any subsidies ... in giving its advice, the West proceeds from its own standards, from western salaries' (U4).

Patriotic and traditional cultures were losing out:

'formerly, children were educated on the war hero Meresiev ... [now] our young people are largely influenced by the West ... the generation now in school do not even try to remember those traditions' (U20); 'when I was young, there were forests around our village and people enjoyed themselves ... they gathered and sang ... now, they do not communicate' (C0); 'nobody listens to traditional music ... most listen to popular songs or western music ... uniquely Korean music is vanishing' (K2).

Styles in dress and food were globalising:

'in the past, we focused on the family but nowadays, it depends on each individual ... some live on their own before getting married or change their dressing style or behaviours' (V4); 'students dye their hair and wear blue jeans' (K23); '[adopt] Japanese culture and hair-dyeing' (K12); 'the clothes of the young are too liberal ... pierced ears, eyebrows, even mouths ... those are all from foreign countries like Japan ... they ruin our traditional thoughts of Confucianism' (K28); 'traditional foods are healthy but fast foods, hamburgers are threatening our health' (K22); 'older generations are not affected much, but younger generations or college students are greatly affected by the Internet ... they do not like our food such as rice cakes, they do not understand what respect for the old means ... it is hard to have a common basis with them' (K32); 'language is a problem, too ... they mix Japanese and English with Korean ... it is difficult even to communicate' (K23).

Standards of behaviour were declining through exposure to foreign cultures, violence and pornography on the media:

'young people especially, come easily into contact with foreign cultures through movies ... they think of foreign things as natural in every respect ... it is getting much worse in little kids' (K10); 'when I organise a trip to the theatre, children do not know how they should behave' (C29) ... 'we were taught how to behave' (C25); '[even] public broadcasting [now includes] programmes that are not good for young kids' (K15); 'just think about the news programme ... all about killing and violence' (C28); 'rubbish shown on television ... gangster films, horror films, downright pornography ... it must be banned, regulated by the state .... when kids scuffled with each other in the past, traditional fisticuffs were prevalent ... now, their legs jerk to strike a blow to the kidneys, to the face ... horror films [make] children nervous and aggressive' (U30); '[instead of Russification] now we have Europeanisation ... brutalisation ... hostility is not only the result of our great impoverishment, it is the result of the influence of our television' (U28); 'cultural censoring bodies are not strict enough' (V16); 'we have to keep depraved foreign culture out of Vietnam and create healthy recreation in the schools for the young people' (V33).

Threats have to be read together with the importance that the public put on the differing aspects of their national culture. Overall, the media was cited by 27 per cent as under threat, but by only 9 per cent as important to them personally. Even in Ukraine, where 47 per cent cited the media as particularly threatened, only 11 per cent cited it as important to them. In Vietnam, 22 per cent cited their dress code as under threat, but only 8 per cent said it was important to them personally. These are threats that can be ignored by most people.

Social relationships were cited by large numbers *both* as most important (42 per cent) *and* as most under threat from foreign influences (33 per cent). The national language was cited by 28 per cent as important but by only 15 per cent as under threat. That may underestimate the degree of linguistic resentment: 40 per cent of Czechs cited their language as most important and 28 per cent as most under threat. More generally, the fear is often not that a language itself will be threatened so much as its status: it might be reduced to a language 'of hearth and home' and cease to be a language 'of business, work, and employment' – a low-status 'language of identity' rather than a high-status 'language of communication'. Thus only 5 per cent of Vietnamese felt their language was 'under threat', but 64 per cent 'completely agreed' that their children needed English 'to succeed in the world today' – and our evidence suggests such perceptions are an index of parochial or nationalist resentment rather than an emotion-free index of cosmopolitan awareness.

So we have three (or four if we include dress codes in Vietnam) aspects of national culture and traditions that are widely perceived to be under threat from abroad, but only two of them – language and social behaviour – are perceived as under threat and also cited as personal priorities by large numbers of the public. Both are part of 'identity culture'. Some aspects of 'consumer culture' are perceived to be under threat, but they are not felt by many to be important to them personally.

Table 4.9. *English domination*

| | Officials % | Public % | Public within each country | | | |
			Czech R %	Korea %	Ukraine %	Vietnam %
Children need to learn English to succeed in the world today						
completely agree	62	60	59	47	67	64
mostly agree	34	32	33	46	24	27
mostly disagree	2	3	4	5	4	0
completely disagree	0	1	2	1	1	2

Note: Per cent of all respondents. Per cents giving other/mixed/'don't know' responses not shown.

4.5   Xenophobia

Fear of foreign culture (whether homogenising or divisive in its impact) is only one aspect of a much wider and deeper fear of 'the foreign' – a fear that includes not just foreign ideas and culture in the narrow sense, but fear of foreign aggression, and fear of foreigners-as-such – in short, xenophobia in its many forms. That includes foreign countries, foreigners at home as well as abroad, even 'foreigners' and 'strangers' who may have lived in the area long before the currently dominant ethnic 'nation': indigenous minorities as well as immigrants.

Territorial threats America was perceived as the primary threat to *territory* as well as to *culture*. More people in Korea (30 per cent), than anywhere else viewed the US as a territorial threat. But Koreans felt uniquely insecure: 40 per cent cited North Korea as the primary threat, while another 17 per cent cited Japan. Only 2 per cent of Koreans did not fear territorial threats from some quarter. No doubt there is some spillover effect from perceptions of territorial threats that reinforces the feeling of cultural threat, but the Korean responses demonstrate that the public does discriminate between the prime sources of cultural threats (Japan – see table 4.4) and territorial threats (North Korea – see table 4.10) – though they rate the US a close second on both. Elsewhere, although many (37 per cent in Vietnam; 56 per cent in East Europe) did not feel territorially threatened at all, those that did cited the US as the primary territorial threat (though Germany came a close second for Czechs).

Ukrainian focus group participants dismissed the very idea of a territorial threat, however, because 'no one needs our abject poverty' (U30). In Kharkiv, the whole focus group was reportedly 'amazed' by the question: Ukraine they insisted was 'threatened by Bank Street [the seat of the Ukrainian Presidency]!' (U12, supported by U16) not by foreign countries. Russian claims on Crimea were dismissed as 'rubbish' (U13), though one far-sighted participant was uncomfortably aware that 'the main channels for delivering fuel from Russia to the EU run through Ukrainian territory' (U8) which posed an ill-defined 'threat' to Ukrainian 'independence'.

Incomers On balance, the public felt that foreigners who come into their country were 'on the whole, good' rather than 'bad' for the country, but views about incomers were much more positive in East Asia than in East Europe – and they were actually negative in the Czech Republic.

Table 4.10. *Territorial threats*

	Officials %	Public %	Public within each country			
			Czech R %	Korea %	Ukraine %	Vietnam %
National territory threatened by ...						
not threatened	42	39	53	2	59	37
America	13	16	8	30	10	18
North Korea	11	10	1	40	0	0
Japan	5	4	0	17	0	0
Russia	3	3	5	1	5	0
China	3	2	2	5	1	2
France + Germany + Britain	2	2	6	1	0	0
other Asian countries	2	3	5	0	3	3
other non-Asian countries	1	1	1	0	1	2

Note: Per cent of all respondents. Per cents giving other/mixed/'don't know' responses not shown.

Attitudes were affected by the origin and purpose of incomers. In Ukraine, Russians were rather more welcome than westerners. Skilled experts and rich tourists were very welcome everywhere. International businessmen were only slightly less welcome – except in the Czech Republic where they were much less welcome, however. Backpackers were less welcome than 'rich tourists' – and dramatically so in Vietnam. On balance attitudes to all kinds of incomers were positive, except for attitudes towards 'low-skilled workers from poorer countries' – which were slightly positive in East Asia but very strongly negative in East Europe.

Focus group participants talked with great passion and at great length about incomers to their land. Mostly their comments reflect the patterns in the survey: incomers' skills and resources, their purpose, and their place of origin all affected their welcome. Those from advanced countries, with business or technical skills, or with wealth to spend or invest, were generally welcome – though even the good could be bad if not watched:

'every foreigner comes to Vietnam for his own purpose, which could be good or bad ... even good foreigners coming to Vietnam could be bad, if the host is not prudent enough' (V18).

History mattered to Vietnamese participants who claimed:

'the Americans and French do not have good will ... and Russians do' (V21); 'Russians left a good impression on Vietnam ... for those having wars with us, it is

Table 4.11. *Welcoming foreigners*

	Officials %	Public %	Public within each country			
			Czech R %	Korea %	Ukraine %	Vietnam %
On the whole foreigners who come to (COUNTRY) are good/bad for (COUNTRY)						
net positive: per cent						
'good' minus 'bad'	+51	+42	−14	+73	+48	+65
Specific kinds of foreigners (net positive: per cent 'good' minus 'bad') ...						
... highly skilled experts from advanced countries	+88	+81	+76	+84	+82	+80
... rich tourists	+79	+76	+76	+68	+85	+72
... international businessmen	+74	+62	+23	+85	+67	+74
... backpackers	+59	+55	+68	+66	+60	+24
... low-skilled workers from poorer countries	−22	−19	−49	+16	−44	+3
... Russians (asked in Ukraine only)	+68				+65	
... westerners (asked in Ukraine only)	+66				+50	

Note: Per cent of all respondents. Per cents giving other/mixed/'don't know' responses not shown.

difficult to have good feelings' (V4); 'for those countries with which we have had long-term [good] relations – such as Russia – we do not have to worry about their people ... [but] for countries like China or America we should be cautious' (V16).

Three decades after the cessation of hostilities some qualified their personal antagonism – yet without either forgetting or forgiving:

'there was time when we thought that all Americans were bad, but now many Americans come here to help ... even in a foreign country, there are both good and bad people ... if we are prudent and clever, we can make good persons better and bad ones good' (V18); 'in the past we hated invading countries but we should forget the past and look forward to the future' (V8); '[though] we still worry about America because we are not sure whether they really want to help us or not' (V5).

Many Koreans accepted the need for US troops to remain in Korea, but no Korean participant in any focus group had a good word to say about them – they were at best an unwelcome necessity and at worst simply unwelcome. Harmful foreigners included:

'soldiers' (K10); 'especially GIs' (K26); 'I am scared of the US ... they are sly ... Korean employees in foreign companies do not know their future' (K25); 'Do you

have special distrust of Americans among other foreigners?' (moderator) ...
'Yes ... US troops should be withdrawn as soon as possible' (K25).

Opinion was most divided about low-skilled, poor incomers. Reflecting
the survey, Koreans were the most sympathetic towards 'low-skilled
workers from poorer countries' who did '3D' ('dirty, dangerous, difficult') work:

'those engaged in 3D type industries' (K28); 'jobs that we avoid' (K23; K19
agrees); 'hard and difficult work' (K30); 'on construction sites where we avoid
working' (K16); 'labourers are good' (K13; K27, K10 similar);

– though:

'without them, the phenomenon of avoiding 3D work would not have emerged ...
we might have returned to such work ... but now companies prefer to employ
foreigners' (K26; K33 agrees).

In East Europe there was far more resentment towards low-status incomers from under-developed countries:

'[we should exclude] manual workers' (C22) ... 'perhaps we would not be able to
find any other people for some kinds of work' (C17) ... 'given our rate of
unemployment, it seems that we do not need much labour [from abroad]'
(C22) ... 'but [unemployed Czechs] mostly do not want to work' (C18).

There were 'too many':

'Ukrainians' (C29); 'Slovaks, Ukrainians, Russians, and similar nationalities ...
nobody sets any limits on their numbers' (C0); 'the Vietnamese work hard, but
they are beginning to expand ... they know how to work, but it is too much' (C25);
'they are skillful people and hard working ... [but] they bring tonnes of clothes
here which ... could be manufactured in our own factories ... this is how our
people lose their jobs' (C9); 'there used to be a normal shop here, Prior [a classic
department store in the socialist period], where they used to serve *knedlo zelo vepøo*
[dumplings, roast pork, cabbage, a typical Czech dish] and now it's a Chinese
restaurant' (C31); 'lots of foreign labourers take much money from us' (K6); 'lots
of foreigners come to buy land ... that is bad' (U19); 'nothing good comes from
those foreigners' (U20); 'no one comes here with good intentions' (U28; all in
group agree) ... 'our legislation creates unusual privileges for them' (U28).

East Europeans criticised low-skilled incomers for being tax-evaders and
petty criminals even if they sold goods cheap:

'the Vietnamese all seek ways to avoid paying taxes' (C27); '[they sell cheaply]
because they do not pay taxes as they should' (C16).

There was a particularly lively altercation in one Ukrainian group:

'If you visit Kyiv's Troyeshchenskiy Market, you will see plenty of people from
such countries as Pakistan, Afghanistan, Lebanon, Iran, Algeria' (U7) ... 'Good'

(U2) ... 'What is good about it?' (U7) ... 'What is bad about it?' (U2) ... 'The bad aspect of it is that they live and work illegally and promote corruption around themselves ... if a policeman' (U7) ... 'catches such a person, in the hope of getting a bribe' (U3, interrupting) ... 'well, catches him because his documents are not in order or he has no trading licence or something else is not right, such a person can tuck some $50 or 50 hryvnias into the policeman's pocket and the cop will happily go away. The foreigner continues to work, he does not pay taxes, he does not pay fines for not registering his whereabouts with the local police office, he does not pay for anything. So he treads our land, breathes our air, and does all this for free. What is good about it for us?' (U7) ... 'He still does work' (U2) ... 'But he works for his own benefit, we do not profit from it' (U7).

That shaded into sheer racism:

'My neighbour comes from Kharkiv ... she says that we Ukrainians are so humiliated ... there are whole blocks of buildings inhabited by Koreans ... they have their own schools, hospitals, shops, everything you can think of ... they strut about so proudly [shows how] ... and our people [with horror] hire themselves out to them as housemaids [claps her hands] ... perhaps they receive good payment ... but it is such a shame!' (U32); 'the main thing is that no Muslims should come ... as to others, let them come ... unpleasant people [referring to Muslims]' (U12); 'Muslims are cads' (U15); 'Chechens ... fleeing from their country ... [are a] fairly acute problem, because if anything crops up there, they may draw Ukraine into this conflict' (U5); 'perhaps we are [culturally] closer to Europe after all' (U11) ... 'our culture is more compatible with the West than with Vietnam, Korea and such like' (U16).

The discussion of corruption in Kyiv's Troyeshchenskiy Market among 'people from such countries as Pakistan, Afghanistan, Lebanon, Iran, Algeria' continued:

'not everybody should be let into Ukraine ... how can such people lead a normal life? ... they are scum who pollute the city ... [on the other hand] if they came from ... the United States or Canada ...' (U5) ... 'from developed countries ...' (U7) ... 'who live like normal people ...' (U5) ... 'yes, from the developed countries ...' (U6).

Czech participants suggested:

'it does not bother little children ... they grow up with it and are different ... when I was a child, we were shocked when we encountered a black, but now it is not anything strange ... children are used to it ... the Vietnamese [clearly 'black' in this context!] are for them, like Czechs' (C6) ... '[but] there will not be any great change, parents do not view [Asians] very positively ... they would point out [to their teenage children], look you are going out with a Chinese' (C8) ... 'I do not think so, it is not like that' (C7).

Yet for C8 if not C7 it clearly was just 'like that'.

While the Czechs worried about Vietnamese incomers who might evade small taxes on their market stalls, back home the Vietnamese worried about unscrupulous and insensitive foreign – and primarily Asian – employers:

'the Vietnamese are fed up with Taiwanese investors in Vietnam because their treatment is very bad … [though] the Japanese treat Vietnamese labourers well' (V21); 'Taiwanese and Chinese [employers] treat Vietnamese workers badly' (V32).

In very sharp contrast, however, to their more general comments about foreigners which were so negative, almost all the comments about *personal* contacts with foreigners were *positive*: foreigners they had met were 'like us' (C0, U16); 'normal, alright' (C17, C7); 'decent people' (C12, C15, U16); 'friends, good friends' (C3, C5, K18,); 'no problems or conflicts' (C0, C18); 'I liked them, very much' (K10, K11, K12, K19, U15); 'fun' (K11); 'simply good' (K26); 'nice and approachable' (K30); 'respectful' (U15, V18).

Rights for incomers Some of the same prejudices emerged from participants' consideration of the specific question of employment rights for immigrants: whether 'people who move to this country should have the same right to take jobs as citizens'. Some felt access to 'the labour market must be closed' (U14) to incomers; or at least 'limited' (U20, C26), because 'the money flows elsewhere' (C26), 'they leak our money to their country' (K29).

Many felt local citizens should get preference in the market:

'we should distinguish' (K27); 'preference for our people, only then jobs to foreigners' (C15); 'Skoda are currently dismissing 2,000 people and foreigners are the first to go! That's good!' (C14); '[at least for] blue collar jobs … foreigners should be dismissed first' (C15); 'not jobs for any loafers … but still I think jobs should be given primarily to Czechs' (C12); 'our workers should have certain advantages' (U3; all in group nod in agreement) … 'because this is our country' (U5) … 'because everything here is ours' (U1); 'we cannot give foreigners fringe benefits such as family allowances' (K26) … 'native [Korean] people are more trustworthy' (K30).

Indeed:

'we should consider a provocative wage system which is rather oppressive to immigrants … giving them only 800,000 Won whereas giving Koreans 1,000,000 Won … we need to stimulate immigrants to be aware of their miserable situation' (K26).

Some backed more equal access to employment:

'as for employment, we should treat them equally' (V31); 'there are lots of Korean Chinese who work in factories or construction sites ... some [native] Koreans exploit them ... [but] they are our brothers ... we should give them rewards, not exploit them' (K16); 'yes, the same rights as we have' (C2); 'I would make [employment rights] the same for the whole of Europe ... apply the laws to everybody in the same way' (C28).

Invoking 'Europe' of course implies a degree of reciprocity. Others made reciprocity explicit:

'according to diplomatic relationships ... reciprocally' (K18); 'rights should be the same everywhere, if I go to a foreign country and they come here ... not that I would be allowed to work in an EU country until after a period of three years [as required by EU accession treaties]' (C3).

Reciprocity could justify discrimination:

'an immigrant to the United States is not given the US citizenship until they have lived there for five years' (U4) ... 'and until they learn the language' (U3); 'we do not have the same rights abroad, either, for example, in Saudi Arabia' (K13).

More remarkably, some Koreans argued for equal rights even in the absence of reciprocity:

'what if other countries do not give our people equal rights to take jobs?' (moderator) ... 'that is unjust' (K25) ... 'So although they are unjust, we should be just? Is that your point?' (moderator) ... 'exactly ... they will learn [justice] from us' (K25); 'when Koreans migrated to America in the early days, they suffered lots of unreasonable treatment ... we should not do the same things in spite of our experiences ... if so, we would be the same as Americans ... let us treat foreigners equally' (K10).

For others, equal treatment was a threat to immigrants, not a promise:

'the same conditions as our people, even the same taxes' (C29); 'we should treat them equally ... they have to obey [the laws of] Vietnam' (V16); 'foreigners have higher living standards and they cannot accept our rules ... if we are not careful, we will make our own people unhappy' (V13); 'we should tax foreigners' (V12); '[only] if foreigners accept Vietnam tradition and custom, we should welcome them' (V25).

One Czech claimed access to the labour market was a purely economic question:

'not any sort of xenophobia' (C26);

– but for others it was:

'I would not want eastern nationalities here ... they feel the same way in Germany' (C4); 'we need specialists ... but that refuse – of course I apologise for this harsh word – but I am sick of those Vietnamese, Afghan and other communities that have conquered practically all city quarters already' (U16); 'Vietnamese [immigrants] have created some jobs ... so let them give those jobs to Ukrainians ... after all, it was in Ukraine that they created them' (U11) ... 'let it be so ... three per cent of the jobs go to the Vietnamese and let the rest go to Ukrainians' (U14); 'we are at such a [low] level that specialists from the West do not come to us ... those who come here are precisely the Vietnamese, Afghans' (U13) ... '[or] Nigerians, who have already started selling heroin here' (U12).

A lone voice argued that exclusion from the labour market:

'must not depend on skin colour ... it is necessary to pay attention to professional qualities ... if he is of more benefit then it is all right if he is a Negro' (U28);

– but others argued for the exclusion of incomers:

'from Arab countries, from Asian countries' (U17) ... 'they cannot bring anything worthwhile' (U22) ... 'nothing, worthwhile' (U20).

Indigenous minorities It was not only incomers that constituted an 'other' which is so significant for nationalism. Czechs focused on the Romany families (Roma). A few denied that the Roma were a minority – a little too vehemently to be convincing:

'Roma are not a minority ... it is propaganda ... they are not a minority' (C6); 'no they are not, but they abuse it [the claim to be one] whenever they can' (C0).

There were few positive references to Roma – and they were mostly conditional:

'some of them decent, civilised' (C30); 'some of them are quite decent and others cause problems' (C5); 'some are good ... I am not afraid of them at my place, but those in Prostejov ...' (C32); 'I know [Roma] who live decently, but others do not ... it is impossible to caution any of them when they do something wrong' (C0); 'near the railway station I saw a small [Roma] boy riding a bicycle on the pavement and I told him that he should not do it and he told me to fuck off' (C25); 'there are two [Roma] families in our village ... they are good, but not the others ... I am scared by them ... the mayor of our village saw to it that all empty houses were sold and that no more [Roma] families could come to live here' (C29); 'no Roma are allowed to move to Český Krumlov ... the Roma have their boss there and he decides whether a given Romany family may or may not move in' (C14);

– which apparently counts as good inter-ethnic relations since:

'Český Krumlov, a town near České Budějovice, is widely admired for relationships between Roma and Czechs ... the large Romany community there has its own leader, who looks after employment opportunities and ensures good relations with its Czech inhabitants' (translator).

Some Czechs resented what they saw as preferential treatment of Roma:

'in the communist period, too much consideration was shown to them, and now the minority abuses it ... they take advantage' (C2); 'take advantage' (C7); 'they are lawyers [laughter]' (C4); 'the EU are only concerned with the whites' attitude toward Roma ... they do not care about the Roma's attitude toward us' (C0).

Mostly however, Czechs simply criticised Roma behaviour:

'I used to work with Roma ... some complained that they did not have any job and when we found one for them, they did not want it ... a mother came to us and said she wanted a job for her daughter, but the daughter refused to do such work and the mother then said that she did not raise her daughter to work in a factory' (C8); 'Roma assault people on the street' (C27) ... 'assault people when they are fourteen' (C29) ... 'a major problem for Prostejov' (C28).

The Vietnamese had much to say about ethnic minorities but, in complete contrast to the Czechs, Vietnamese comments were characterised by sympathy and guilt. Without denying their minorities' status as ethnic minorities they asserted that:

'they are Vietnamese and we should help them' (V26); 'ethnic people are Vietnamese ... we are more advanced than them, so we have to help them ... the Party and state should have assistance programmes for them' (V30); 'ethnic minorities are underprivileged and we must help them' (V19); 'we should create better conditions for ethnic people because their life is still difficult' (V9); 'ethnic minorities helped the Vietnam revolution in mountainous areas ... but the government have not taken enough care of them, making their cultural life and education poor ... the enemy [unspecified – but possibly Cambodia] will take advantage of this ... the problem is how to raise their living standard' (V5).

It was not just altuistic however:

'ethnic issues are always important in any country ... if we get it wrong the consequence will be uncontrollable ... I know because I was a soldier of Truong Son ... in the West of Vietnam, natural conditions are very tough, economic and cultural conditions for development are very low ... thus local residents have suffered very much in terms of development ... twenty-five years after the liberation, the state has not yet focused on improving this area ... the state should have channeled at least half of what it has spent on developing the economy into this area ... but the state ignored this area and even assigned border soldiers up there ... it is not a good idea, the state should take care of all Vietnamese ethnic minorities and bring their living standard up to equality with Kinh people ... without this, there is no equality in society, which is the basis for social stability ... if I were ethnic and I saw you are rich, that you drive a car, that you have a brick-built house while I am poor, I would not be friendly' (V18) ... 'I agree' (V24); 'ethnic minorities are good ... we should pay more attention to them because they are poor and have many difficulties ... [that way] we can avoid unnecessary civil wars' (V4).

These critics of the Vietnam state were not to be satisfied by policy alone:

'state policy is very clear and gives priorities to ethnic minorities, but this policy is still just on paper ... there has just been ethnic chaos because of discrimination ... the National Assembly has a committee taking care of ethnic issues but it is not working well ... it lets bad people manipulate it ... some ethnic minorities have not had suitable land for settlement, they are pushed to remote areas without irrigation' (V21).

Against a background of remarkable Vietnamese optimism, remarkable satisfaction with progress, and remarkable reluctance to criticise anything (as much perhaps out of politeness as fear), this criticism of the Vietnam government's failure to provide sufficient help for ethnic minorities stands out very sharply indeed.

4.6   Cultural protection

Concept, content and responsibility Although a large majority of survey respondents expressed great pride in their national culture and declared a wish for more emphasis on their distinctive national culture and traditions (Table 4.1), in our extended focus group discussions it seemed that the *concept* of a national culture or tradition was often more popular than its *content* – and popular because culture was seen as a marker, perhaps even a guarantee, of national identity rather than for its own intrinsic content. Without national traditions:

'we will lose our national character' (U28); 'we lose identity' (K32); 'national holidays ... should be maintained [because] that helps us have ... a sense of being one nation' (K19); 'Ukraine should preserve its originality ... though it is beneficial to assimilate other cultures while preserving national traditions' (U3); 'there is no need to stroll along the streets in *sharovary* [Ukrainian wide trousers] but I believe that it is necessary to preserve our culture' (U5; U6 agrees).
'Vietnam has a cultural tradition of thousands of years ... although there are changes in individuals and families as people are exposed to new things, Vietnamese identity is unchangeable ... if it is changeable, there will be no more Vietnamese' (V5) ... 'I agree with V5, we should maintain Vietnamese national identity' (V6); 'culture is very important and it distinguishes this nation from another ... if you are assimilated culturally, you lose yourself' (V21; V24 agrees); 'we should keep our identity while gathering the good things from other societies' (V19); 'preserve our national identity, accept good things and keep away from bad things' (V22); 'maintain Vietnamese national tradition but choose positive aspects of foreigners to learn from in order to develop' (V10); 'keep Vietnamese national identity by all means because we have been fighting and peacemaking just to keep Vietnamese national cultural identity' (V15); '[we should] believe in Vietnam' (V31); 'accept foreign cultural influences, but do it so as not to erode

Table 4.12. *Who is responsible for changes in respect for national cultures?*

	Officials %	Public %	Public within each country			
			Czech R %	Korea %	Ukraine %	Vietnam %
Do you feel that changes in respect for the (COUNTRY) language, culture and traditions have been caused more by ...						
... the changing attitudes of (COUNTRY) people and officials	60	58	44	57	70	62
... foreign influences from outside (COUNTRY)	29	31	45	36	14	23

Notes: Per cent of all respondents. Per cents giving other/mixed/'don't know' responses not shown.

In Ukraine the '(COUNTRY) language etc' question read 'the *Ukrainian* language etc' even for Russian-speaking areas and respondents.

Vietnamese traditional culture ... it is essential to consider Vietnamese culture to be the main staple food and foreign culture the spice' (V33).

In short, national culture was so very important to Ukrainians and Vietnamese *not* for the intrinsic qualities of the painting, the dancing, the carving, the music, the literature, the family values or the customs – none of which are mentioned here at all – but as a necessary foundation for a distinctive 'identity'. If traditional culture did not exist it might have to be invented or re-invented to protect what really mattered: identity.

Overall, twice as many survey respondents attributed changing respect for their national culture to national attitudes rather than to 'foreign influences', but there were very significant differences between countries. In Ukraine and Vietnam, where the public were so sure that their culture was strong and increasingly respected, they were 22 per cent less likely (than in the Czech Republic or Korea) to attribute it to foreign influences, and 16 per cent more likely to attribute it to internal influences.

Explaining the strength of public support for cultural protection There was overwhelming public support for cultural protection in every country. A large majority everywhere agreed that 'our way of life needs to be protected against foreign influences'. However, the strength of that support varied sharply: the numbers who 'completely agreed' ranged from just 27 per cent in the Czech Republic, through 36 per cent in Korea and 38 per cent in Ukraine, to a remarkable 70 per cent in Vietnam. Very few,

Table 4.13. *Public support for cultural protection*

	Officials %	Public %	Public within each country			
			Czech R %	Korea %	Ukraine %	Vietnam %
Our way of life needs to be protected against foreign influences:						
completely agree	41	42	27	36	38	70
mostly agree	41	39	46	54	34	22
mostly disagree	12	12	19	9	17	1
completely disagree	3	3	4	1	5	3

Note: Per cent of all respondents. Per cents giving other/mixed/'don't know' responses not shown.

even in the Czech Republic disagreed (15 per cent). That pattern of cross-national variation in support for cultural protection correlates strongly and *positively with the importance* attached to culture in the different countries but strongly and *negatively with cultural fright* or pessimism about the status and prospects for the national culture. In itself, that is significant, but it raises the question of whether support for cultural protection among individuals within the same country follows a similar pattern and also correlates positively with the importance that individuals attach to culture and negatively with their sense of cultural fright.

Among individuals within countries, the key influence on public support for 'protecting *our way of life* against foreign influences' was commitment to the national culture rather than cultural fright or opposition to opening up the economy which was so widely recognised as likely to threaten national culture. By far the strongest correlation with support for cultural protection was the public feeling that 'though their people were not perfect, their culture was superior to others'. That correlated with support for cultural protection at around 0.40 in the merged data sets and within every country. A correlation of that size is suspiciously high, however, and was probably inflated by the unfortunate proximity of the two questions in the interview; so we should perhaps discount it. However, the second and third highest correlations with support for cultural protection were other measures, based on less proximate questions, of the importance that the public attached personally to their culture: how important their country's 'culture and traditions were to them personally' and whether they would prefer their country to become 'more like other countries' or 'to emphasise its own culture and traditions'. On average within countries, the impact on the balance of support

Table 4.14. *Public support for cultural protection is based on positive commitment not fright*

	Public and officials R . 100	Public R . 100	Public within each country			
			Czech R R . 100	S Korea R . 100	Ukraine R . 100	Vietnam R . 100
Correlation between strength of support for protecting 'our way of life' and ...						
Positive commitment to culture:						
our culture is superior	40	42	46	37	40	40
importance of culture to me personally	28	32	37	18	16	15
want more emphasis on cultural differences	19	22	29		19	19
have exclusively national rather than dual identity	22	19	19		16	
Cultural fright:						
fear our traditional way of life is getting lost			10			−10
fear 'our culture and way of life' will become more like other countries if we open up our economy[1]						
Opposition to opening up the economy:						
opening up the economy has more disadvantages			23		22	
opening up the economy is bad for our country			22		22	
opening up the economy is *not* the only way to go			20		18	

Notes: Correlations less than 0.10 are not shown. All correlations shown are significant at the one per cent level.

[1] No correlation with fears of cultural homogenation exceeded 0.06.

for cultural protection of opposition to homogenisation was 16 per cent, the impact of the importance of culture 'to me personally' was 30 per cent, and the impact of claims to cultural superiority was 46 per cent.

Exclusively national rather than more supra-national identities also correlated quite strongly with support for cultural protection. Those with 'exclusively national' identities backed cultural protection more than those with 'dual' identities – identities that simultaneously embraced

Table 4.15. *Explaining the strength of public support for cultural protection*

Our way of life needs to be protected against foreign influences	All four countries		Public within each country			
	Public and officials	Public	Czech R	S Korea	Ukraine	Vietnam
RSQ =	20	19	22	3	14	14
	beta.100	beta.100	beta.100	beta.100	beta.100	beta.100
Our culture is superior (excluded for technical reasons – see text)	n/a	n/a	n/a	n/a	n/a	n/a
importance of culture to me personally	16	21	29	18	12	11
want more emphasis on cultural differences	11	13	15		14	14
dislike foreign films and TV	12				14	
opening up the economy has more disadvantages	11	13				
market economy does not deliver prosperity			15		10	
dislike foreigners			14			
opening up the economy is bad for our country					13	
have exclusively national rather than dual identity					10	
family living standard below average						16
crime increasing						15
no moped						15
market economy is unfair						11
Legacy: Vietnam	24	19				
Legacy: Asia	15	12				

Note: Betas less than 0.10 are not shown. All betas shown are significant at the one per cent level.

both country and a wider region such as 'Europe' (in the Czech Republic and Ukraine) or 'East Asia' (in Vietnam and South Korea). The correlation with exclusive versus dual identities was greater within East European countries, however.

Very significantly, support for 'protecting our way of life' did *not* correlate well with indicators of cultural fright – with feelings that 'our traditional way of life is getting lost' or that it was 'inevitable that our culture and way of life will become more like other countries if we open up our economy'. So it was positive commitment to the national culture, and *not fear for its future* that drove support for cultural protection.

Even if we exclude pride in culture on the technical grounds of question proximity, a multiple regression analysis using all the many potential predictors we used in Chapter 3 highlights two indicators of positive commitment to national culture as having a strong, independent and cumulative impact: the importance of national culture 'to me personally' (beta = 0.21) and to a lesser extent the wish to put more emphasis on national culture (beta = 0.13). The first of these had an influence within every country, and the second within every country except Korea. Beyond that, regression also confirms that, even after taking positive personal commitment to culture into account, there was greater commitment to cultural protection in East Asia (beta = 0.12), and especially Vietnam (beta = 0.19 over and above the Asian impact). Other influences were less powerful or consistent.

4.7   Conclusions

The public recognised that opening up the economy was a Faustian bargain in which they must trade cultural distinctiveness for economic development. However they wanted to drive a hard bargain with the devil: maximising the economic gain and minimising the cultural loss. As we found in Chapter 3, cultural perceptions and attitudes did *not* have an important impact on support for opening up the economy, but there was widespread support for cultural protection: it only varied in intensity. The public attributed changing respect for their culture more to internal than foreign influences. Where the public felt their national culture was more secure – in Ukraine and Vietnam – they were even less inclined to blame foreign influences.

The culture that the public regarded as important 'to them personally' was what we have termed 'identity culture' rather than 'consumer culture'. Globalised consumer culture was very visible, and simultaneously welcomed and despised. In itself it was not important to the public – though previous state-imposed restrictions on personal choice were remembered and resented. Yet when the public had the opportunity to discuss their culture at length, it seems that they valued even their 'identity culture' more for reasons of identity than for reasons of culture: the actual content of their culture was less valued for itself than for its utility as a marker of identity. Indeed, national traditions were often irritating in themselves though valued as a mark of identity.

Our main conclusion, however, must be that public support for cultural protection rested on personal respect for culture, not on perceptions of cultural decline, not on whether people were economic winners or losers, not on social background, not on contact with foreigners, and only very little on xenophobia. Public support for cultural protection at the level of individuals – as well as in cross-national comparisons – reflected positive rather than negative considerations. It reflected confidence, hope and respect rather than fear. Surprisingly perhaps, public support for cultural protection was not a response to cultural fright. Our individual-level regression analyses suggest it is no accident that, cross-nationally, support for cultural protection was outstandingly strong where people felt their culture was already best preserved and most secure.

Since this is an important but perhaps surprising finding let us illustrate it with a simple tabulation of public support for cultural protection by a combination of cultural commitment and cultural fright (Table 4.16). In the merged data set of the public in all four countries, that shows the impact of cultural commitment was 34 per cent; and the impact of cultural fright was not only much lower, at 7 per cent, but had the 'wrong' sign: public support for cultural protection was *higher* among

Table 4.16. *Per cent of public who 'completely agree' on 'need to protect our way of life'*

| | ... if (COUNTRY) culture and traditions are ... | |
	... 'very' important to me personally	... not 'very' important to me personally
Public (all four countries merged)		
... if think our traditional way of life is getting lost	58	30
... if think our traditional way of life remains strong	70	31
Czech		
... if think our traditional way of life is getting lost	49	24
... if think our traditional way of life remains strong	41	20
Korea		
... if think our traditional way of life is getting lost	52	27
... if think our traditional way of life remains strong	55	31
Ukraine		
... if think our traditional way of life is getting lost	50	35
... if think our traditional way of life remains strong	47	34
Vietnam		
... if think our traditional way of life is getting lost	74	53
... if think our traditional way of life remains strong	83	61

Percentages exclude 'don't know', mixed, and other responses.

those who thought their culture 'remained strong', not lower, as a cultural fright model would predict.

Within each country the impact of cultural commitment (averaging 20 per cent) far exceeded that of cultural fright. In the two East European countries there was evidence of a slight cultural fright effect which raised support for cultural protection only by an average of 4 per cent, however, among those who feared their traditional way of life was 'getting lost'. In the two East Asian countries the impact was in the opposite direction and slightly greater: it raised support for cultural protection by an average of 6 per cent among those who felt their traditional way of life 'remained strong'!

5   Protest and resistance

In Chapter 3 we found the public were evenly divided on their attitudes towards an internal market, though more positive towards opening up to world markets. Even those who had, on balance, positive attitudes nonetheless had plenty of criticisms. Contentment was mixed with discontent. This chapter looks at public attitudes towards the articulation of that discontent, towards resisting the downsides of internal markets and economic openness – low wages, unsafe working conditions, pollution, or unfair international regulations.

International companies have faced both local and international protests against their alleged pursuit of global wealth at the expense of local interests. Oil companies like Shell have faced persistent local protests against their operations in Africa. Brands like Nike (in 2003 the largest private employer in Vietnam) have faced strikes by badly paid or badly treated workers across Asia – backed up by consumer boycotts and court actions in more developed countries. But the most spectacular 'anti-globalisation' protests have been the series of protests at meetings of international organisations or self-designated groups of 'world leaders', beginning with the Seattle riots of 1999.

The violence and disorder of 'Seattle' methods of protest provoked adverse reactions in the affluent West. Yet they might resonate with the frustrations of ordinary people in relatively poor, developing or transitional countries. Indeed anthropologists such as Scott (1985; 1990) have suggested that poor people in poor countries might be willing to use what he called the 'weapons of the weak' against their oppressors. These 'weapons of the weak' go far beyond peaceful protest or even the 'ritualised demos' of Seattle, Prague, Genoa or Gleneagles. They include forms of protest that are more private, personal, and less visible – including sabotage by deliberately sub-standard work, by theft, or by damage to property or machinery. We investigated the limits of public support in our four countries for a wide range of 'anti-globalisation' protest and protest methods: including sabotage and violent or disorderly demonstrations, as well as the more peaceable methods; and including methods that involve foreigners as well as local people.

Few actively participate in protest. Does it matter what the general public think about protest, or even the tools and methods of protest, if they do not themselves participate? From a democratic perspective of course public attitudes are intrinsically important. But they are also important from the perspective of public order – and ultimately from a development perspective as well. Both elites and counter-elite activists operate against the background of the wider public, and the attitudes of that wider public – approval or disapproval – create a climate that may significantly promote or inhibit the actual activity of potential activists. Potential activists are propelled into action by a combination of their own internal attitudes and the sense they have of broader tolerance or even approval among the less active bulk of the public – and approval not for their objectives alone, but also for their methods (Muller 1979). The number of actual protestors is usually very small, but they are sensitive to the presence or absence of this 'oxygen of approval'. Disorder, undertaken by the few perhaps, but with the approval and encouragement of the many, discourages risk-averse investors (Alesina and Perotti 1996) and thus development.

In Barnes and Kaase's (1979) or Parry, Moyser and Day's (1992) terms we focus *not* on 'actual participation' ('have done'), nor on 'potential participation' ('would do') but on 'justification' – that is, on the broad public feeling that it '*would be right*', even '*morally right*' for someone to protest, or protest in a particular way, or in particular circumstances. Personal participation may be restrained by lack of opportunity, by infirmity, or by fear of the personal consequences (a significant inhibition in most of our countries). But that does not affect the moral status of protest, and the broad moral status of protest defines the climate in which potential protesters decide to take action.

Of course fear may also affect even the contributions of focus group participants and the answers of survey respondents to our questions about justified protest, especially in tightly controlled Vietnam, though probably far less than it affects actual physical participation. We asked enough questions, in enough different ways, to have some confidence that our findings accurately portray the 'climate of approval' – which necessarily requires some overt expression – if not the most private and secret feelings of individuals.

5.1   The alleged utility of disorder

The Third World Trade Organisation (WTO) Ministerial Conference held in Seattle in December 1999 ended in three days of violence as protestors fought riot police on the city's streets. It was the biggest protest in the US since the Vietnam era: with more than 500 arrests and several million dollars of damage. A 'state of civil emergency' was declared and the police used plastic bullets, tear gas, pepper spray, truncheons and water cannon. More than 100,000 protestors took part in the demonstration. Most were not involved in the violence, but it was the violence that made world headlines.

That was followed by similar protests at the World Bank/International Monetary Fund (WB/IMF) meeting at Washington DC in April 2000, when 1,300 people were arrested. In September that same year, violent protestors forced an early end to the WB/IMF meetings in Prague; 400 were arrested. In January 2001 the police used armoured vehicles and water cannon to keep protestors disguised as skiers away from the conference centre in Davos, Switzerland where the World Economic Forum was meeting. In April, 400 protestors were arrested at the Summit of the Americas in Quebec City after petrol bombs were traded against tear gas and rubber bullets. In June, at the European Union (EU) Summit in Gothenburg, three protestors were shot and over 500 arrested as stones and fireworks were thrown at the police. For the July 2001 G8 Summit in Genoa security preparations included a new missile-defence system at the local airport. One demonstrator was shot dead and others severely injured as activists overturned cars and stoned the police.

G8 leaders developed a preference for meeting in remote and heavily fortified places. The 2002 G8 meeting was held in Kananaskis, two hours away from Calgary, Canada, and surrounded by a thirteen-mile wide security cordon. The 2003 G8 Summit in Evian, France, was protected by a ten-mile exclusion zone. When the US hosted the 2004 G8 Summit they retreated to a remote island off the coast of Georgia. In July 2005, the UK hosts took the G8 to the remote Gleneagles Hotel in Scotland, its land surrounded by miles of security fence and thousands of armed police with large military transport helicopters.

During our fieldwork in 2003, the WTO met at Cancun, Mexico. It was lobbied by poor farmers rather than urban European radicals. Lee Kyung-Hae led a march of 300 Korean farmers up to the security fence around the exclusion zone, pulled out a knife and committed suicide. Earlier in the year he had protested outside the WTO offices in Geneva under a banner reading 'WTO Kills' (*Guardian*, 12 September 2003). His suicide had a detectable, though very brief impact on public perceptions in our Korean survey (see below). Generally, however, the most widely-publicised protests took place in affluent western surroundings. Protests were *for* the poor, but not generally *by* the poor. The participants – Lee Kyung-Hae notwithstanding – were mainly drawn from the West. Despite the ritual assertion that the protests were 'largely peaceful' it was the violence that caught the media's attention. For many on both sides of the argument about globalisation, the protest and the violence, not the plight of the developing world, became the story.

By far the largest transnational protest in 2003 was remarkably peaceful and not overtly an 'anti-globalisation' protest. That was the February 2003 'anti-war' demonstration against the invasion of Iraq. Estimates put the number of participants worldwide between 7 million and 30 million. Despite the overt focus on Iraq, however, a survey of over 5,000 participants in eight western countries found that 89 per cent 'identified with the anti-globalisation movement', 55 per cent of them 'strongly' (Walgrave and Verhulst 2003: p. 19; see also Bursens and Sinardet, 2003). On the surface it was a protest against the hegemonic global power of the US in military matters rather than economic, but nonetheless it was arguably the largest and most peaceful anti-globalisation protest of all – though in its own terms, completely *in*effective.

Veteran anti-globalisation polemicist, George Monbiot, was typically ambivalent about violence. Although he distinguished 'two forms of political action', which he characterised by the Arabic words 'hamas – enthusiastic but intelligent anger', and 'hamoq – uncontrolled, stupid anger', he nonetheless declared:

'though I am scared to say it, it is now clear to me that we cannot win without raising the temperature. The disorienting, profoundly disturbing lesson from Genoa is also the oldest lesson in politics: words alone are not enough' (*Guardian*, 24 July 2001)

But many other critics of globalisation were repelled by the violence. Increasingly, they argued that it was counter-productive: while boosting attention for the anti-globalisation movement, violence diminished support for it. After Seattle 'the law of diminishing media returns' applied, and non-governmental organisations (NGOs) were reportedly 'uncomfortable with the increasingly violent trend in the protest movement' (*Guardian*, 20 April 2001). Indeed, despite their name, governments reportedly provide 40 per cent of NGO income (*Guardian*, 24 July 2001), and violent confrontation with governments was not in their interest.

After Genoa, a former *Guardian* Editor, Peter Preston (*Guardian*, 23 July 2001) argued that 'protest must now change'. He claimed that 'ritualised demos' at western summits in western venues attracted newspaper proprietors but repelled the public, particularly the public in rich western countries whose support was needed for a policy switch towards greater global justice. Violent protests he claimed 'do not represent an unstaunchable swell of public concern ... [but] lump third world debt and petrol bombers in the same basket of way-out distaste'. Similarly Clare Short, the then UK Secretary of State for International Development, complained that 'violent protesters' were not only 'nasty in what they do' but 'confusing international debate'. Even the Global Social Forum complained that it was caught between 'state and anarchist violence' (*Guardian*, 21 July 2001). The utility of disorder was questionable.

5.2   Public support for protest

Globally, the most newsworthy anti-globalisation protests were more often in developed countries and owed more to elites and activists than to the wider public. Not surprisingly, we found that the public in our developing or transitional countries were more aware of protests in *other* countries than in their own. We set the scene for interviews or discussions about anti-globalisation protest by noting that:

in many countries throughout the world people have protested against damage caused by international companies or international organisations;

some protests have been directed against *international companies* for causing local problems – like polluting the local environment, taking land away from local people, paying low wages, forcing local companies to close, or bribing local officials;

other protests have been directed against *international organisations* like the WTO, the IMF and the World Bank for being biased towards richer or more powerful countries.

We then asked:

'Have you heard of any such protests here in (COUNTRY)? And have you heard of any such protests in other countries?'

Only half the public had heard of anti-globalisation protests in their own country, but two-thirds had heard of such protests elsewhere, though officials were more aware of such protests both at home and abroad.

Awareness varied very sharply from country to country. Reflecting perhaps the traumatic 'trashing of Prague' in September 2000, four out of five Czechs remembered hearing of anti-globalisation protests both at home and abroad. By contrast, awareness was much lower in South Korea where rather less than half remembered such protests either at home or abroad. The third Asia-Europe Meeting (ASEM) took place in Seoul a month after the IMF/WB meeting in Prague and the Korean government mobilised 30,000 police to deal with potential protests. The number of protesters was limited, they were mostly Korean, most demonstrations took place well away from the conference centre, they were not so violent as in Prague, and they proved less memorable. Korean protests were often against indigenous Korean firms rather than international firms or organisations. Even the suicide of Lee Kyung-Hae at the

Table 5.1. *Aware of 'anti-globalisation' protests*

		Officials %	Public %	Public within each country			
				Czech R %	Korea %	Ukraine %	Vietnam %
Heard of any such							
protests here in	yes	60	49	78	45	26	41
(COUNTRY)?	no	36	46	17	54	69	50
Heard of any such							
protests in *other*	yes	79	64	81	46	55	65
countries?	no	17	31	14	52	38	29

Note: Per cent of all respondents. Per cents giving other/mixed/'don't know' responses not shown.

WTO meeting in far-away Cancun on 10 September 2003 – in the midst of our Korean interviews – had only a short-term impact on public awareness. In the 724 interviews before his suicide 44 per cent of Koreans said they had noticed anti-globalisation protests outside Korea. Immediately after his suicide that leapt to 64 per cent but thereafter it dropped sharply, and by 21–23 September it was back to 44 per cent or less. The impact on Korean awareness seemed to last just ten days.

The pattern of public awareness was significantly different in Ukraine and Vietnam. In these countries it was not so much a matter of whether awareness was high or low, as of the huge contrast between public awareness of *internal* and *external* protests. Far more Vietnamese had heard of such protests outside Vietnam (65 per cent) as inside (41 per cent). Even more strikingly, over twice as many Ukrainians had heard of such protests outside Ukraine (55 per cent) as inside (26 per cent). In focus groups, Ukrainians revealed their awareness of anti-globalisation protests in South Africa, the EU, and America but:

'in Ukraine, [ordinary people] do not manifest themselves loudly . . . they wield no significant influence' (U28).

Neither Ukrainians nor Vietnamese drew much comfort from the relative lack of anti-globalisation protests within their own countries, however. Some focus group participants explicitly depicted protests as a 'normal' characteristic of fully developed democracies and rather envied places where such protest was more frequent:

'Vietnamese people are different from foreigners – in Europe people are freer' (V21); 'such protests are normal and they are good for such countries because they prompt government officials and international organisations to review whether what they have done is right and suitable or not' (V4); 'I support such protests' (V12; V14 agrees);

'we should have such protests in Ukraine, and more often – our people are very inactive … scared, immobile – they should protest more often' (U4; U7 agrees).

In every country, there was overwhelming support in principle for protests against international companies or organisations that behaved badly. Around 86 per cent of the public (and slightly *more* among officials!) thought it was 'morally right' to protest against 'an international company causing serious local problems', or against 'international organisations such as the WTO, IMF or World Bank' when their actions were 'damaging poorer countries' – though around 10 per cent volunteered the comment that they could only support peaceful protest (Table 5.2). A mere 5 per cent thought protest would be wrong in these circumstances and 3 per cent that it might be dangerous to protest.

With the partial exception of a small minority of Koreans (around 13 per cent), public support for the principle of protest against global injustice was near universal. That is particularly significant in Vietnam where the public express so much enthusiasm for globalisation – and for their government – that we might suspect them of being unduly reluctant to voice criticism. But they certainly have no inhibitions about openly voicing

Table 5.2. *Morally right to protest*

	Officials %	Public %	Public within each country			
			Czech R %	Korea %	Ukraine %	Vietnam %
If international company causes serious local problems …						
morally right to protest	80	78	74	76	83	78
(VOL) only peaceful protest	11	9	13	7	7	8
(VOL) too risky to protest	2	3	3	3	3	2
morally wrong to protest	4	5	4	14	1	2
If WTO/IMF/WB etc damage poorer countries …						
morally right to protest	76	75	72	79	79	69
(VOL) only peaceful protest	12	10	14	6	7	10
(VOL) too risky to protest	2	3	4	2	3	2
morally wrong to protest	5	5	3	11	3	4

Note: Per cent of all respondents. Per cents giving other/mixed/'don't know' responses not shown. VOL indicates that a particular answer was not offered by the interviewer, but was spontaneously volunteered by some respondents.

support for the *principle* of anti-globalisation protest against international firms or organisations. That suggests that Vietnamese expressions of enthusiasm for globalisation itself are largely genuine and not merely 'politically correct'.

In focus groups, the overwhelming majority of Koreans thought:

'there is no choice but protest' (K6); 'such protests are necessary' (K23); 'otherwise, we just let them do whatever they want' (K9, K15); 'to restore our rights, we have to organise' (K13); 'protest is justified even if it causes some loss' (K7) ... 'even if the company withdraws?' (moderator) ... 'yes' (K14).

One Vietnamese participant re-defined so-called *anti*-globalisation protests to make them in a very important sense *pro*-globalisation and therefore legitimate:

'we should protest if we do it to ensure equality – but not if we do it to obstruct integration' (V31).

In other words, protests against the abuse and distortion of globalisation by foreign interests should be encouraged, but nonetheless, Vietnam's goal should still be global integration.

Despite near universal support for the principle of protest in the survey, some Ukrainian focus group participants viewed actual protests with good-humoured scepticism. In Kharkiv, they thought anti-globalisation protests were:

'organised events' (U12); 'there will be about twenty per cent of fools there, and the rest is just a show' (U16); 'nothing but a performance ... just like all those international forums of students and young people used to be – in the main the people there are youngsters – they know that there is a conference in America or in South Africa – they go there to have fun – someone pays them' (U13); 'money was also paid for the rally against our McDonald's restaurant – for carrying a poster 15 hryvnyas, for appearing on camera 30' (U15) ... 'it would just be interesting to find out who pays them' (U13) ... 'then we could take part too – there you have it, the Ukrainian mentality' (U16).

Elsewhere in Ukraine, however, attitudes towards anti-globalisation protests were unambiguously positive. Ukraine itself was criticised for its unresponsive bureaucracy and its servile population. Protests were certainly regarded as a foreign phenomenon, but one that should be emulated, even if they would probably be ineffective in Ukraine:

'in democratic countries such protests bring good – there, they listen to them – here, you may dance naked!' (U17); 'but let it be a voice in the wilderness ... attention may be paid to it' (U30).

In Kyiv they could cite some small success:

'even judging by a small action – we had a protest against the rise in transport fares' (U4; U7 agrees) ... 'the action was not very massive but this protest apparently made the Mayor reconsider his decision' (U4).

But are local bus fares really a 'globalisation' issue? Apparently so, because of:

'IMF interference in the issue of raising transport fares – they dictate the rules of the game to us – however, they do not dictate that our government should provide jobs or increase our salaries' (U4; again backed by U7).

Prague had been the scene of large and violent battles between anti-globalisation protesters and the police in 2000. Two years later anti-globalisation protesters were still regarded by focus group participants as:

'professional demonstrators ... here ten days before and ten days after' (C21) ... 'paid' (C20) ... 'directed and paid from abroad' (C22) ... 'troublemakers' (C21) ... 'permanent protesters ... willing to protest against protesting!' (C18);

and the bill for damages had to be met by Czechs (C22, C24, C18).

Prague participants agreed there were problems of globalisation – running from 'enormous differences between the rich and the poor world' (C21), to the spreading culture of 'hamburgers' (C19, C18), but protesters:

'should protest in a decent way ... not destroy Prague' (C19); 'let them stage rallies but do not let them destroy Prague' (C14); 'we are for demonstrations even with slogans, but not with violence' (C8).

There was scepticism about protesters who 'make use of the benefits' of 'globalisation' (C24):

'they protest against all kinds of things and then they go home by metro and switch on TV and use mobile phones' (C18).

Yet that unqualifiedly negative view of globalisation protesters was limited to Prague. Even in the rest of the Czech Republic views were more mixed. Some refused to take sides:

'I did not side with anybody' (C11); 'I cannot judge who was in the right' (C14).

Others expressed complex views, combining positive and negative elements. In particular they distinguished: (i) between protesters' methods and their ideas; and (ii) between the IMF and the local police. These two distinctions were linked. Czechs tended to condemn the protestors' violence but support their ideas; or at least support the need for the protesters' ideas to be considered and debated if not accepted. While they supported the Czech police in their hand-to-hand fighting with the mainly foreign protesters, they were at the same time more favourable to the protesters in their battle of ideas with the IMF or World Bank.

'I was not there and the TV showed only the worst shots ... so of course [I was] on the side of the police' (C2; supported by C5, C7 and others);

– but some of these same participants then went on to insist on reformulating the question:

'I am on the side of the ideas' (C2; C8 agrees);

– and others were as ambivalent as Monbiot:

'I am against violence but I must say that I was on the side of the protesters' (C12); 'I hate violence but I have read something about the IMF and I agree that it is a criminal organisation – but those who throw paving stones are downright nuts' (C26) ... 'you mean that stones should not be thrown?' (moderator) ... 'but without this violence I could walk there with a poster and they would take a photo of me and place it in a paper and that would be all – this would not change anything – I am afraid that violence is necessary in this context' (C26).

5.3   How? Acceptable methods of protest

Public support for protest against global injustice was near universal but in both survey interviews and focus group discussions some of the public spontaneously qualified their approval of protest by insisting it should be 'peaceful' or 'orderly'. So we asked everyone to address this issue explicitly:

'Suppose an international company here in (COUNTRY) treated its workers badly or polluted the local environment. Should protesters: (1) never use disorderly or violent forms of protest; (2) only use disorderly or violent forms of protest after peaceful protests have been ignored; or (3) use any form of protest they think will solve the problem quickly?'

Overall, half the public completely ruled out disorderly or violent methods and another fifth would accept them only as a last resort. Opinion was most polarised in the Czech Republic, but generally most favourable to the use of disorderly methods in Ukraine.

The classic studies of public attitudes towards protest and 'direct action' throughout western Europe and America during the turbulent 1960s (Madgwick 1973; Marsh 1977; Barnes and Kaase 1979) used a seven-point 'scale of protest action' that ran from very mild actions such as 'signing a petition' through successively more aggressive actions: (1) petitions; (2) 'lawful' demonstrations; (3) boycotts; (4) refusal to pay taxes; (5) 'unofficial' strikes; (6) occupying buildings; and (7) blocking traffic. It

Table 5.3. *Only peaceful protest?*

	Officials %	Public %	Public within each country			
			Czech R %	Korea %	Ukraine %	Vietnam %
Suppose an international company here in (COUNTRY) treated its workers badly or polluted the local environment. Should people ...						
(VOL) not protest at all	1	1	1	0	1	4
... never use disorderly or violent forms of protest	57	51	58	58	37	46
... use disorderly or violent forms of protest only after peaceful protests have been ignored	16	19	9	31	24	16
... use any form of protest they think will solve the problem quickly	19	20	28	7	26	16

Note: Per cent of all respondents. Per cents giving other/mixed/'dont't know' responses not shown.

Index of support for disorderly or violent protest calculated by scoring 'never' as zero; 'as a last resort' as 1; 'unconditionally' as 2. VOL indicates that a particular answer was not offered by the interviewer, but was spontaneously volunteered by some respondents.

was never a universally successful 'scale' (in strictly statistical terms) and these authors rearranged the order of their items in different countries. They also excluded altogether from their scale such items as 'damaging property' or 'personal violence' (which averaged only 2 per cent and 3 per cent respectively across the five countries in Barnes and Kaase), restricting their scale to what may be called 'democratic protest' (Miller *et al.* 1982) rather than 'violent protest'.

'Democratic' protest, typified by peaceful demonstrations, is very much part of the normal democratic process. Democracy would be less complete without such protests. Our focus group participants in Ukraine and Vietnam who lamented the lack of popular protest in their own countries and felt such protests were 'normal' in democratic countries were entirely correct. But 'violent' protest – 'damaging property' and 'personal violence' – generally does not contribute towards a more vibrant democracy. These are not just more extreme positions on a scale of increasingly strong protest. They are an alternative to democratic protest, not a stronger form of democratic participation. In 1970s Britain, for example, high education or trade union membership increased support for democratic protest methods such as peaceful demonstrations but not for violent direct action. Conversely, political distrust, and even social distrust, *decreased* support for peaceful methods of protest, while *increasing* support for violent methods (Miller *et al.* 1982).

To measure public attitudes towards acceptable methods of anti-globalisation protest in developing and transitional countries we use some items modeled on the work of Marsh, Barnes and Kaase but take care to include what they excluded – some of what Scott (1985) calls the 'weapons of the weak' in developing countries – deliberately working slowly or badly, stealing from the factory, or damaging company property and machinery. We also add 'using the internet' to the long-established, but broadly equivalent, methods of signing petitions and writing letters to the press.

We specified two scenarios. First, where:

'an international company here in (COUNTRY) did not have safe working conditions in its factory, or paid very low wages'

and second, where:

'an international company here in (COUNTRY) is damaging or polluting the local environment'

Among the possible forms of protest open to the workers in a company with unsafe working conditions or low wages, we asked respondents to consider whether the '*workers* should retaliate' by:
1. signing petitions, writing to newspapers, or using the internet to criticise the company;
2. holding peaceful marches, rallies or demonstrations;
3. going on strike;
4. doing as little work as possible;
5. doing their work badly;
6. stealing what they can from the factory;
7. damaging the company property or machinery.

Our second scenario – 'polluting the local environment' – affects more than the workforce. So respondents were asked to consider whether '*people who live in the locality* should retaliate' by 'signing petitions' etc; 'holding peaceful marches' etc; or 'damaging the company property or machinery' (work-related methods of protest were inappropriate in this case).

These methods of protest were posed as separate possibilities, not a scale, and not alternatives. They can be grouped into *complaining* (signing petitions etc), *collective action* (demonstrations, strikes), and *sabotage* (bad work, stealing, damaging company property or machinery). Doing as little work as possible – a 'go-slow' – does not quite fit into any of these categories. It is a disruptive act on the margin between collective action and sabotage, depending to some extent on whether it is done openly, primarily as a demonstration of collective discontent as is sometimes the case, or secretly and privately as a personal act of sabotage or revenge.

There was steadily declining support as the focus shifted from petitions and complaints, through 'peaceful demonstrations' and then strikes, to 'go-slows' and sabotage (though little to choose between support for the various methods of sabotage). That reflects the public's general reservations about any kind of 'disorderly or violent' protest. Those who explicitly condemned 'disorderly or violent' protest were almost as willing to support the use of 'petitions' and 'peaceful demonstrations' as anyone else (and slightly more willing than others to complain to government or trade union officials – methods of protest that we discuss in Chapter 6). But they were much less willing than others to support strikes (18 per cent less), go-slows, or indeed sabotage in any of its forms. Even though support for sabotage was very low among those who said they were willing to accept 'any form of protest' (just over 9 per cent), it was over three times as much as among those who ruled out disorderly or violent protest (under 3 per cent).

Although the sequence of declining support is the same everywhere, the steps down that sequence occur at different points in different countries (Table 5.4). Around 86 per cent of Czechs, Koreans and Ukrainians back the use of petitions, letters to the press or internet websites (especially relevant in Korea) to ventilate grievances – but only 66 per cent of Vietnamese. Around 80 per cent of Czechs, Koreans and Ukrainians support 'peaceful' marches, rallies and demonstrations – but only 42 per cent of Vietnamese. Twice as many Czechs and Ukrainians as Koreans or Vietnamese back strikes, or 'go-slows'.

Few of the public back any of the methods of sabotage – though rather more in Korea and Ukraine than elsewhere. Given all the pressures to keep quiet about support for sabotage, we should perhaps focus on those who fail to consistently condemn it, or even occasionally support it. We asked four questions about sabotage – three in relation to poor working conditions, plus one in relation to pollution. Altogether, 11 per cent of the public (rising to 14 per cent in Ukraine) supported it on at least one of the four times they were asked; and 23 per cent (rising to 27 per cent in Ukraine) failed to condemn it on all four occasions. So there were very few enthusiasts for sabotage, but a surprisingly large number who failed to consistently rule it out in all circumstances – even when talking to a stranger taking notes. There was very much more support for sabotage in our study of developing or transitional countries than in the classic studies of West European protest by Barnes and Kaase.

Support for all methods of protest – from signing petitions to damaging machinery – was consistently a few percentage points higher under the

Table 5.4. *Methods of protest*

	Officials % yes	Public % yes	Public within each country			
			Czech R % yes	Korea % yes	Ukraine % yes	Vietnam % yes
If an international company ...						
... did not have safe working conditions in its factory, or paid very low wages (was damaging or polluting the local environment) ...						
... should the workers (local people) protest by ...						
Complaining: signing petitions, writing to newspapers, or using the internet to criticise the company	79 (84)	79 (83)	84 (89)	81 (82)	88 (92)	65 (67)
Collective action: peaceful marches, rallies, demonstrations	70 (75)	68 (72)	77 (82)	77 (79)	78 (84)	40 (44)
strikes	47	51	72	36	64	31
Go slow: doing as little work as possible	14	17	13	20	27	9
doing their work badly	3	6	6	6	7	6
Sabotage: stealing what they can from the factory	2	4	3	6	5	3
damaging company property or machinery	3 (4)	4 (7)	3 (6)	5 (9)	4 (9)	5 (5)
% who support sabotage on at least one of four questions	7	11	9	13	14	8

Note: Figures in brackets indicate responses to the pollution scenario.
% yes = number saying 'yes' as a percentage of all respondents.

'pollution' scenario than the 'bad working conditions' scenario. The difference is most significant with respect to sabotage where the level of support, though still very low, was almost twice as high under the pollution scenario.

If we accept the distinction between 'democratic protest' and 'violent protest' (Miller *et al.* 1982), then both the Vietnamese and the Ukrainians look rather weakly committed to the conventions of democracy, though for diametrically opposite reasons: the Vietnamese because they give *so little* support to the democratic tool of 'peaceful marches, rallies and demonstrations', and the Ukrainians because they give *so much* support to the undemocratic tools of disruption and sabotage.

Vietnamese support for the various methods of protest starts relatively low even at the most peaceable end of the spectrum (petitions etc) and it declines across the spectrum of protest more rapidly than elsewhere. That may reflect greater fear of the state. It certainly reflects greater reliance upon the state (which we discuss in Chapter 6) and unusually high levels of contentment with economic progress. Conversely, across the spectrum of protest methods, support starts and finishes relatively high in Ukraine. Our focus groups not only reinforce that finding, showing considerable Ukrainian support for sabotage, but also indicate that it reflects extreme disenchantment with economic progress and with the performance of the Ukrainian state (which we also discuss in Chapter 6).

In focus group discussions, Vietnamese participants were brief but to the point: they condemned sabotage and expressed faith in collective action – including faith in action by state authorities. Should workers retaliate by doing as little work as possible, doing work badly, stealing, or damaging the company's property or machinery?:

'they should not behave in those ways' (V19); 'it is not good to protest like that' (V13); 'workers retaliating is wrong' (V25).

But that did not rule out a more collective response:

'we should negotiate through labour unions' (V15); 'it is true that there are joint ventures or foreign-owned companies that ill-treat Vietnamese workers. But retaliating is not good. They should let labour unions and authorised agencies solve the problems. That is good for both the workers and the foreign partners' (V4; V5 agrees).

Most Korean participants felt workers should oppose unsafe working conditions or low wages, but 'only through laws' (K27), using 'due process' (K9) or 'proper procedures' (K4, K6, K23, K33) emphasising the restraints imposed by both personal and national self-respect.

Personal self-respect was important to Koreans:

'would the workers be right to retaliate by stealing what they could from the factory?' (moderator): 'by no means' (K6); 'that is blatantly wrong' (K30); 'I am sympathetic but theft is not allowed' (K7); 'one should do one's duty' (K23); 'one has to do one's duty' (K30) . . . 'only then can you claim your request legitimately' (K33).

More surprising was the way Koreans invoked the national interest and even *national* self-respect as a constraint on sabotage:

'I do not think sabotage is justified – workers should claim their rights in a proper process – sabotage weakens our economic power' (K4); 'if we consider it from the national perspective, if inferior products are exported to foreign countries [through badly done work] then that is a shame on our country – from that perspective, we have to make good products' (K14).

Sabotage by 'for example, screwing nuts only four turns when five turns are necessary' (moderator) was dismissed by one Korean participant as 'South Asian' (K22).

Koreans were by no means unwilling to resist, but they expressed remarkable faith in institutions and in:

'collective action' (K10, supported by all in the group); 'it is better for workers to demonstrate than to sabotage, even if they suffer bad conditions' (K11); 'sabotage is not allowed but there are two rights to resist, the right to build a labour union and the right to negotiate with an employer' (K26; K23 agrees).

The 'government', 'state' or 'Ministry of Labour' should 'not neglect these problems' (K23, K29, K32).

Koreans, two-thirds of whom had access to the internet, suggested using:

'internet anti-sites to disclose the wrongdoings of a company' (K22); 'internet-prompted boycotting is much better than breaking machines or stealing products' (K33).

Czech participants were also opposed to sabotage, emphasising peaceful collective action: 'protest – if everyone does it then it could be effective', but only if the protest was 'peaceful' (C0): 'a signed letter' (C0); or better, 'writing to the newspapers, that is an effective weapon' (C2); or 'switching to another job, that is a solution' (C3); 'I would leave the job if they did not stick to safety regulations' (C30).

But unlike Korean participants, Czechs felt more inhibited by fear than by any moral considerations. They felt completely powerless:

'people have to work even under these conditions – it is not possible to do anything else' (C25); 'they cannot do anything because if they gripe, they will get sacked' (C14); 'my Mum once expressed her dissatisfaction and she was the first to be sacked' (C0).

Even collective protest could be dangerous: workers 'will never stage any joint protest – employers would sack them in an instant!' (C12). Strikes were an option only for the indispensable like 'doctors, or people in high positions' who 'are not within two years of retirement – they can afford it' (C7). When sabotage was raised explicitly by the Czech moderator, it evoked the same fear of being sacked that had emerged in other responses:

'what if the employees steal?' (moderator) . . . 'then they would *get sacked*' (C18) . . . 'they *would not dare*' (C0).

In Ukraine, too, such constraint as was expressed was based not on morals but merely on fear or 'intimidation'. But Ukrainians went further than Czechs on the morality of sabotage: they asserted explicitly that sabotage was at least morally justified. In Ukrainian focus group discussions, unlike the less flexible survey interviews, there was much more support for sabotage by working badly, stealing, or damaging machinery: 'those protest actions would be very good' (U21; U20 agrees). In the Kyiv group everyone agreed that such sabotage 'would be right' (U7; supported by all). One participant seemed to waver: 'no, it is not right to steal' (U3) but even that participant then came back on track by adding: 'but if working conditions are not safe then they should' (U3).

In Kharkiv, several participants at first declared, like the vast majority of Ukrainian survey respondents, that 'there should not be any stealing'. But one participant argued that:

'it depends on what those violations are, because the people's patience is not infinite – if someone spent half a year working and his wage was not paid, he might well break something there – he would be justified in his own way' (U14).

Others then warmed to the idea of violent retaliation:

'it seems to me that it is not the equipment that should be whacked – it is necessary to whack the manager – what does the equipment have to do with it?' (U16; U11 agrees);

– and no moral restraint was evident:

'but if he hit the manager, the latter would report the incident to the militia' (U15) . . . '[so] the equipment should be cautiously unscrewed' (U12; with burst of laughter from rest of group) . . . 'then pocketed and carried away' (U16).

There was support for violent retaliation in another Ukrainian group:

'let them smash those pieces of iron, provided that they do not hit each other . . . from the viewpoint of law they are wrong doing all that, but if the law does not protect them then one can understand their actions' (U28).

In complete contrast to Korean moral restraint, Ukrainians lamented their fellow citizens' servility and criticised them for it:

'our people would not damage company assets, unless they were really upset' (U22) ... 'our people do not even go to demos' (U19) ... 'because the people are intimidated ... afraid to get sacked' (U20) ... 'our people will bear and forbear' (U22) ... 'yes, our people are like that' (U21).

5.4   Who? Acceptable protestors

Anti-globalisation protestors are noted for protesting globally. They themselves have a global perspective. But to a nationalist public, global protests can threaten national autonomy as much as any other aspect of globalisation. The broad issue is whether to accept – or even request – foreign help to combat global injustice. Also, there is a subsidiary issue: whether foreigners should be welcome to join *local* protests, as well as provide *help from afar*.

Foreign boycotts One method of globalising resistance to global injustice is the use of foreign boycotts. It has the advantage of avoiding an invasion of foreign protestors of the kind that so upset the citizens of Prague. Western critics of third world exploitation have argued in favour of boycotting imported goods produced by methods that pollute the environment or are a danger to workers in the countries where they are produced. In our scenario about an international company polluting the local environment, we asked the public whether local people 'should retaliate' not just by petitions and demonstrations but by 'asking international environmental groups in foreign countries to boycott the company's products'. Overall, this method of protest won around 60 per cent support among both public and officials. In Vietnam it won almost as much support as peaceful marches and demonstrations by local people, though neither got very strong backing in Vietnam.

Later in the interview we asked further questions about international boycotts, and about boycotts from both sides. There was remarkably wide support for banning *imports* from other countries (Table 5.6) but much less public support for a ban on their own country's *exports* (Table 5.7). So although a majority supported local appeals for international boycotts (Table 5.5) only a minority felt it would be helpful if foreign governments imposed a ban on imports from their country (Table 5.7). These are, however, very different kinds of foreign boycotts. The public might trust local people to request boycotts only when it was in their own local interest; but they suspected foreign governments would

Table 5.5. *Globalising protest*

If an international company here in (COUNTRY) was damaging or polluting the local environment, should people who *live in the locality* retaliate by . . .

| | | Officials % yes | Public % yes | Public within each country | | | |
				Czech R % yes	S Korea % yes	Ukraine % yes	Vietnam % yes
Taking collective action:	peaceful marches, rallies, demonstrations	75	72	82	79	84	44
Going international:	asking international environmental groups in foreign countries to boycott the company's products	61	58	61	60	73	37

Note: % yes = number saying 'yes' as a percentage of all respondents.

use a ban to favour foreign interests – a view that was articulated very explicitly and indignantly in our Ukrainian focus groups (see below). It matters *who calls* the boycott, and especially whether the boycott is at the *request* of local people or is *imposed* by foreign competitors.

First, we asked two questions about a ban on *imports* from other countries:

'should we ban the import of goods into (COUNTRY) if they are produced by methods that pollute the environment or are a danger to the workers in the countries where they are made, even if those products are good value to us?'

'Should we ban the import of goods into (COUNTRY) if they are produced by children, even if families in the countries where they are made depend upon children's work for their income?'

(In each case our interviewers were instructed to note any replies of the kind that such a ban 'would only be an excuse to protect our businessmen from competition'.)

There was wide public support (70 per cent) for a ban on imports produced by dangerous methods, but opinion was much more divided about a ban on imports produced by child labour (only 53 per cent support). On either criterion, however, East Europeans were 11 per cent more willing than East Asians to impose import bans.

Table 5.6. *A ban on imports*

	Officials %	Public %	Public within each country			
			Czech R %	Korea %	Ukraine %	Vietnam %
Ban *imports* produced by methods that pollute the environment or are a danger to the workers in the countries where they are made?						
yes	75	70	75	65	76	60
no	13	15	9	26	9	20
(VOL) excuse to protect our businessmen	3	4	5	4	4	2
Ban *imports* produced by children?						
yes	55	53	60	47	58	43
no	28	28	19	43	19	36
(VOL) excuse to protect our businessmen	4	4	5	3	5	2

Note: Per cent of all respondents. Per cents giving other/mixed/'don't know' responses not shown. VOL indicates that a particular answer was not offered by the interviewer, but was spontaneously volunteered by some respondents.

We then asked two similar questions about a ban (by foreign countries) on the respondents' own country's *exports*:

'suppose foreign countries banned imports of goods from (OUR COUNTRY) that were produced by methods that polluted *our* environment or were a danger to *our* workers here in (OUR COUNTRY) even if those products were good value to them. Would that help to improve conditions in our country or make things worse for us by excluding our products from world markets?'

'Suppose foreign countries banned imports of goods from (OUR COUNTRY) that were produced by children here in (OUR COUNTRY), even if their families depend upon the children's work for their income. Would that help to improve conditions in our country or make things worse for us by excluding our products from world markets?'

(Again, in each case interviewers were instructed to note any replies of the kind that such a ban 'would only be an excuse to exclude our products' or that 'things are not made that way in our country'.)

Two-fifths of Czechs and one-fifth of Ukrainians insisted that child labour was not used in their country, though they did not deny that dangerous production methods were used. Irrespective of whether the foreign ban was to stop dangerous working methods or to stop child

Table 5.7. *A foreign ban on our exports*

	Officials %	Public %	Public within each country			
			Czech R %	Korea %	Ukraine %	Vietnam %
Ban *exports* produced by methods that pollute our environment or are a danger to *our* workers?						
help	44	39	32	53	33	36
make things worse	27	31	29	39	31	28
(VOL) excuse to exclude our products	7	6	10	1	7	5
(VOL) not made that way here	9	8	12	3	4	8
Ban exports produced by *our* children?						
help	37	34	23	56	26	30
make things worse	23	25	18	35	22	29
(VOL) excuse to exclude our products	6	5	7	1	5	7
(VOL) not made that way here	22	19	38	5	20	10

Note: Per cent of all respondents. Per cents giving other/mixed/'don't know' responses not shown. VOL indicates that a particular answer was not offered by the interviewer, but was spontaneously volunteered by some respondents.

labour, there was far less support for a foreign ban on exports than for the corresponding ban on imports. Only in Korea was there a majority who felt that foreign bans on their exports would help.

In focus group discussions participants were asked only about foreign countries imposing an export ban on goods produced in the participants' country. As in the survey, Koreans accepted that restrictions on their exports could help, while the Vietnamese were divided. More significantly, both Czechs and Ukrainians wilfully misinterpreted the question, though in different ways.

Korean participants generally accepted the right of foreign countries to restrict imports from Korea if they were produced by methods that polluted the Korean environment or were a danger to Korean workers. In general they did not think such restrictions would just be an excuse to exclude Korean exports. None of the participants in Seoul and Yechon, for example, thought that 'foreigners would take advantage of this restriction' just to exclude Korean exports:

'we should accept the restriction' (K8) ... 'we have to admit our faults' (K7, supported by everyone else).

Some Koreans emphasised reciprocity:

'if other countries export such products to us, we cannot help rejecting them (K18); 'it might be a different story, if foreign countries themselves did not follow the rule' (K5) ... '[or] find fault with our products alone' (K4, supported by K8).

But other Koreans disagreed even with that condition:

'even if they do the same in their countries too, we have to revise our faults – if there is environmental pollution, that is our damage, not theirs' (K6).

There was some mild scepticism: accepting such restrictions as 'appropriate' because the 'fault was on our side' was 'true in terms of morality but in practice, it is more appropriate to regard it as an excuse' (K20). Yet restrictions would be acceptable if they were:

'grounded on facts instead of excuses – we have to change so that we may export our products proudly' (K18); 'there must be reasons' (K14) ... 'clear reasons' (K10) ... 'proper reasons' (K14); '[even if] a product is of good quality but is made in a bad way there should always be restrictions whether we are exporting or importing – the world is in a process of globalisation and humanisation ... those products should be categorically rejected' (K30).

'Reciprocity' was not always an excuse: in Yoju everyone agreed when the moderator asked:

'without any consideration of reciprocity – when our products are rejected for such reasons, then we should accept it?'

Czech participants could not imagine such restrictions on their products and insisted on discussing import bans, not export bans – though they expressed doubts about the utility even of import bans. As an 'accession state' to the EU there were more problems of competition from EU products flooding into the Czech Republic than problems of Czech products being excluded from world markets, and Czechs focused their discussion around whether they should boycott shoes made for Nike by children in Thailand. They felt the problem should be:

'solved by the state where it happens' (C17; C18 agrees); 'what would children do if they did not do this kind of work?' (C18) . . . 'I think they would not go to school' (C21); 'they are glad to earn some money' (C17).

In any case an import boycott:

'would not work here, not from the position of the customer' (C0) . . . 'given that Nike is a well-known brand' (C19) . . . 'people here will buy their goods anyway' (C17) . . . 'if a mother is to decide between shoes that cost 500 or 200 crowns, she buys those that cost 200 crowns' (C8).

Ukrainians also wilfully misinterpreted the question – but in a very different way. Despite the moderator's question which stressed damaging *methods of production*, Ukrainian participants insisted on interpreting it as a question about *sub-standard products*, and they were offended:

'if goods are low quality then let them impose restrictions to keep Ukraine from doing it again, but if the goods are OK . . .' (U3); 'if it is an attempt to sell some products that really pollute the environment then that should be restricted – but if it is only an excuse on the foreign side not to buy something from us, then . . .' (U10).

Their insistent focus on sub-standard products was reinforced by a foreign example spontaneously introduced by one participant in Kharkiv:

'there was that mad cow disease in England last year – trade restrictions were a normal thing – that is how it should be' (U11).

Ukrainians were notably apprehensive about their product quality. But what most set them apart from others was their extreme suspicion and resentment of potential restrictions:

'it is only an excuse' (U28); 'to buy Ukrainian goods for next to nothing' (U25); 'to reduce our exports and to humiliate our Ukraine – we are humiliated far and wide!' (U32); 'how can our products be environmentally polluted? Our enterprises are at a standstill – fertilisers are not spread over the soil – the Chernobyl accident was long ago and it did not cause damage to this country alone – for some reason there is no talk of environmentally polluted products from Poland despite the fact that more regions suffered from Chernobyl in Poland than in Ukraine. It has been proved, there is scientific data indicating that our products are really environmentally clean but they are exploiting our dead-end situation to buy all those products from us for next to nothing' (U28; supported by U26, U29).

Ukrainians felt exploited by stronger powers:

'that scandal around those CD disks – our disks are not any worse than theirs ... but those countries do not want the same product there so they put pressure on us – said they would block any import from Ukraine – Ukraine must obey' (U19) ... 'this just cannot be avoided' (U17; supported by U22, U24).

In the few instances where they did not willfully misinterpret the question, Ukrainian participants looked to the state rather than foreign consumers to protect them, but blamed the state for failing to do so:

'above all it is the policy of the state [deep sad sigh] – if the plant in question is advantageous to the state and brings large profits to businessmen then that plant will go on functioning all the same – and as to how many people remain in that village, what is the health of the children born there, no one will be interested in such things' (U30; supported by U31, U32).

Vietnamese participants fully understood the question, but their opinions were nonetheless divided, complex and on balance opposed – though not so helplessly resentful as in Ukraine. Vietnam had some very poor and underdeveloped hill regions where the whole family traditionally joined in domestic production – much of it craft work by children. So some supported restrictions (V19, V24, V12) and gave reasons:

'yes, they should restrict – thus child abuse and deforestation could be limited' (V19)

But others, equally concerned for the hill people, advised caution, and also gave reasons:

'it should be considered carefully because we can create jobs for children with this production' (V21); 'it is nonsense to ban those products – it is a way of making things difficult for us – it is obviously not good to exploit children but it creates jobs' (V26) ... 'each nation should have its own policy ... it is not good to ban goods like that' (V31).

The moderator also drew attention to American complaints against Vietnam 'for selling catfish at a price lower than the 'real' [i.e. American] cost, arguing that 'workers here in Vietnam get low wages'. But a Vietnamese participant rejected that argument:

'the living cost here in Vietnam is not expensive and this payment is acceptable for Vietnamese fishermen' (V31); 'it is just an excuse not to import our goods' (V13) ... '[imposed by the US] to harm us' (V15).

Welcoming foreign protestors? As a supplementary to our question about whether it would be right to protest against the WTO, IMF or World Bank damaging poorer countries, we asked:

'should sympathetic people from richer countries protest – or only people in the poorer countries damaged by these policies?'

As a supplementary to our question about whether it would be right to protest against an international company causing local problems, we asked:

'should sympathetic people from other countries join in the protest – or only people who live in (COUNTRY)?'

In both cases the question was essentially whether protest should be limited to people from the country, or even the locality, directly affected. But the second question implies that foreigners might come into the respondents' country to 'join in' the local protest. The impact of this difference is clearly detectable in the responses and seems more significant than whether the target of protest was international firms or organisations.

Only around 14 per cent in all countries thought protests against international organisations such as the WTO, IMF or World Bank should be limited to people from the poorer countries adversely affected by their policies. But positive support for people from rich countries protesting on behalf of poorer countries was noticeably higher in the richer countries and lower – though still high in absolute terms – in relatively poor Ukraine and Vietnam. Public opposition to foreign participation in protests against international companies was higher and less uniform – only 12 per cent in Vietnam and around 20 per cent in Korea and Ukraine, but peaking at 28 per cent in the Czech Republic which had the most experience of foreign protestors – even if the Prague protests had not been about international companies so much as about international organisations.

Vietnamese focus group participants stressed that local people – but also the state – should be involved:

'those who directly suffer those problems can protest' (V4); 'not only local people can protest – the state and people all over the country can interfere too' (V12).

But Korean participants generally accepted the right of people from outside the locality to protest – even if they were foreigners:

'foreign residents in Korea should have the right' (K32) ... 'if the company affects the foreign residents' (K18; K8 agrees) ... 'although they are foreigners, they are living in Korea now' (K10);

Table 5.8. *Welcoming foreign protestors?*

	Officials %	Public %	Public within each country			
			Czech R %	Korea %	Ukraine %	Vietnam %
Who should protest if WTO/IMF/WB etc damage poorer countries?						
only people in the poorer countries damaged by these policies	12	14	13	16	15	13
sympathetic people from richer countries	72	68	71	80	64	53
If an international company is causing serious local problems … should sympathetic people from other countries join in the protest, or only people who live in (COUNTRY)?						
only people who live in (COUNTRY)	15	19	28	21	18	12
people from other countries	73	66	58	75	64	65

Note: Per cent of all respondents. Per cents giving other/mixed/'don't know' responses not shown.

– and even foreigners from foreign countries:

'also have the right – it is about affairs of human beings – if there is something wrong in foreign countries, we may blame them, so likewise . . . ' (K22, supported by K19, K20; though opposed by others).

In Ukraine, participants supported people 'from other regions' joining in local anti-pollution protests:

'yes, let them join us – after all, we are all human beings' (U25) . . . 'I think so too, because it will reach our neighbours anyway' (U27, supported by all others in the group).

Even foreigners were welcome:

'protest should not be limited to the specific locality – this should concern the entire Ukraine' (U3, with everyone else nodding agreement) . . . 'and people from other countries?' (moderator) . . . 'yes, it is normal' (U3; again supported by everyone else).

But while in principle Ukrainians accepted foreigners' rights to protest, the group in Kharkiv doubted whether foreigners cared. Protests should:

'first be local people – if no one listens to local people, then the whole of Ukraine' (U10) . . . 'and people from other countries?' (moderator) . . . 'none of them will join in' (U15) . . . 'there is a Ukrainian proverb "my home is on the outskirts" [meaning: "that is none of my business"]' (U13).

Even within Kharkiv itself there was allegedly very little community spirit:

'for example, that dumping ground for garbage that people have been protesting against – do you support those people? Do you participate in those protests? No, you do not – apart from those directly affected it is nobody's concern' (U13).

5.5   Explaining public support for protest methods

We have found near universal public support for protest – of some kind – against global injustice, in particular against badly behaving international companies or organisations. Very few (5 per cent) actually said there should be no protest in these circumstances. The only issue was therefore about *acceptable methods* of protest – in particular whether to accept disorderly or even violent protest, and whether to accept or even request the *participation of foreigners* in these protests.

Explaining support for robust methods What made half the public insist on only peaceful protest while the rest refused to rule out disorderly and violent protest? There are two possibilities: structured cleavage or probabilistic prejudice. Structured cleavage is the unspoken assumption underlying most social science analysis: the assumption that different views about disorderly protest reflect different kinds of people – different backgrounds, different experiences, different prejudices. But on an issue so far removed from everyday experience, so dependent on unspecified details, and so beset by conditions and caveats, the structured cleavage approach may be wrong. Possibly there is no structural explanation at all. Conceivably the ambivalence about disorderly protest lies within each individual rather than between them – so that each has probabilistic tendencies, that they are 'switherers' (to use the precise Scots term) on the issue of disorderly protest, albeit *biased* switherers, somewhat more likely to opt for orderly protest than disorderly. If that is the case then the overall percentages opting for orderly and disorderly protest have a real meaning at the level of *society* but they do not define one *individual* as pro-order and another as pro-disorder.

Regression analyses using all our measures of background and experience, perceptions of development and satisfaction, attitudes towards national culture and xenophobia, plus attitudes to the market economy and opening up, do not provide very powerful explanations of why one individual accepted disorderly methods of 'anti-globalisation' protest and another did not (RSQ never exceeds 6 per cent in any country). Nonetheless, they do highlight a few factors that have more influence than any others on support for disorderly protest. As usual, what was not highlighted by the regression analyses is as significant as what was. The key factors behind support for 'disorderly or violent' protest against global injustice were *not* socio-economic background such as income, education, or rurality, but attitudes towards globalisation itself, and specifically towards international companies.

Apart from uniquely high Ukrainian support for disorderly protest (to which we return in later chapters), these factors mostly reflected general attitudes towards foreigners, foreign companies, foreign businessmen or foreign guest workers, rather than more abstract support for the market economy or opening up: those who generally distrusted or disliked any or all of these were much more willing to support disorderly or violent methods if and when international companies or organisations behaved badly; conversely, those who had more generally favourable attitudes towards foreigners were more likely to opt for no more than peaceful protest even when protest might be appropriate.

The single best predictor of public support for more disorderly or violent methods of protest was the perception that foreign companies did more to 'exploit' than 'help' the country. That was the best predictor in the merged four-country data set, and it was the best within Ukraine

Table 5.9. *The impact of perceptions of exploitation on public support for violent protest*

	Officials and public %	Public %	Public within each country			
			Czech R %	Korea %	Ukraine %	Vietnam %
% '*never* use disorderly or violent forms of protest' minus % 'use whatever is effective', among those who feel foreign companies ...						
... help a lot	+48	+47	+52	+45	+39	+50
... help a little	+44	+43	+50	+57	+22	+35
... exploit a little	+32	+28	+25	+50	+10	+17
... exploit a lot	+5	0	−6	+33	−9	+33

Note: Based on the percentages who: (1) completely reject 'disorderly or violent forms of protest'; (2) accept them 'only after peaceful protest has been ignored'; and (3) support the use of 'any form of protest that protestors think will solve the problem quickly'.

The exact balance overall between extreme views among those who feel foreign companies 'exploit a lot' is the product of strong support for peaceful methods among the few East Asians who regard foreign companies as exploiters, and the small bias in the opposite direction among the much larger number of East Europeans, especially Ukrainians, who feel that way about foreign companies.

and close to best in the Czech Republic and Vietnam. (In Korea, unlike the other countries, the impact of more general attitudes towards opening up supplanted that of more specific attitudes towards foreign companies.)

The balance between those who would never accept 'disorderly or violent' protest and those, at the other extreme, who would support whatever methods of protest were effective, shifted towards support for disorderly methods in line with general perceptions that foreign companies tended to 'exploit' more than 'help' the country – by 47 per cent in the merged data set and by slightly more than that within both of the East European countries. In East Asia the effect was much smaller but still clearly visible.

Perceptions that foreigners were generally good for the country, or that opening up had more advantages than disadvantages, also shifted public opinion towards the exclusive use of peaceful methods of protest – though by only about half as much (20–25 per cent) as perceptions that foreign companies were generally helpful.

Explaining support for foreign participation in local protests Foreign participation, especially in local protests, constitutes a different dimension in methods of protest and one that is particularly relevant to

Table 5.10. *The impact of xenophobia on public support for foreign participation in local protests*

| | Officials and public % | Public % | Public within each country | | | |
			Czech R %	Korea %	Ukraine %	Vietnam %
% agree minus % disagree that sympathetic people from other countries should join in a protest about an international company which is causing serious local problems ...						
... if feel foreigners are generally good for (COUNTRY)	+69	+64	+45	+60	+66	+74
... if feel foreigners are generally bad for (COUNTRY)	+30	+28	+25	+21	+37	+63

'anti-globalisation' protests. In contrast to the basis of support for robust protest which correlated best with adverse perceptions of foreign companies and to a much lesser extent with adverse perceptions of foreigners as people, support for foreign participation in local protest correlated best with positive perceptions of foreign people and to a lesser extent with general support for opening up – but not at all with perceptions of foreign companies as such.

The balance between those who would welcome foreign participation in local protests and those, at the other extreme, who would oppose foreign participation, shifted towards support for foreign participation by 36 per cent (in the merged data set) if general perceptions of foreigners were positive; and by 23 per cent if general attitudes towards opening up were positive. Irrespective of other factors, however, Czechs were distinctively less enthusiastic about foreign participation in local protests: they were uniquely opposed to roving anti-globalisation protestors.

5.6   Conclusions

We have found almost universal support – in all four countries, and among officials as well as the public – for protest of some kind against international companies that cause serious local problems, or against international organisations whose policies damage poorer countries. These circumstances were sufficient to justify protest. So in these circumstances the issue for most people was not *protest itself*, but the *method of protest*.

After the clashes in Genoa, George Monbiot had argued that 'words are not enough' (*Guardian*, 24 July 2001). But critics complained that violent protest simply confused international debate and gained publicity at the expense of sympathy – especially among the public in rich countries whose sympathy was needed if policies were to be changed. We have found that disorderly, disruptive and violent methods of protest were also rejected by the majority of ordinary people in our developing or transitional countries (though they were supported by a sizeable minority). These publics had their discontents and they did support protest; but like western publics they valued order. Even in principle, more of the public opposed than supported disorderly protest in every country except Ukraine.

Moreover, when asked about specific methods of protest, public support for anything other than peaceful protest is very low. Two-thirds would support a peaceful demonstration but only one-sixth would support a 'go-slow' by aggrieved workers, and only one in nine ever explicitly supported sabotage despite being asked about it four times (though twice as many failed to consistently condemn it). Many participants in Ukrainian focus groups expressed extreme frustration and some expressed moral support for sabotage. But in the more formal and isolated setting of a survey interview, although only a minority of Ukrainians were completely opposed to violent or disorderly protest, only one in seven Ukrainians explicitly supported sabotage (though over a quarter failed to consistently condemn it).

Public support for more robust methods of protest reflects something more than commitment to the classic liberal-democratic concept of a general right to protest, however. Indeed, the liberal-democratic concept of legitimate protest is normally limited to peaceful methods of protest. Support for 'disorderly or violent' protest clearly varies with attitudes towards the issue of globalisation itself, particularly with feelings of global injustice and xenophobia. When international companies or organisations behave badly, even those who generally trust and like foreigners and foreign companies are likely to support protest. But those who generally *dis*trust and *dis*like foreigners, or more especially foreign companies, are significantly more likely to back the use of disorderly and violent methods for that protest.

There is also widespread acceptance of a global dimension to protest, though the notion of protestors from richer countries aiding protest in poorer countries is more popular in richer countries, and import boycotts are far more popular than export boycotts. Those with a xenophobic distrust of foreigners-as-people are not only more willing to back robust methods of protest, they are also less willing to accept the participation of foreigners in local protests – more willing therefore to back a combination of *self-reliance* and disruptive or *violent methods*.

Beyond general tendencies, that are visible in all our countries, the national setting remains important. Even when attitudes towards global-isation were taken into account, the Ukrainian public remained notably unwilling to condemn disruptive protest. Conversely, Czechs were nota-bly reluctant to accept foreign participation in local protests. While the Vietnamese supported the *principle* of anti-globalisation protests as much as people from other countries, they were very much less willing than others to back specific forms of protest including relatively peaceable methods.

The obvious explanations of these residual national differences are history, culture, and development – in the case of our four countries, the possibilities include the legacy of communist and authoritarian regimes, or authoritarian 'Asian' versus liberal 'European' values, or recent experience of rapid development versus stagnation or decline. But such grand explanations are less coherent when their details are spelt out and, in any case, they fail to explain our findings. All four of our countries have a history of communist or authoritarian rule: by itself that cannot explain differences between them. The concepts of 'Asian', 'European' or 'western' values are vigorously contested, and liberal European values hardly explain why Czech officials should be the least tolerant of disorderly protest. Conversely, the long experience of Czarist and communist rule in Ukraine hardly explains why Ukrainians should be the most tolerant of disorderly protest. Asian values or Vietnam's indig-enous communist legacy might be brought up as explanations of the Vietnamese reluctance to endorse the various methods of protest we have considered. But Ukraine also has an indigenous communist legacy. We have found no reluctance to endorse the principle of protest in Vietnam, nor an unusual reluctance to accept disorderly protest – if only in the abstract. Falling living standards sounds a more plausible explanation. Since their post-communist economies were opened up, Ukrainian living standards have been falling rapidly. But even if we compare the (relatively few) Ukrainians who report rising family living standards with similar people in other countries, Ukrainians stand out as much less willing to condemn disruptive methods of anti-globalisation protest.

Some less obvious or perhaps less routine explanations seem more plausible. First, the trashing of Prague: the Czech Republic was the only one of our four countries whose iconic capital had suffered several days of violent battles between (largely foreign) anti-globalisation protestors and the local police. That did not reduce Czech commitment to the principle of protest but it left a peculiar distaste for violent methods – and for foreign participation. Hence Czechs were particularly reluctant to accept foreign protestors in their own country. Hence, too, the strong opposition of the Czech public, and the quite outstanding opposition of Czech officials, to 'disorderly or violent forms of protest'. It is not the historic or culturally embedded authoritarianism of the Czechs, but recent bruises that most obviously fits their peculiar attitudes towards anti-globalisation protests. They may have sympathised with the cause that prompted the disorder. They continued to express some sympathy for the cause, but they were hurt and offended by the manner of the protest. Peter Preston was right to warn that disorder provokes an adverse public reaction (*Guardian*, 23 July 2001).

Second, the desired and perceived role of the state – and the connection between desire and perception: Ukrainians were uniquely disappointed by their post-communist state, which they criticised for being ineffective, no longer concerned about governing, and merely a front for self-serving criminals – in their view a 'failed state'. By contrast, the Vietnamese regarded their state – postcommunist in content though not in form since 1992 – as much more effective, still very much 'in charge', and still committed to public rather than private goals. The Vietnam state might therefore be sensitive to protest and particularly resent disorderly protest, while the Ukrainian state would be insensitive, unresponsive, and disengaged. Right or wrong, and they are not entirely without foundation, such perceptions encourage the Vietnamese to focus their protests on and through government and to regard other methods of protest as inherently disorderly. Conversely, they encourage Ukrainians to feel that direct action is more necessary, though likely to be ignored unless it employs relatively robust methods.

Chapter 6 explores public attitudes towards the role of the state in a globalising economy and the possibility of expressing the discontents of globalisation *through* the state, rather than by direct action.

6   The role of the state

With an internal market economy, exposed externally to world markets, and with a plethora of international organisations deciding political and economic policy, what role is left for the nation state? This chapter looks at public perspectives on the state: the role that the public in developing or transitional countries feel it should play in the life of their nations, and their perceptions of its actual role and performance in practice. They see at least four possible roles for the state in an era of globalisation: as national economic entrepreneur, as physician or protector, and as advocate – all of which they would support; and as a conspiracy against the public, which they condemn. To explore that fourth role more fully, we take a closer look at the differences between public and officials.

6.1   'Decline of the state' or transformation?

Robertson (1985: p. 307) suggests that 'the State may be the most commonly-used and the most opaque term in the whole of political vocabulary'. Its meaning certainly varies according to context. It can be distinguished from transient 'government' in the narrow sense of a small group of ministers. But it is not so different from 'government' in the wider sense of the ministry plus all the civil and military servants at their command. In Vietnam it is equated with the Party, and both Party and government are regarded as permanent insofar as any socio-political structure is ever permanent. When we look at public perceptions of, and attitudes towards, the 'role of the state' in the context of globalisation we focus on what the public want government – in the wider sense of political elites right down to junior officials – to do, and what the public think government (in this wider sense) actually is doing. There is likely to be some difference between what the public want from government or the state, and what they get.

There has been a vigorous academic debate over the impact of international economic integration, and of globalisation more generally, on the role of the state. Some argue that globalisation has made the state *impotent* – unable to perform its traditional role of raising taxes and redistributing income; or *irrelevant* – because its citizens now earn their living and take their leisure in a world where state frontiers contribute nothing towards their welfare or happiness. At street level especially, critics go further and claim that as globalisation has forced the state to retreat from its role of providing public welfare it has focused more on its own private welfare, and developed its (always latent) role as a corrupt, *self-serving* conspiracy of officials against the public.

   The 'decline of the state' It is alleged that the nation-state is in 'decline' (Bauman 1993; Hutton 2002; Monbiot 2000; Hirst and Thompson 1996; Lee 2000); that states are 'victims of the market economy' (Strange 1996; p. 14); that 'impersonal forces of world markets . . . are now more powerful than the states' (Strange 1996: p. 4). Even if globalisation were not inherently anti-state, 'the way that globalization has been managed has eroded the ability of the state to play its proper role' (Joseph Stiglitz, *Guardian* 12 March 2004). States 'can no longer manage national economies in isolation; they cannot protect their citizens from the effects of financial deregulation; they cannot prevent unemployment when transnational corporations decide to move operations or find new supplies elsewhere' (Horsman and Marshall 1994: p. 176). All that states can do is provide, at the lowest possible cost, the infrastructure and public goods that business wants (Hirst and Thompson 1996: p. 175).
   Indeed, it is alleged that states are increasingly irrelevant (Ohmae 1990); 'losing their meaning-generating capacity' (Bauman 1998: pp. 2–3). 'The unfettered movement of [industry, information technology, and individual consumers] makes the middleman role of nation-states obsolete . . . traditional nation-states have become unnatural, even impossible business units in a global economy' (Ohmae 1995: p. 5) and 'unable to put . . . the true quality-of-life interests of their people first in any of the decisions they make' (Ohmae 1995: p. 42). Some of those most sympathetic to the ideal of a globalised world argue that the capacity of the state to govern effectively and command the loyalty of the public has been so eroded that the only way forward is through a 'new global covenant' (Held 2004) to an even more global system of governance.
   Opening up economies is said to undermine policies aimed at promoting national economic growth as well as reducing the state's ability to expand 'fiscal and social protection' (Weiss 2003: p. 2). The interventionist state of the late twentieth century is threatened by the new mobility of capital (Kudrle 1999: p. 213) and 'classical national economic management now has limited scope' (Hirst and Thompson 1996: p. 199). Politically also, state autonomy is threatened by the growing role of

international organisations such as the World Bank and International Monetary Fund (IMF), the World Trade Organisation (WTO), or the United Nations (UN); by regional organisations like the European Union (EU); and by military blocs such as the North Atlantic Treaty Organization (NATO), (Holton 1998).

A decline overstated On the other side, it is argued that the downsides of globalisation have been overstated (Bhagwati 2004). In particular: 'the proposition that globalization makes the state unnecessary is even less credible than the idea that it makes states impotent ... as the source of order and the basis for governance, the state will remain in the future as effective, and will be as essential, as it has ever been' (Wolf 2001: pp. 188, 190; see also Wolf 2004); the nation state 'is not disappearing, and the scope of government, taken overall, expands rather than diminishes as globalisation proceeds' (Giddens 1998: p. 32); 'public goods [including] the maintenance of the market mechanism itself ... can only be provided by a political process' (Soros 2002: p. 6). Sadly, 'by far the most important causes of misery and poverty in the world today are armed conflict, oppressive and corrupt regimes, and weak states – and globalisation cannot be blamed for bad governments' (Soros 2002: p. 14). So for good or for ill, the state remains important.

'Failed states, disorderly states, weak states, and corrupt states' are not the product of globalisation. Indeed, they are incompatible with it: an effective, orderly, strong and 'honest' state is necessary 'to take advantage of the opportunities offered by international economic integration' (Wolf 2001: pp. 189, 190). The limits on states' ability to impose taxes and redistribute income are imposed by internal 'electoral resistance, not globalization' (Wolf 2001: pp. 185, 188). If they and their public so wish it, 'states have significantly more room to manoeuvre in the global political economy than globalisation theory allows' (Weiss 2003: p. 26), especially in relation to 'social protection and wealth creation'.

One study of East Asian states in particular confirms their autonomy by showing that their responses to the 1997 currency crisis varied considerably: 'while the dynamics of globalisation involve strong pressure to transform economic policy in neo-liberal directions, it is not inevitable that this will be the outcome. Indeed, our work suggests that national governments continue to have room for manoeuvre' (Henderson and Hulme 2002: p. 9). The decline of the state is a 'European delusion' without applicability to East Asia: 'building a strong nation state has been the central objective' in the post-colonial world and 'in East Asia ... the project has been hugely successful: the vast majority of [East Asian] nation states have seen steady accretion of power – the opposite to the European experience' (Martin Jacques, *Guardian*, 29 July 2004). In contrast to the supra-national EU, the 'strictly intergovernmental' (Sweeney 2005: p. 404) Association of South-East Asian Nations (ASEAN), 'is a conscious attempt to enhance the power of its member states through the creation of a regional body' (Martin Jacques, *Guardian*, 29 July 2004).

Indeed globalisation itself 'is not destined, it is chosen' (Wolf 2001: p. 182); 'the acquiescent state ... has not been a passive victim of globalisation ... state *governments* have engineered their own reduced roles ... it is [state] *governments* ... that shape EU policies ... *governments* that shape other international bodies with a global brief, such as the UN or the WTO ... *governments* [that accepted] the Washington consensus ... *governments* [that] created globalisation as we currently experience it' (Sweeney 2005: pp. 351–7, our emphasis).

The state transformed But 'discussions of loss of sovereignty miss the point, being based on a zero-sum interpretation of international relations ... [while] action by governments with a commitment to cooperation [is seen by them] as the only way to enhance their own legitimacy' (Sweeney 2005: p. 415) both internally and externally. Sovereignty 'has been displaced as an illimitable, indivisible and exclusive form of public power, embodied in an individual state, and [is now] embedded in a system of multiple, often pooled power centres and overlapping spheres of authority. There has been ... a [voluntary and purposeful] reconfiguration of political power' (Held and McGrew 2002: pp. 125–6).

That transformation applies to the notion of military power also: shifting the emphasis to 'soft power': 'hard power ... grows out of a country's military and economic might. Soft power arises from the attractiveness of a country's culture, political ideals and policies ... soft power will become increasingly important' (Nye 2003: p. 64). So the notion of a 'powerless state' is a 'myth' (Weiss 1998). 'Globalization ... is far from making the nation-state obsolete ... [though] any emerging pattern of governance will have to be networked rather than hierarchical ... minimal rather than highly ambitious ... [and] legitimacy in international regimes will derive in part from delegation from elected national governments' (Nye and Donahue 2000a, b: pp. 36–8).

Nye and Donahue's benign vision may now require some revision. 'Hard power' is back in fashion. But their fundamental claim that states remain strong still holds. Indeed it has been reinforced by the return to 'hard power': 'the emergence of the USA as the sole superpower, and its turn towards unilateralism, thereby weakening the trend towards multilateralism and global governance, is a quintessential demonstration of the power of the nation state, in some respects in excess of anything seen before' (Martin Jacques, *Guardian*, 29 July 2004).

The re-definition of a strong state There is no generally agreed definition of what constitutes a 'strong', 'weak', or 'failed' state (Orchard 2004). During the 1990s the US Central Intelligence Agency (CIA) sponsored two major studies of 'state failure' without ever defining the term. Proposed definitions for its '2020 Project' now place states on a four-point spectrum of categories – 'strong', 'weak', 'failed' and 'collapsed' – based on their ability to 'deliver a full range and high quality of political goods' (Rotberg 2003: p. 2; see also Rotberg 2004). Naturally, those advising the CIA put 'security' at the top of their list of 'political goods'. But even CIA advisors list other 'indicators' of strength, including 'GDP per capita, the UNDP *Human Development Index*, Transparency International's *Corruption Perceptions Index*, and Freedom House's *Freedom of the World Report*' (Rotberg 2003: p. 2). States may be considered 'strong', it is now argued, only if they deliver these other 'political goods' – and 'weak' or 'failed' if they do not. Even in a world of economic interdependence and military domination by a single hegemonic superpower, therefore, states large and small may be judged 'strong' or 'weak' – and judged not only by their own citizens – according to their success in delivering public welfare. They may be judged no less strong if they achieve that success by honest, efficient and responsive (rather than oppressive) bureaucracy at home and by a cooperative (rather than belligerent) negotiating stance abroad. The exercise of 'hard power', whether internally or externally, is no longer regarded as the sole indication of a 'strong state'.

6.2   What boosts public support for government

The academic debate about the role of the state is clearly vigorous. But it may not represent opinion on the street in developing countries. As a starting point for consideration of the roles that the public want the state to perform, we can look at how government popularity is related to public perceptions of change and public attitudes towards openness. That will not tell us everything about the public's attitude to the role of government but it will indicate some of the things that really matter most to the public, and on which governments – and thus 'government' itself – are judged.

Overall, the public were evenly divided on whether their government and its policies were good or bad (just 2 per cent net negative) while officials were far more satisfied (21 per cent net positive). In both East European countries, the public were highly critical of their governments

Table 6.1. *Good government – and bad*

	Officials %	Public %	Public within each country			
			Czech R %	Korea %	Ukraine %	Vietnam %
On the whole, would you say that the present government and its policies are ...						
very good for (COUNTRY)	10	13	1	5	2	47
good for (COUNTRY)	44	31	24	38	18	41
bad for (COUNTRY)	27	35	47	42	50	1
very bad for (COUNTRY)	6	11	18	7	17	0

Note: Per cent of all respondents. Per cents giving other/mixed/'don't know' responses not shown.

(40 per cent net negative in the Czech Republic; 47 per cent net negative in Ukraine). But in Korea they were on balance only slightly critical (only 6 per cent net negative), and in Vietnam they were wildly enthusiastic: a total of 88 per cent praised their government as being at least 'good for Vietnam'; and 47 per cent said it was 'very good' – compared with a mere 5 per cent in Korea and 2 per cent or less in East Europe.

But more important than the *levels* of public support for governments is to understand *what influences* public support. That provides at least a clue as to what the public really want the state to do. We use multiple regression to assess the impact of all our indicators of background, experience, and perceptions of both cultural and economic change on public support for the 'government and its policies'.

In the merged data set of the public in all four countries, that regression highlights a major difference between those in East Asia and East Europe (beta = 0.31): public support for the government and its policies was much higher in the Asian countries than in the two East European countries, even after taking into account all other influences. Cross-national patterns of support for the government can be explained by a legacy model reflecting varying national standards of judgement together with the competence of governments themselves. But what else had an impact? And what explains variations in government support between individuals *within* the same country?

In the merged data set the impact of this extremely powerful Asian/European legacy model was matched by a winners and losers model based, however, on perceptions of national economic trends (beta = 0.30) rather than personal or family gains and losses – which also had an impact but a much smaller one (beta = 0.12). Perceptions of international justice (beta = 0.11) also had a weak impact, and perceptions of domestic justice (beta = 0.05) even less.

But public perceptions of cultural trends – whether the national 'language, culture and traditions' were 'gaining or losing respect' – came a good second (beta = 0.19) to perceptions of national economic trends. The impact of cultural perceptions was particularly weak in the Czech Republic. But the impact of cultural perceptions was one of four roughly equal influences on government support in Ukraine – where personal or family gains and losses mattered much more than anywhere else. The impact of cultural perceptions ran very slightly ahead of the impact of national economic perceptions in Korea, however, and was by far the most important explanation of why some Vietnamese were even more enthusiastic than others about their government and its policies.

So while cultural perceptions have very little impact on public attitudes towards the market economy or towards opening up (as we noted in Chapter 3), they had a major impact on public support for the government and its policies.

Perhaps we should include public attitudes towards the internal market economy and towards opening up as themselves a potential influence upon support for the government and its policies (see Table 6.3). If we do that, then cultural perceptions remain the second most powerful explanation of government support – somewhat closer behind the national winners and losers model than before (betas now 0.25 and 0.17 respectively, instead of 0.30 and 0.19). Cultural perceptions remain by far the most important factor in Vietnam, and they become relatively more important in Korea and Ukraine than before. But perceptions that the market is fair move into third place (beta = 0.13), ahead of a personal or family based winners and losers model. Whether the market economy produces prosperity or whether opening up has more advantages than disadvantages are relatively unimportant for explaining government support, once we have taken into account perceptions of national economic and cultural trends.

So whatever the mechanisms, whatever the technicalities, whatever the theories that governments employ, they win the support of the public if the *national economy* and the *national culture* prosper – and to a lesser extent – if the internal market operates fairly.

The claim of neo-liberals is that internal market economies and externally open economies automatically generate wealth and that government interference merely disrupts – and often corrupts – them: that government cannot take the credit for them. Indeed the claim of extreme liberals is that government interference damages or degrades market mechanisms: that these are not the proper responsibilities of governments but

Table 6.2. *The twin bases of public support for government*

The government and its policies are good for (COUNTRY)		All four countries		Public within each country			
		Public and officials	Public only	Czech R	Korea	Ukraine	Vietnam
RSQ =		49	52	19	14	21	13
		beta.100	beta.100	beta.100	beta.100	beta.100	beta.100
MODEL	INDICATOR						
Winners and losers – national	national economy got better	33	30	29	17	20	8
Culture	more respect for national culture	21	19	6	18	15	30
Winners and losers – family	family income got better	11	12	6	11	18	
International justice	foreign companies help	7	11	12	14	15	13
Domestic justice	think winners have more skill and luck	6	5	8		11	
Legacy	Asian						
Elite	officials	29	31				

Note: All betas shown are statistically significant at the five per cent level.

Table 6.3. *The twin bases of public support for government (extended analysis)*

The government and its policies are good for (COUNTRY)		All four countries		Public within each country			
		Public and officials	Public only	Czech R	Korea	Ukraine	Vietnam
RSQ =		50	54	21	15	24	15
		beta	beta	beta	beta	beta	beta
MODEL	**INDICATOR**						
Winners and losers – national	national economy got better	28	25	26	15	17	7
Culture	more respect for national culture	20	17		17	14	28
Pro-market on fairness	think market economy is fair	11	13	13	12	10	
Winners and losers – family	family income got better	9	10		10	15	
International justice	foreign companies help	5	9	12	12	12	12
Pro-market on prosperity	think market brings prosperity	3	5			13	16
Domestic justice	think winners have more skill and luck	4	3			10	
Pro-opening up	think opening up is advantageous	2					
Legacy	Asian	28	29				
Elite	officials						

Note: All betas shown are statistically significant at the five per cent level.

essentially alternatives to state or government control. But judging by the patterns of public support for their governments in Tables 6.2 and 6.3, the public hold their governments responsible for national prosperity, for the respect accorded their national culture, and to a lesser extent for the fairness of the market economy. These are the public's criteria, consciously or unconsciously, for rewarding government with their support. Yet these analyses suggest the public do not hold their governments responsible to the same degree for their personal or family circumstances on the one hand, nor for the injustices of international companies or international organisations on the other.

In general, it seems governments are held responsible for outcomes rather than theories or ideologies. Public support for government seems to reflect the sentiment attributed to the late Deng Xiaoping: 'it does not matter what colour a cat is, as long as it catches mice'. But for the public, on our data, 'catching mice' seems in this context to mean delivering on fairness to some degree, and more especially it means delivering cultural respect, as well as national economic growth.

Public perceptions of declining respect for their national culture do not erode their support for opening up as much as they erode public support for their government. Conversely, governments can win favour with the public by successfully defending national culture while at the same time opening up the economy to the world. National culture is therefore *not a problem* for governments bent on opening up, but a resource, a compensation to be weighed against other discontents.

6.3 Public perspectives on the state

As an alternative to inferring public attitudes towards the role of the state from an investigation of the factors that influence government support, we asked the public more direct and explicit questions about what they thought the role of their state should be in dealing with opportunities and problems of the international economy; and about what its role actually was in practice.

Their answers point to public support for a 'mentor state', guiding rather than commanding, but able to play the roles of entrepreneur, physician or protector and advocate. As national *entrepreneur*, the public hold the state responsible for improvements in the national economy. Though they accept the need to open up to world markets, they also expect the state to act as *physician and protector* – remedying the ills of globalisation by intervening to provide help for losers, and by protecting (though *not* primarily by tariffs or trade barriers) farmers, workers, local businesses, national culture and their traditional 'way of life'. Not least the combination of public support for joining international organisations and public distrust of those same organisations, suggests they see a need for the state to act as an effective *advocate* of their national interest within them. Strong states are not seen by the public as incompatible with globalisation but, especially in East Asia, as necessary to reap the advantages of globalisation and minimise the disadvantages.

In practice, however, the public sometimes see another role for the state: as a criminal *conspiracy against the public* – not part of their hopes, of course, but part of their perceptions or fears.

The state as entrepreneur

The public see a major role for the state as 'national entrepreneur' with responsibility for 'growing' the national economy. Asked explicitly, the public in every country gave credit or blame for recent trends in the economy to the government and people of the country (70 per cent) rather than to foreign businesses and international organisations (18 per cent). Within every country, they gave credit or blame to government (60 per cent) rather than to their country's businessmen and workers (26 per cent). The public did not doubt the capacity of the state to influence economic development – for good or ill.

In Korean focus groups, government intervention to improve economic performance was more a technical matter than an ideological issue:

Table 6.4. *Responsibility for national economic trends*

			Public within each country			
	Officials %	Public %	Czech R %	S Korea %	Ukraine %	Vietnam %
Economic trend due to						
government and people of						
[COUNTRY]	72	70	61	71	72	77
foreign businesses and international organisations	16	18	29	21	15	6
Economic trend due to						
the government	51	60	53	63	67	55
the people – [COUNTRY] businessmen and workers	33	26	36	28	21	20

Note: Per cent of all respondents. Per cents giving other/mixed/'don't know' responses not shown.

'one should not value too much one way of running the economy . . . the USA does not leave everything to the market . . . it is a problem of degree' (K18); 'I prefer a mixed economy . . . in a [purely] market economy public goods and social overhead capital can be poor but creativity can be ignored if the state is entrusted with everything' (K12).

State intervention was not always considered helpful. One rural participant felt 'prices of agricultural products should increase' but that 'state intervention has left rural communities bankrupt . . . the state paralyses the market' (K14).

Czech participants were divided over state intervention and they qualified any support they gave:

'it should intervene more' (C12) . . . '[but] without silliness' (C9) . . . 'with certain limits set' (C11) . . . '[and] not throw away money on useless things' (C14); 'Czech agriculture has . . . been liquidated . . . and it is our politicians who had it liquidated' (C25); 'the state should not intervene' (C24) . . . 'not intervene too much' (C27).

Even in Vietnam, participants' support for state intervention, though extensive, was qualified and conditional:

'current economic management can be considered successful' (V26); 'before 1985 life was tough because we did not open up' (V31); 'the state should be the watchdog to limit bad activities . . . but not directly involve itself in business activities [and end] as soon as possible the monopoly in electricity, water and telephone services' (V18); 'the state is indispensable. The state should reinforce its role in managing and regulating the national economy . . . [its] guidance role in the economy, to maintain stability and concrete benefits' (V31); 'avoid too many factories and enterprises existing in some provinces and too much unemployment in other provinces' (V16); 'without the regulation of the state, equality and tranquility in the society will not be guaranteed' (V26).

For Ukrainians this was not a technical matter however, not a question of fine-tuning the degree of intervention, not even a matter of qualified support. While in principle they wanted more state intervention, they criticised and condemned actual state intervention as corrupt. What they wanted was state intervention to take care of its citizens and to impose order in the market – but not state intervention merely to line the pockets of power holders:

'there was a state – it provided farms with everything . . . now we have to pay cash for everything' (U21); 'in our village we have some surpluses but there is no place where we can sell them . . . we used to have a state procurement station and I could go and sell my surplus there' (U32; U31 agrees); 'the state should play a bigger role . . . because prices are out of control' (U1); 'everybody sets their own markup' (U6); 'it is necessary to establish order within the state' (U9); 'prices must be controlled by the state' (U25) . . . 'it is necessary to get back to how it was before, to have the same prices in all the shops' (U29) ... 'I also think so – the state must establish order in every sphere' (U32); 'establish prices' (U21); 'regulate prices' (U19; U18 agrees); 'there should be one price' (U22); 'all of us here agree that the economy has got to be of the market type ... but there is no order' (U13).

Although the public held the state responsible for economic development, it was blamed for failure more than praised for success. The state was held responsible for economic trends by around 65 per cent in Ukraine and Korea where public perceptions of economic trends were strongly negative (even if the official statistics were positive in Korea); but by an average of only 55 per cent in the Czech Republic and Vietnam where perceptions were mixed or strongly positive. Among individuals within countries, the same pattern was even more evident. Cross-tabulating the assignment of responsibility by personal perceptions of state performance shows that people were far more likely to see the government as influential if they thought the economic trend had been negative. In Vietnam, the vast majority of respondents saw the economic trend as positive and credited the government. But in the Czech Republic, only 25 per cent of those who said the economy had improved credited the government, while 74 per cent of those who said it had worsened blamed the government. Similarly, the government was credited when the trend was rated positively by only 46 per cent in Korea and 51 per cent in Ukraine, but blamed by many more when the trend was rated negatively (by 70 per cent in Korea and 82 per cent in Ukraine).

The less-structured format of focus group discussions allowed participants to express more complex views about the respective roles of state and individuals in economic development, however. They thought positive action by both was best, with the state providing opportunities and individuals seizing them – a view regularly expressed in Vietnamese discussions:

'firstly, the boat rises as the tide rises, secondly it is because of our efforts' (V26); 'we have to lean on the national economy ... but if we are not agile in taking opportunities and chances we cannot improve our family's standard of living' (V16); 'the dynamic of my family in combination with state regulation' (V5; V6 agrees); 'the direction of the Party and the State, as well as the efforts of each family' (V15).

But both could contribute negatively:

'Who made our economy worse?' (moderator) ... 'first of all, it is government ... but ultimately it is our people' (K31) ... 'if we were wiser in electing politicians, things would be different' (K33); 'the government on the whole ... however nowadays ordinary people are not sincere either ... they seek shortcuts' (K16).

Or, as many felt in Ukraine, individuals could exert themselves to salvage something from the wreckage left by the state. In that peculiar sense both were responsible for economic trends – though their contributions were in opposite directions:

'I have found a job "on the side" . . . a way to extricate myself somehow . . . it is very difficult to subsist on the [state] salary alone . . . it is not the state helping us, it is the people looking for work on their own' (U13); 'the common man always keeps fighting for survival . . . he can overcome anything but he must get some help . . . if the state does not help him, what is he to do then?' (U11); 'my husband is an excellent mechanic . . . but the *kolkhoz* [collective farm] has disintegrated and he has been unemployed for five years' (U30); '1991 began the active collapse of agriculture . . . while all were in a state of euphoria over independence, desolation began . . . those [privatisation] laws brought about the collapse' (U28; U27 agrees).

The state as physician and protector

As well as holding the state responsible for economic trends, particularly negative trends, people across all four countries had high expectations that the state should act to reduce or offset the potential downsides of economic integration and development – including increasing crime and corruption, pollution and environmental damage; the intrusion of foreign culture; and especially the loss of jobs and businesses that proved uncompetitive in world markets.

Crime and corruption Overall, the public felt crime and corruption were increasing though they were equally divided on whether to hold the government or people responsible for it. But there were sharp differences between countries. Ukrainians were the most likely to feel there had been a great increase in crime and corruption and at the same time the most likely (66 per cent) to attribute responsibility to the government. Within three of the four countries, the worse the public's perceptions of trends in crime and corruption, the more they were likely to attribute responsibility to government. Vietnam was the exception. There alone the pattern was reversed: the *better* the Vietnamese public's perceptions of trends in crime and corruption, the more they were likely to credit the government.

Pollution and environmental damage Overall, the public felt pollution and environmental damage was increasing, but on balance they held the people rather than the government responsible. Again there were sharp differences between countries, however. Ukrainians were by far the most likely to feel there had been a great increase in pollution and environmental damage and they were also the most likely (59 per cent) to hold the state responsible. Again, within the Czech Republic, Korea and Ukraine, as with crime and corruption, the worse the public's

Table 6.5. *Shared responsibility for crime and corruption*

	Officials %	Public %	Public within each country			
			Czech R %	S Korea %	Ukraine %	Vietnam %
The trend in crime and corruption is due to ...						
government	32	42	45	45	66	11
changing attitudes of people	48	43	45	49	23	51

Note: Per cent of all respondents. Per cents giving other/mixed/'don't know' responses not shown.

Table 6.6. *The public and pollution*

	Officials %	Public %	Public within each country			
			Czech R %	S Korea %	Ukraine %	Vietnam %
The trend in pollution and environmental damage is due to ...						
government	31	37	33	37	59	23
changing attitudes of people	53	49	55	57	27	51

Note: Per cent of all respondents. Per cents giving other/mixed/'don't know' responses not shown.

perception of trends in pollution, the more they attributed responsibility to government. But again, the pattern was reversed in Vietnam: the worse their perception of trends in pollution, the more they blamed the people themselves.

The intrusion of foreign culture We found universal public support for cultural protection, though its intensity was weakest in the Czech Republic and strongest in Vietnam. In the countries where respect for national culture was seen to be declining most, Korea and the Czech Republic, three-quarters attributed the trend to the 'changing attitudes of the people'. But in the countries where respect for national culture was perceived to be increasing, Ukraine and Vietnam, the public were more likely to credit the state.

Industrial protection We asked a series of questions about whether the state should protect particular industries or businesses 'from foreign

Table 6.7. *Varying responsibility for cultural trends*

	Officials %	Public %	Public within each country			
			Czech R %	S Korea %	Ukraine %	Vietnam %
The trend in respect for national language, culture and traditions is due to ...						
government	28	32	16	23	46	41
changing attitudes of people	62	58	74	74	43	37

Note: Per cent of all respondents. Per cents giving other/mixed/'don't know' responses not shown.

competition' until they had a chance to become competitive, or whether protection would just encourage them to be inefficient and globally uncompetitive. We instanced 'farmers'; 'small businesses – until they are strong enough to compete'; outdated 'businesses with old methods or machinery – while they modernise'; and, 'because it is so important for our culture, our media – our newspapers, television, books and films'. Despite the high level of public support for opening up the economy to world markets, there were high levels of support for protection, most of all for farmers (77 per cent), followed closely by 'small businesses' (72 per cent), and somewhat further behind by the media (63 per cent). There was even support for protecting out-of-date businesses while they modernised (60 per cent).

Public support for protecting *farmers* ranged from 71 per cent in the Czech Republic to around 81 per cent in Vietnam and Korea. (In the 724 Korean interviews before the suicide of Lee Kyung-Hae at the WTO meeting in Cancun on 10 September 2003, 18 per cent opposed protection for farmers. That dropped to only 9 per cent in the week after his suicide, but rose to 14 per cent in the following week and was back to 19 per cent in the week after that.)

Public support for protecting *small businesses* ranged from 62 per cent in the Czech Republic to 74 per cent or more elsewhere. Support for protecting the *media* ranged from only 40 per cent in the Czech Republic to 78 per cent in Vietnam. Support for protecting *out-of-date businesses* ranged from 50 per cent in the Czech Republic to 74 per cent in Korea.

One striking feature of focus group discussions about agricultural and industrial protection was the extent to which participants emphasised methods of 'non-tariff' protection – they backed 'support' or 'privileges', rather than 'protection' in the narrow sense of a 'closed economy'. They cited tax breaks, special loan finance, state technical assistance, preferential

Table 6.8. *Public support for economic protection*

	Officials %	Public %	Public within each country			
			Czech R %	S Korea %	Ukraine %	Vietnam %
Protect farmers						
Yes	75	77	71	82	75	80
No	15	14	16	16	14	9
Protect small business						
Yes	69	72	62	79	74	75
No	21	18	23	18	16	13
Protect media						
Yes	60	63	40	72	66	78
No	29	26	46	24	22	12
Protect out-of-date business						
Yes	54	60	50	74	65	59
No	32	27	32	21	22	26

Note: Per cent of all respondents. Per cents giving other/mixed/'don't know' responses not shown.

planning, preferential state procurement, and cheap sales of state land, among other methods. Moreover they claimed that foreign rather than local firms were sometimes granted exactly these favours, or even that markets were rigged against local firms. Participants tended to combine support for open international markets with preferential treatment for local businesses – a not unfamiliar concept in the affluent West.

One Ukrainian (U28) did cite the high tariff regime of Catherine II (Czarina of Russia, 1762–96) as a success but that was unusual. In general, state protection or support for local industry and agriculture were seen as an increasingly important part of the state's role under globalisation, *not as an alternative* to globalisation.

Some Czechs argued against any import restrictions:

'otherwise we will never get into the EU ... [and] if something is produced at a high cost here, why should it not be imported?' (C32).

Those Czechs who did support protection tended to impose conditions. Local companies should be protected only:

'until they are able to compete' (C26) ... '[and] under consistent monitoring of where the funds go' (C0); 'we should protect at least that part of our agriculture – vineyards, hops – that part which is quality' (C22); 'it is the content of the newspapers that matters ... a question of objectivity – it does not matter who owns it, but the content should be protected' (C2);

– and treated equally:

'a plot of land near Brno [was sold] for one crown [i.e. given to a foreign company]' (C3); 'Mlada Boleslav [Skoda, now owned by Volkswagen] also got more advantageous conditions – there could be corruption behind it ... Czech firms should [get] the same conditions' (C2); 'there are state subsidies for farmers abroad and not here' (C25).

One Korean participant dismissed support for large-scale enterprises:

'they are morally and socially irresponsible ... abuse their advantages ... speculate in land and disturb politics with soft money ... it is absurd to favour them ... [but] there are some industries we should protect, agriculture for instance' (K22).

In the focus groups generally, as in the survey, there were universally high levels of support for agricultural protection:

'a rural area is like a patient who cannot stand up without protection' (K22); 'farming is not fully effective anywhere in the world and has to be subsidised everywhere' (C15); '[the state] should provide some subsidies for agriculture; agriculture is subsidised all over the world' (U21); 'adapting land to other purposes would come much dearer than support for farmers who carry out the demanding task of taking care of it' (C18); 'people would take social benefits and the state would lose money' (C9); 'the market mechanism is good but ... the state should find outlets for farmers' products ... and also take care of other aspects like culture' (V13) ... 'At present, the state always takes care of farmers in terms of capital. But the state is not able to control the prices and output. The state should strengthen its role in [agricultural] price regulation and market control' (V12).

In Korea and Vietnam support for agriculture was often linked to the view that farmers were suffering special hardship and therefore deserved special support:

'unlike the old days, it is difficult to buy even one pyong [six square feet of land] in Seoul for the money you are paid for all your possessions in the countryside ... the gap between the urban and rural economy has deepened' (K14); '85 per cent of our population are farmers [an exaggeration] and their current living standard is very low. While the average salary of a state office is 500,000 dong, the farmer can earn only tens of thousands of dong because farmers' products are very cheap. So the state should protect them' (V4); 'it is very difficult for farmers if there is no [financial] assistance to change plants and stocks ... new kinds of plants are being grown but the fruits cannot yet be sold' (V21) ... '[and similarly, since] domestic enterprises are at a disadvantage in technology and capital, the government should have special treatment for them' (V19).

Food was at the base of Maslow's (1970) 'hierarchy of needs' and paradoxically therefore it was as much a psychological as a material need. It must not only be available but be seen to be available, and reliably available in the foreseeable future. Koreans in particular could anticipate problems:

'self-sufficiency in food is important – especially after [Korean] unification we will need more food supply than now and without sufficient food supply basic life is not guaranteed' (K20).

Ukrainians lamented the decline of their industrial base:

'barring foreign goods from the Ukrainian market [would not help] because domestic enterprises would begin to produce low-quality goods' (U5) ... '[but] privileges are needed' (U6) ... 'to enable enterprises to stand on their own – look how many enterprises are closed, people laid off, specialists lost from the industry ... precious equipment wasted ... it hurts to see that' (U4).

Yet Ukrainians frequently voiced their perception that their state was not only incompetent:

'state bodies ought to provide assistance and see to it that the law is obeyed ... they should not insert their "wise" ideas into matters that they do not understand at all' (U28);

– but also corrupt:

'nowhere in the world will you find a state that does not support its manufacturers to some extent, but support for domestic manufacturers must *not* be provided according to the principle: "whose pipe-manufacturing plant is this one?" ... only to those who need it' (U12; U14 agrees) ... '[it needs] the toughest control – only I do not know who will exercise this control because I do not trust any police, no one' (U17).

We might expect that the old, the poor, the less educated, and globalisation-losers in general, would favour protection. But in addition we might expect that those who were sceptical about the benefits of open markets would be particularly favourable to state protection for obsolescent industries; and that cultural nationalists would be particularly favourable to protection for their national 'way of life'. The old and the less well-educated were indeed somewhat more favourable than others to protecting both obsolescent businesses and the national 'way of life', but the correlations were weak. General attitudes towards opening up or towards national culture provide a somewhat more powerful, albeit more proximate, explanation, however.

Even though it could be argued that 'protecting businesses with old methods or machinery from foreign competition until they are strong enough to compete' is not inconsistent with a general policy of opening up to world markets (or is even a wise, temporary precaution during a period of readjustment) public support for protecting obsolete businesses correlated best with negative attitudes towards opening up $(r = 0.17$ overall, rising to 0.28 in the Czech Republic); and only slightly less well with perceptions that foreign companies 'exploited rather than helped' the country. By contrast, however, as we noted in Chapter 4, the key influence on public support for 'protecting *our way of life* against foreign influences' was not so much commitment to open markets as commitment to the national culture.

Healing the wounds Overall, a large majority (63 per cent to 24 per cent) wanted more rather than less state intervention to help the casualties of globalisation by 'controlling wages and prices or protecting jobs'. Opinion in Korea was evenly divided but there was a two-to-one majority in the Czech Republic and a seven-to-one majority in Ukraine and Vietnam.

In particular, 70 per cent thought the state should do more to help globalisation-losers and only 21 per cent thought losers should do more to help themselves. Opposition to state help for losers was strongest in the Czech Republic (30 per cent) and Korea (27 per cent) but much less in Vietnam (16 per cent). Ukrainians, however, made the strongest demands on the state: 85 per cent wanted more state help and only 8 per cent opted for leaving losers to do more to help themselves.

Although Ukrainians *wanted* helpful state intervention:

Table 6.9 *State intervention and state help for losers*

	Officials %	Public %	Public within each country			
			Czech R %	Korea %	Ukraine %	Vietnam %
Do you feel the state should intervene in the market economy – for example, to control wages and prices or to protect jobs …						
more than it does now	58	63	54	50	78	69
less than it does now	30	24	28	45	11	10
Although opening up our economy to international markets may be good for some people it may be bad for others. Do you think the state should do more to help [COUNTRY] people who lose their jobs or businesses because of opening up our economy? Or should people do more to solve their own problems?						
more state help for losers	67	70	60	69	85	68
losers should do more to help themselves	25	21	30	27	8	16

Note: Per cent of all respondents. Per cents giving other/mixed/'don't know' responses not shown.

'the state should in the first place assume the function of taking care of its citizens . . . strictly speaking, that is the main purpose of the state' (U16);

– they complained that its actual intervention was corrupt and self-serving (see section 3.3 in Chapter 3).

In the survey we asked specifically about more state help for losers:

'Do you think the state should do more to help [your country's] people who lose their jobs or businesses because of opening up our economy? Or should people solve their own problems?'

In focus groups we found evidence of the national debate in South Korea about this which Henderson and Hulme (2002) claimed was one result of the 1997–9 Asian financial crisis. Korean participants were not only particularly vocal on this issue but discussed it in quite complex, well-thought-out terms. Some held the state responsible for creating problems and so under an obligation to help those who suffered as a result:

'people suffer without their own responsibility' (K5); 'the state made the decision on the open economy, so the state is responsible for its negative effects' (K2); 'having made the decision to open up, the state should take the responsibility for that' (K9); 'the very reason why the unemployed lost their jobs lies with the state or politicians' (K10); 'if the state does not help them out, we cannot avoid an increase in crime' (K22).

Others linked taxes to welfare:

'it is the government's duty is to redistribute collected taxes, isn't it?' (K27); 'taxes should be used for helping redundant workers instead of investing public funds in state-owned enterprises' (K19).

And others linked social welfare to 'advanced' countries, a category to which Koreans aspired but did not feel they yet belonged:

'our social welfare policies are in the lower level in comparison with advanced countries . . . the state should help people to enjoy fundamental human rights' (K8) . . . 'our country is not described as "advanced" precisely because the state is not doing that' (K4).

In Vietnam some focus group participants backed state help for global-isation-losers:

'the state ought to assist them – this is the role of the state in keeping balance in a society' (V21); 'the state should open up the economy but pay attention to domestic employment, farmers in particular' (V4); 'I hope that the Party and state will pay more attention to the lives of labourers' (V15); 'the state should do more to help those who suffer losses and create jobs for them' (V9).

But others argued, more conditionally:

'for those who are honest in their business but failed in international competition, we should help them to survive in the market mechanism; for those who do no good for the economy and cheat as well, we should not help them with money' (V5); 'we should help bankrupted but good-intentioned Vietnam companies to develop' (V33).

Some were suspicious of creating dependency:

'unsuccessful companies cannot ask the state to help them. It is the same with individuals who are unemployed for not having ability. Helping them means backing lack of education and laziness' (V26).

Direct help for losers is more consistent with the concept of open markets than many other forms of protection, especially if it is targeted at unemployed workers rather than struggling businessmen. But, more than tariffs and trade barriers, it requires popular support for higher and more visible taxation. Indeed Wolf (2001: pp. 185, 188) argues that the state's ability to tax and redistribute is limited not by globalisation but by the willingness of its citizens to pay. To the contrary however, we found that almost two-thirds of the public in our four countries felt the state should redistribute from globalisation-winners to globalisation-losers by 'increasing taxes on those whose incomes have increased, in order to help those who have lost their jobs or businesses because of opening up our economy.' We recognise the difference between supporting higher taxes on globalisation-winners in principle, and being personally willing to pay higher taxes. Nonetheless mindless scepticism about willingness to pay taxes is as unrealistic as mindless credulity, and the support that we found for increased taxation – albeit as a mere opinion in survey interviews – is significant.

In the Czech Republic the numbers demanding more state help for globalisation-losers (60 per cent) and the numbers who supported a tax increase to fund that extra help (62 per cent) were very similar; and in Korea support for a tax increase on winners (79 per cent) actually exceeded demands for extra state help for losers (69 per cent). By contrast, however, in Vietnam and Ukraine, demand for more state help exceeded support for a tax increase – by 14 per cent in Vietnam and by a remarkable 29 per cent in Ukraine. More than others, Ukrainians combined a demand for more state help with a refusal to pay more taxes to provide it. Everything we know about public opinion in Ukraine suggests that this reflects well-founded Ukrainian suspicion of the state rather than mere logical inconsistency.

Help was never synonymous with handouts, however. 'What kind of help', we asked, 'should the state provide to people who have lost their jobs or businesses because of opening up the economy?' Overall, the

Table 6.10. *Helping losers*

| | Officials % | Public % | Public within each country | | | |
			Czech R %	S Korea %	Ukraine %	Vietnam %
Should the state increase taxes to help globalisation-losers?						
yes	61	63	62	79	56	54
no	30	26	29	19	27	28
Preferred type of state help: mainly ...						
advice and retraining to help them compete for new jobs	67	58	67	61	30	63
direct payments to unemployed people to help them survive	12	19	14	8	47	10
subsidies to keep unprofitable companies in business	14	15	11	28	14	8

Note: Per cent of all respondents. Per cents giving other/mixed/'don't know' responses not shown.

public opted overwhelmingly for 'retraining' (58 per cent), with 'unemployment benefits' far behind (19 per cent) and subsidies to local companies still further behind (15 per cent). 'Retraining' was the top choice in Korea (61 per cent), the Czech Republic (67 per cent) and also in Vietnam (63 per cent); but it came a poor second in Ukraine (with only 30 per cent). 'Direct payments to unemployed people to help them survive' was the top choice in Ukraine (47 per cent). That makes Ukrainian reluctance to tax winners in order to help losers, all the more remarkable.

Outside Ukraine, focus group participants, like survey respondents, were reluctant to back cash handouts:

'the state should protect farmers – which does not mean give them money, but rather upgrade the fields, create conditions for them to produce on a larger scale, provide new breeds to raise productivity' (V4).

Korean participants were as eloquent about the kinds of state assistance that should be provided as they were about state assistance itself. One declared:

'there are many things that state can do ... create jobs by establishing a special company for collecting garbage ... provide vocational education ... subsidise living expenses for the time being ... [though in the end] instead of monetary aid, it is necessary to create more jobs' (K22).

Another specified strict limits:

'the state should provide employment insurance and occupational education for six months or one year, so that people may be capable of living a basic life' (K4).

Providing work was better than giving handouts to the unemployed:

'the state should do more to ... create jobs because the compensation will soon run out' (V9); 'the state should increase jobs by creating public employment' (K27); 'forced to leave their position, they have nowhere to go. However hard they try, they will not be hired. For that reason, the state should create jobs, and accept them' (K11); 'the state should give them a benefit like a stable job. They should have jobs ... [otherwise] they will be exhausted and lack living ability later' (K16); 'lots of jobs should be created [for example in education] by decreasing the number of students in a class, or [in industry] by decreasing working hours [which were exceptionally high in Korea]' (K9).

Others stressed training rather than public employment:

'in addition to economic aid, government should help them have better opportunities by educating and training them' (K29; C5, C20 similar); 'motivate people in some way – so they look for work themselves and do not rely on social services' (C2).

More brutally:

'I think they lost their jobs because they were incompetent. The state can help them get education so that they may find jobs. It is important they have competitive ability' (K12).

Or invest in the children:

'offering public employment is not enough. Most unemployed are over 40 and 50. They have children of middle school, who are going to college soon. The state should subsidise [the children's] educational expenses' (K26).

Similarly for businesses:

'technology support is the most urgent [type of assistance for businesses]' (K31).

Again, we might expect that the old, the poor, the unemployed, the unskilled or those with obsolescent skills, and globalisation-losers in general might want the state to play a stronger role in healing the wounds of globalisation by taxing winners to compensate losers. But that disregards any sense of community. That model would work best in a well-informed and self-consciously individualistic society where only the losers themselves had any concern for losers. It works best in the Czech Republic and not at all well elsewhere. Being personally a winner or a loser mattered more than the social background variables (age, education etc) that themselves affected the chances of being a winner or loser. But even being a winner or loser had a relatively weak impact outside the

Czech Republic, and particularly so in East Asia. The correlation between support for taxing winners to compensate losers and actually being a loser (with family living standards getting worse rather than better) was 0.19 in the Czech Republic and 0.12 in Ukraine, but a statistically insignificant 0.02 in the East Asian countries.

Community was significant in two ways. First, as we saw earlier, support for taxing winners was uniquely high in Korea where the public had an ideal that equated an advanced state and economy with effective social welfare on a Scandinavian model. Second, a more 'sociotropic' model works as well as the 'egocentric' model in the Czech Republic and rather better than the egocentric model elsewhere. Although Czech support for taxing winners correlated at around 0.20 with being a loser, it also correlated at 0.20 with the perception that recent changes had benefited the rich more than the poor. And support for taxing winners also correlated with perceptions of growing inequality at 0.16 in Korea and 0.13 in Vietnam – where correlations with personally being a winner or loser were negligible. Only Ukrainian attitudes towards taxing winners seemed to be driven exclusively by personal misery: they scarcely correlated at all with the perception that the rich had gained more than the poor, though that perception was so widespread and so strongly held in Ukraine that its explanatory power was bound to be minimal; but they correlated at 0.12 with being a loser, and at 0.19 with being a pensioner or unemployed.

The state as advocate

The third role that our respondents proposed for the state under globalisation was to act as advocate for the country and its citizens in dealing with foreign companies and international or supranational organisations.

Against foreign companies The most popular suggestion for dealing with an international company that treated local workers badly or damaged the local environment was to 'complain to government officials'. It was even more popular than signing petitions, writing to the press, or using the internet to criticise the company – by a few per cent in Korea and the Czech Republic, but by 21 per cent in Vietnam, though not at all in Ukraine. Ukrainian views about government officials were so negative that they could have had little confidence that complaints to officials would be effective, but at least they thought officials should hear about their discontent. The exception was the Vietnamese: they were uniquely unwilling to back protest by any other means than through the state. Vietnam was still a (one) party-state where the public might feel petitions would be frowned upon and the press would take little notice of

Table 6.11. *Protest through the state*

	Officials % yes	Public % yes	Public within each country			
			Czech R % yes	S Korea % yes	Ukraine % yes	Vietnam % yes
If an international company did not have safe working conditions in its factory, or paid very low wages. Should *the workers* …						
complain to government officials	91	87	87	86	88	86
complain to trade union officials	91	86	90	86	81	86
sign petitions, write to newspapers, or use the Internet to criticise the company	79	79	84	81	88	65
If an international company here in [COUNTRY] was damaging or polluting the local environment, should people who *live in the locality* …						
complain to government officials	94	90	93	87	91	87
sign petitions, write to newspapers, or use the Internet to criticise the company	84	83	89	82	92	67

Note: % yes = number saying 'yes' as a percentage of all respondents.

their complaints. Nonetheless the Vietnamese were not at all reluctant to support complaining through the state, or through the semi-official trade unions (in the case of workers' conditions), just more reluctant than others to back complaints though non-state channels.

Within international organisations Even though few (18 per cent) felt their country could 'usually' expect fair treatment from international organisations (see Chapter 2), the public felt on balance that they could neither ignore nor reject membership. That combination suggests they saw a need for their state to assume the role of advocate of the national interest within these organisations.

Overall, only 20 per cent thought it better to be 'completely independent' rather than join 'unfair' international organisations 'like the WTO, World Bank or IMF'– or regional organisations 'like the EU or ASEAN'. But in the Czech Republic, well over a quarter volunteered the unenthusiastic – and unprompted – response that their country had 'no choice' in this matter. In focus groups, too, perceptions of inevitability were particularly marked in East Europe, especially the Czech Republic where EU accession loomed large:

'when our neighbours enter the [European] Union, there will not be any other option for us – if we stayed outside, we would have huge problems exporting our goods' (C18); 'we are a small country and if we were not in the EU then we would be good for nothing' (C6).

If we focus on positive support, rather than mere acquiescence, then the two East Asian publics were clearly the most enthusiastic about joining (70 per cent) and the two East European the least (45 per cent). But enthusiastic or not, a large majority in every country felt they should join.

In East Asia and especially in Vietnam, joining international organisations was seen as a matter of calculation and choice, not bowing to the inevitable:

'we have to calculate carefully' (V5).

Moreover the choice was the responsibility *of the state* rather than the public:

'the state should weight the pros and cons to maximise the benefit' (V4); 'the Party and the state have considered this' (V16);

and there was no whiff of supranationalism as distinct from internationalism:

Table 6.12. *Joining unfair organisations*

	Officials %	Public %	Public within each country			
			Czech R %	S Korea %	Ukraine %	Vietnam %
Should we join international organisations (WTO, IMF, WB etc) ...						
(VOL) no choice	13	13	28	5	13	3
yes	66	56	42	67	45	66
no	14	20	19	24	27	11
Should we join regional organisations (EU/ASEAN etc) ...						
(VOL) no choice	10	11	26	3	11	2
yes	71	60	50	66	45	81
no	14	20	19	26	30	8

Note: Per cent of all respondents. Per cents giving other/mixed/'don't know' responses not shown. VOL indicates that a particular answer was not offered by the interviewer, but was spontaneously volunteered by some respondents.

'we should not consider this as sacrifice' (V18); 'in joining international organisations we have to accept some conditions on our control and independence' (V27); 'in working sessions we have to protest against issues that affect our country severely but accept shared issues' (V5).

The cross-national pattern of attitudes towards appealing internationally 'beyond the state' was the inverse of the pattern of attitudes towards relying upon the state as an advocate of the national interest within international organisations. In Europe, we noted:

'There is a European Court of Human Rights. Governments in European states allow their citizens to appeal to that Court if those citizens feel their own government has treated them badly',

– and asked:

'do you feel it is a good idea or a bad idea for governments to allow their citizens to appeal to an international court like that?'

While the Vietnamese were outstandingly enthusiastic about joining international organisations in which they would be represented by their state, they were outstandingly reluctant to concede power to an international court designed to overrule their state. Overall, net approval for a supranational court ran at plus 45 per cent. It was highest in East Europe (plus 74 per cent); much lower in Korea (plus 53 per cent); and significantly *negative* in Vietnam (*minus* 25 per cent) – though a large number of Vietnamese expressed no view or mixed views. Of course there may be an element of European familiarity with the specifically European Court in this. But perhaps Martin Jacques (*Guardian*, 29 July 2004) is right and this familiarity with supranational European institutions merely reflects

Table 6.13. *Appealing beyond the state*

	Officials % yes	Public % yes	Public within each country			
			Czech R % yes	S Korea % yes	Ukraine % yes	Vietnam % yes
International court of human rights is ...						
a good idea	64	62	77	73	80	16
(VOL) impractical – too						
difficult to appeal	11	10	15	4	9	9
a bad idea	17	17	3	20	6	41

Note: Per cent of all respondents. Per cents giving other/mixed/'don't know' responses not shown. VOL indicates that a particular answer was not offered by the interviewer, but was spontaneously volunteered by some respondents.

the peculiarly European phenomenon of weakening states. What is clear is that where the state was seen as most corrupt and self-serving, support for appeals beyond the state was strongest. And where it was seen as most effective with respect to the benefits of globalisation, only a minority supported appeals beyond the state.

6.4   Officials: vanguard or conspirators?

Our evidence suggests that the public wanted the state to play a role as national entrepreneur, protector or physician, and advocate within international organisations. But it also suggests they feared it had another, darker role: as a criminal conspiracy against the public – with government officials 'using public office for private gain' rather than to advance public welfare. Throughout millennia of history that has probably been the main role of government, and theorists and polemicists from Robert Michels (1911) to Michael Moore (2004) allege that it remains a significant, if subsidiary role, within modern democratic regimes. On the street it is a remarkably widespread assumption about government.

We have seen that the public cited government officials as the chief beneficiary of opening up, especially in East Europe, though less in Korea and much less so in Vietnam (see Chapter 2). Participants in focus groups often articulated views of the state as self-interested and corrupt as well as incompetent:

'the state mishandles finances' (C14); 'people's distrust increases because they see that government pursues only its own interests' (K31).

Even in Vietnam, where criticism was mild and infrequent by Ukrainian standards, at least one participant in every discussion alleged that officials were the chief beneficiaries of opening up. Only the degree and extent of the conspiracy seemed open to debate.

But the sense of scandal was most widespread, most explicit, and most bitter in Ukrainian focus groups where participants alleged that officials even discouraged foreign investment in order to make profits for themselves. There is no need to repeat at length the comments we have already cited in earlier chapters, but participants alleged that 'everything was done to discourage' anyone except the friends and acquaintances of officials from coming in to set up businesses locally (see Chapter 2). And they spontaneously talked of 'the state' as well as particular officials: the 'state which keeps robbing us', the 'state which we do not need' (see Chapter 4). These participants were not complaining about the globalisation of their local economy but arguing *in favour of globalisation* and *against their officials* who they alleged had obstructed and perverted globalisation for their own benefit. In the view of many Ukrainians, their state was not merely weak in terms of state capacity (Way 2002) but an all-too-powerful criminal conspiracy against the people – what one Ukrainian journalist described as 'a regime that blends sinister authoritarianism with banana republic-style bungling' (Askold Krushelnycky, *Independent*, 12 August 2004).

On a turnout of 77 per cent in the Referendum of April 2000, over 90 per cent of Ukrainians voted to remove their parliamentary deputies' limited immunity from criminal prosecution (www.electionguide.org). It was the most popular of four propositions in that referendum. That vote did not solve the problems of the state in Ukraine, but it does corroborate our more detailed evidence on the Ukrainian public's attitudes towards their state.

Public perceptions that the state was a conspiracy against the public were sufficiently widespread to suggest we should look more closely and systematically at the differences between officials and their public. We interviewed at least 500 junior officials in each country, 2,014 in all. Half the officials in the Czech Republic, Korea and Ukraine were elected deputies at regional or local government (but not national) level; the rest were appointed officials in economic affairs, education, social services, environmental affairs, or general administrators. In Vietnam, just over one-fifth were elected officials, and the rest were divided equally between these five categories of appointed officials. Samples were spread right across each country roughly in proportion to the general population. They were of course too numerous to be the top elite, but they were important because they reflected the perceptions, attitudes and opinions of the 'apparatus', the governing machine. Junior or middle-ranking officials are also more likely to express their real views than top political or administrative elites, if only because their numbers make them so much less 'newsworthy' and therefore so much more anonymous.

Throughout previous chapters we have contrasted the views of these officials with those of their publics in the merged data set comprising all interviews with the public and officials. There were consistent differences. But these were seldom very large, and regressions never highlighted the differences between public and officials. There are two reasons for that, however. *First*, we only contrasted officials as a whole, taken together across all four countries, with publics as a whole. That averages out small differences in one or two countries with larger differences in others. Closer inspection reveals that officials were fairly representative of their public in our two East Asian countries, but not in our two East European countries. *Second*, regression would not highlight officials as such, if officials differed from their publics on the independent (predictor) variables as well as on the dependent variables. For example, in a winners and losers model of satisfaction with 'the way things are going', officials were more likely than the public both to be winners and to be satisfied. So a simple winners and losers model could then explain satisfaction without distinguishing officials as such from other winners among the general public. Again, however, closer inspection suggests that while officials were generally more likely to be winners than their public, that was especially so in East Europe.

Moreover, the most important question about the differences between publics and officials is not the *size* of these differences, but the *nature* of the differences. We can take it for granted that officials are unlikely to be demographically representative of the public. Nor should they be so. Instead they should represent the interests of the public, which may require greater than average skill, insight and education. The question is whether the differences suggest that officials are a 'development vanguard', in the forefront of public opinion, setting out a vision for their country that the public themselves would endorse, if only they were better informed and more aware of the possibilities for national development. Or whether the differences suggest a conscious or unconscious conspiracy by officials for private advantage.

The vanguard model Even junior officials might usefully be better educated, more open and more cosmopolitan than the general public. That might foster commitment to a development process that could benefit the country as a whole. But a 'development vanguard' model might suggest that in addition to having above average education and skills, officials would be:
  i. somewhat more favourable than the public towards economic globalisation;
  ii. more nationalist, more willing than the public to resist cultural globalisation;
  iii. somewhat more opposed than the public towards any expressions of discontent that could disrupt economic development;
  iv. yet not out of touch with public opinion;
  v. not unsympathetic to the casualties and problems of globalisation.
Their objective would be to use globalisation in the national interest, for national advantage, not to throw off their commitment and responsibilities towards their own country and merely enrich themselves.

The conspiracy model A self-interested 'officials-for-themselves' or 'conspiracy' model would also suggest that officials would be favourable to economic openness and willing to resist cultural globalisation. In

contrast to the vanguard model, it would suggest that officials would
be more adversarial towards the public, a 'new class' rather than 'citizen
officials', and thus:

   i. much less sympathetic than the public towards the casualties of
     globalisation;
  ii. much more out of touch with public opinion;
 iii. very strongly opposed to public expressions of discontent;
 iv. more defensive about the government's record;
     This self-interested model would be corroborated by:
  v. evidence – from officials and/or the public – that the benefits of
     opening up were going disproportionately to officials themselves.

The difference between the vanguard and conspiracy models is not so
much a categorical difference as a difference of degree. But as public
allegations against officials increase, as officials confess to greater benefits, and as officials become significantly less representative, more out of
touch with their publics, and less sympathetic towards the casualties of
globalisation, then the 'conspiracy' model becomes a better character-
isation of the role of officials and the state, and the 'vanguard' model
correspondingly less plausible. Of course, the decision whether to accept
the conspiracy or the vanguard model is ultimately a matter of judgement,
but we can at least set out the hard evidence on which that judgement
might be based – and on which the public themselves make that
judgement.

Backgrounds and benefits

The officials we interviewed were indeed better educated and more
cosmopolitan than their publics. Compared to the public, they were 53
per cent more likely to be engaged in professional, managerial or office
work and 50 per cent more university educated. They were 27 per cent
more likely to have been abroad, 24 per cent more likely to have had
at least 'a little' personal contact with foreigners within their own country,
19 per cent more likely to speak English, and somewhat more likely to
speak other languages also. As more educated and cosmopolitan people,
they were more aware than their publics of protests against the downsides
of globalisation within their own countries (11 per cent more) and especially abroad (16 per cent more). Elected officials had an even more
cosmopolitan background than appointed officials – with significantly
more experience of foreign travel and more contact with foreigners within
their own country.

    Greater education and more wide-ranging, cosmopolitan contacts
are largely functional, even desirable, characteristics of political and

administrative officials. But the officials we interviewed, especially elected officials, were much more likely to be male. Even more controversially, officials were much more affluent than their publics. Some degree of greater affluence might be regarded as a just reward for their skill and education. But a jealous public might not take that view, especially if the gap between the incomes and wealth of officials and the public was large and/or increasing.

Officials were less likely to complain that their family income was either inadequate or below average. But the difference was over twice as great in the Czech Republic (14 per cent) as in East Asia (7 per cent), and over four times as great in Ukraine (30 per cent). So in terms either of adequate incomes or of relative incomes, officials in the two East Asian countries seemed fairly representative of their publics; but in the two East European countries officials were, by their own account, very much better off than their fellow citizens.

Moreover, officials were far more likely to feel that they had been 'winners' in recent changes while the public were more likely to feel they had been 'losers'. Again, the difference between officials and their publics was much greater in East Europe than in East Asia: greatest of all in Ukraine (27 per cent) and almost negligible in Vietnam (3 per cent). In explicit comparisons, officials were conscious that their families had benefited more than average: in East Asia they were 11 per cent more likely than their publics to feel they had done better than average, and in East Europe 19 per cent. By their own account, therefore, officials and their families had done better out of recent economic change (irrespective of whether that change had been development or decline) than their publics, especially so in East Europe, and most of all in Ukraine. Their own confessions corroborated the views expressed by the public (see Chapter 2) that officials had gained the most from opening up and ordinary people the least – again, especially so in East Europe, and most of all in Ukraine.

While it may be possible to justify an affluence gap between officials and the public on grounds of greater education and skill, it is very much harder to justify a *widening* gap – harder still against a background of decline than against a background of development. Indeed, where Ukrainian officials and their public differed most dramatically was on the extremes of despair – not having even barely enough to survive, or feeling that their living standards had not just got worse, but *much* worse.

The same pattern emerged in the gap between officials' and the public's perceptions of national progress: the gap was greater in both East European countries (averaging 18 per cent) than in either of the East Asian (averaging 4 per cent); and greatest of all in Ukraine (26 per cent) while almost negligible in Vietnam (under 3 per cent).

Table 6.14. *Unrepresentative backgrounds: more affluent*

	All four countries %	Officials within each country (compared with public)			
		Czech R %	Korea %	Ukraine %	Vietnam %
family income is not enough to survive on	5 (−9)	1 (−1)	7 (−8)	10 (−27)	2 (−1)
not enough, or barely enough	35 (−15)	14 (−23)	55 (−6)	48 (−27)	22 (−5)
family income is a lot below average	3 (−11)	2 (−5)	2 (−6)	7 (−30)	1 (−2)
family income below average	19 (−19)	16 (−26)	19 (−9)	34 (−34)	8 (−11)
family living standards got much worse	4 (−9)	2 (−4)	6 (−7)	9 (−25)	0 (0)
family living standards improved	76 (+19)	78 (+29)	63 (+16)	66 (+28)	97 (+5)
own family has benefited more than average	43 (+14)	44 (+19)	33 (+10)	42 (+19)	52 (+12)

Note: Figures outside brackets refer to officials; figures inside brackets show the difference between officials and their publics.

Table 6.15. *Unrepresentative perceptions of progress*

	All four countries %	Officials within each country (compared with public)			
		Czech R %	Korea %	Ukraine %	Vietnam %
think national economy got better	63 (+13)	51 (+13)	30 (+5)	70 (+32)	99 (+3)
satisfaction with country's progress	45 (+9)	37 (+9)	19 (+7)	35 (+19)	89 (+2)

Note: Figures outside brackets refer to officials; figures inside brackets show the difference between officials and their publics.

All this evidence, from both public and officials, suggests that officials have reaped more of the benefits of opening up and the public have carried more of the burden – especially in East Europe, but much less so in the two East Asian countries. But to fully assess the vanguard versus conspiracy models, we also need to look at the other aspects of those models: differences between public and officials on attitudes towards opening up the economy; towards national culture and identity; towards the casualties of globalisation; towards expressions of public discontent; and towards defending the government and its policies.

Across the whole range of attitudinal questions in our survey, Czech and Ukrainian officials generally stand out as being less representative than Korean and Vietnamese officials. Out of rather more than a hundred questions that might be designated 'perceptions' or 'attitudes', differences of more than 10 per cent between officials and their publics occur only 15 times in Vietnam and 22 times in Korea; but 40 times in the Czech Republic and 59 times in Ukraine. These statistics provide a very crude but nonetheless illuminating index of the varying degree to which the attitudes of officials represent the attitudes of their publics: much better in East Asia than in East Europe; and particularly well in Vietnam but particularly badly in Ukraine.

Moreover, the pattern is more structured than even these country-by-country statistics imply. There are over twenty questions where both Czech and Ukrainian officials differ from their public by over 10 per cent while both Korean and Vietnamese officials do not. Almost inevitably, these are *not* questions on which the overall differences between publics and officials are very large – because large differences in two countries are averaged with small differences (if any) in the other two. So they do not grab our attention in overall contrasts between officials and publics. But they are the most politically significant of all the differences between publics and officials because they provide insight into the differing role of officials in different countries. These questions form a coherent set. They are precisely the ones that deal most specifically with attitudes towards marketisation and opening up. On almost all of these questions the Czech and Ukrainian officials take not only a much more pro-market, pro-globalisation position than their publics, but also a more hard-line attitude towards the casualties of markets – while the views of Korean and Vietnamese officials more closely reflect their public opinion.

Economic globalisers

Perspectives on development   Reflecting their personal family experience, Czech and Ukrainian officials had a much more optimistic view of

Table 6.16. *Unrepresentative on development – but only in East Europe*

	All four countries %	Officials within each country (compared with public)			
		Czech R %	Korea %	Ukraine %	Vietnam %
expect living standards to improve steadily	74 (+12)	68 (+12)	67 (+8)	70 (+29)	92 (0)
rapid economic development is good	61 (+10)	52 (+13)	38 (+4)	74 (+22)	80 (+12)
rich have benefited much more	56 (−7)	47 (−15)	58 (−3)	69 (−12)	50 (−3)

Note: Figures outside brackets refer to officials; figures inside brackets show the difference between officials and their publics.

development than their publics. Compared with their public, Ukrainian officials were 22 per cent more favourable to the concept of rapid development, 29 per cent more optimistic about living standards steadily improving, and 12 per cent *less* likely to agree that the rich have benefited 'much more' than the poor. The same pattern of greater optimism among officials occurs in the Czech Republic, though the difference between officials and public is less sharp. But it is scarcely visible at all in East Asia.

Perspectives on the market economy Judged by their views on whether the market economy delivers prosperity, whether it is fair, and whether it is 'the only way to go', there was scarcely any difference between officials and their publics in East Asia: indeed, compared with their publics, officials were slightly more pro-market on some questions but less so on others. But in Ukraine, officials were 16 per cent less likely than their public to criticise the market economy for failing to deliver prosperity; 23 per cent less to criticise the market economy for being unfair; and 25 per cent more likely to say the market economy was 'the only way to go'. In the Czech Republic the differences between public and officials were similar, though only half as great.

Perspectives on opening up Compared to their publics, officials in East Europe were between 15 and 18 per cent more likely to say opening up was 'good' or had 'more advantages than disadvantages' – but only 8 per cent more in Vietnam and actually *less* likely than the public in Korea. If we include detailed questions about alternatives, about exploitation

Table 6.17. *Unrepresentative on the market economy – only in East Europe*

| | All four countries % | Officials within each country (compared with public) | | | |
		Czech R %	Korea %	Ukraine %	Vietnam %
market economy makes country less prosperous	16 (−10)	28 (−9)	26 (−11)	9 (−16)	2 (−2)
market economy is unfair	46 (−7)	37 (−11)	73 (−2)	43 (−23)	29 (+5)
market economy is only way	50 (+8)	55 (+12)	26 (−3)	54 (+25)	65 (+1)

Note: Figures outside brackets refer to officials; figures inside brackets show the difference between officials and their publics.

Table 6.18. *Unrepresentative on opening up the economy – but only in East Europe*

| | All four countries % | Officials within each country (compared with public) | | | |
		Czech R %	Korea %	Ukraine %	Vietnam %
opening up the economy is good	75 (+9)	71 (+16)	62 (−3)	71 (+18)	94 (+6)
opening up the economy has more advantages	65 (+9)	60 (+15)	48 (−3)	66 (+17)	86 (+10)
opening up the economy is the only way to go	55 (+7)	64 (+14)	41 (−6)	46 (+12)	68 (+9)

Note: Figures outside brackets refer to officials; figures inside brackets show the difference between officials and their publics.

and unfairness by international companies and businessmen or by powerful countries, and about the impact of opening up on the gap between rich and poor, then officials in East Europe were on average 15 per cent more favourable than their publics to opening up their economy to world markets; but only 7 per cent more in Vietnam, and 2 per cent less than the public in Korea.

Cultural nationalists

Differences between officials and publics on nationalism, international-ism and supranationalism were complex, but coherent. Especially in East Europe, officials were *less* likely than their publics to identify exclusively with their country rather than their global region ('Europe' or 'East Asia'). But at the same time officials were *more* likely than their publics to say that their national 'culture and traditions' were important to them personally – especially in Korea and Ukraine. So in Ukraine, officials were 16 per cent less narrowly nationalist than their public in terms of identity, but 24 per cent more nationalist in terms of culture.

In East Europe, but not in East Asia, officials were also around 17 per cent more favourable than their publics towards membership of regional organisations (the EU, ASEAN, or a 'north-east Asian' equivalent of ASEAN). In all countries except Korea, officials were around 14 per cent more favourable than their publics towards joining international economic organisations (WTO, IMF and World Bank).

Harder on the casualties of globalisation

Officials, especially in East Europe, disagreed with their publics on the reasons why some people had benefited (or suffered) more than others from opening up the economy. By a margin of 14 per cent in East Europe

Table 6.19. *Unrepresentative on nationalism – but only in East Europe*

	All four countries %	Officials within each country (compared with public)			
		Czech R %	Korea %	Ukraine %	Vietnam %
national culture is very important to me	58 (+11)	30 (+4)	51 (+18)	70 (+24)	82 (+2)
exclusively local identity, no supra-national element	33 (−6)	15 (−12)	26 (+6)	22 (−16)	69 (−8)
better to be member of international organisations	66 (+10)	56 (+14)	69 (+1)	60 (+15)	80 (+14)
better to be member of regional organisations	71 (+10)	65 (+15)	67 (+1)	65 (+20)	89 (+8)

Note: Figures outside brackets refer to officials; figures inside brackets show the difference between officials and their publics.

(17 per cent in Ukraine) but only 3 per cent in East Asia, officials were more likely than the public to justify the pattern of winners and losers by arguing that the winners' success reflected greater skill and education, rather than power, contacts, corruption or even luck.

Consistent with that view of deserving winners, officials in East Europe took a tougher line than their publics on state aid for the casualties of globalisation. In East Europe they were less willing than their publics to provide unemployment pay for those who had lost jobs through globalisation, more in favour of using state funds for retraining rather than unemployment pay, less favourable to state intervention, less willing to protect obsolete industries, and less willing to tax globalisation-winners to compensate globalisation-losers – on average by around 11 per cent. By contrast, in Vietnam officials differed from their public by half as much, and in Korea not at all.

Intolerant of disorderly methods of protest

Studies of western politicians and officials have uncovered a 'governing perspective' (McClosky and Brill 1983; Sniderman *et al.* 1991; 1996;

Table 6.20. *Harder on the casualties of opening up – but only in East Europe*

	All four countries %	Officials within each country (compared with public)			
		Czech R %	Korea %	Ukraine %	Vietnam %
more skill and education are the main reason why some have benefited more than others	34 (+8)	24 (+10)	26 (+1)	27 (+17)	58 (+6)
main state help should be unemployment pay	12 (−7)	5 (−10)	7 (−1)	31 (−16)	6 (−4)
main state help should be retraining	67 (+9)	78 (+11)	67 (+6)	43 (+13)	78 (+15)
no increase in taxes on winners to help losers	30 (+3)	41 (+12)	13 (−6)	37 (+10)	29 (+1)
state should intervene more in the economy	58 (−5)	45 (−9)	53 (+3)*	68 (−10)	68 (−1)
should provide protection for obsolete businesses	54 (−6)	42 (−8)	71 (−3)	56 (−10)	49 (−10)

Notes: Figures outside brackets refer to officials; figures inside brackets show the difference between officials and their publics.
* officials take a softer line than publics.

Miller *et al.* 1996): officials typically display more support than the general public for citizens' liberties, including the right to protest – providing these protests do not go too far. But at a certain point officials switch from being *more liberal* than the public to being *more authoritarian* than the public. Although the differences are slight and not, in purely statistical terms, compelling, our overall findings concerning officials' attitudes towards anti-globalisation protests are consistent with that general model. On our figures, officials gave 2 or 3 per cent *more* support than the public to the principle of protest, to 'peaceful' marches, rallies and demonstrations; and to appeals to international environmental groups. Officials also gave 4 or 5 per cent *more* support than the public to complaints to local trade unions or government officials. But at the same time, officials gave slightly *less* support than the public to strikes (4 per cent less), go slows (3 per cent less), or sabotage, and officials were 6 per cent more likely than the public to insist that protest should be exclusively peaceful.

East European officials, especially Ukrainian, differed from their public more than officials in East Asia in condemning robust methods such as strikes or go-slows. Ukrainian officials were 8 per cent more likely than their public to condemn strikes or go-slows, and 10 per cent more likely to insist on protest being peaceful and orderly (though that still left Ukrainian officials less likely to condemn disorderly protest than officials in any other country). Czech officials also were 12 per cent more likely than their public to insist on protest being peaceful and orderly (though that made them more intolerant of disorder than officials in any other country).

Unduly defensive about the government

There were large differences between officials and their publics in East Europe, but negligible differences in East Asia, on support for the government and its policies. In East Asia, officials were only 5 per cent more inclined than the public to support their government and its policies – but 12 per cent more in the Czech Republic, and 20 per cent more in Ukraine. Conversely, officials in the Czech Republic were 10 per cent less likely than the public to criticise the government and 34 per cent less in Ukraine (an unusually high 20 per cent of Ukrainian officials had mixed views).

In three of the four countries very few officials or members of the public suggested their government and its policies were '*very*' good: mostly support was moderate rather than enthusiastic. Vietnam was the exception. In Vietnam large numbers did describe government policies as 'very' good – but officials 14 per cent *less* often than the public. This underlines further the enormous contrast between East Europe (especially Ukraine)

Table 6.21. *Intolerant of disorderly protest*

	Overall % yes	Officials within each country (compared with public)			
		Czech R % yes	Korea % yes	Ukraine % yes	Vietnam % yes
If an international company was causing serious local problems, should people *protest*	80 (+2)	73 (−1)	81 (+5)	86 (+3)	81 (+3)
Suppose an international company here in (COUNTRY) treated its workers badly or polluted the local environment. Should people *never* use disorderly or violent forms of protest?	57 (+6)	70 (+12)	58 (0)	47 (+10)	54 (+7)

Notes: Figures outside brackets refer to officials; figures inside brackets show the difference between officials and their publics.
% yes = number saying 'yes' as a percentage of all answers. The remaining percentage includes 'no', 'mixed' and 'don't know' answers.

and East Asia (especially Vietnam). Ukrainian officials were 34 per cent less likely than the public to *criticise* their government and its policies; by contrast, Vietnamese officials were 14 per cent less likely than the public to *praise* it strongly. What the Vietnamese public was praising was, of course, the post-Doi Moi policies, not the former command economy. Nonetheless, the new direction of policy was more popular with the public (than officials) in Vietnam, but more popular with officials (than the public) in Ukraine. Only in East Europe did officials stand apart from the general population as peculiar apologists for their government.

The consequences

Although in earlier chapters officials overall did not appear to be greatly out of touch with their publics, we have discovered that this masks the fact that East Asian officials were very close to their publics, while East European officials – and especially officials in Ukraine – were dangerously out of touch. Taking their uniquely unrepresentative views together with the uniquely strong public allegations that the chief beneficiaries of the open economy in these countries had been officials, power-holders

Table: 6.22. *Unrepresentative on support for the government and its policies – but only in East Europe*

	All four countries %	Officials within each country (compared with public)			
		Czech R %	Korea %	Ukraine %	Vietnam %
The government and its policies are ...					
very good	10 (−3)	2 (+1)	4 (−1)	3 (+1)	33 (−14)
good (incl. very good)	54 (+10)	36 (+12)	46 (+3)	40 (+20)	95 (+7)
bad (incl. very bad)	33 (−13)	55 (−10)	45 (−4)	32 (−34)	1 (0)

Note: Figures outside brackets refer to officials; figures inside brackets show the difference between officials and their publics.

or those 'with contacts' – allegations that were corroborated by East European officials' own reports and perceptions – the 'vanguard model' fits better in East Asia while the 'conspiracy' or 'officials-for-themselves' model fits better in East Europe, and particularly well in Ukraine.

The consequences of public perceptions of government as a conspiracy were considerable. On average across the four countries, public perceptions that the benefits of globalisation had gone specifically to high government officials rather than to ordinary people reduced perceptions that the market economy was fair (by 17 per cent) or delivered prosperity (by 16 per cent); reduced perceptions that opening up was good for the country (by 21 per cent), or had more advantages than disadvantages (by 26 per cent); and even reduced support for 'rapid development' (by 23 per cent).

Public perceptions that the benefits of globalisation had gone specifically to high government officials rather than to ordinary people also reduced satisfaction with 'the way things are going in our country' (by 16 per cent), and had a measurable impact on state legitimacy. It eroded public support for 'the government and its policies' by an average of 17 per cent and increased support for 'disorderly or violent' protests when foreign firms behaved badly by around 10 per cent in the Czech Republic, Ukraine and Vietnam, though by a smaller amount Korea. With the exception of Vietnam, it increased support primarily for the use of disorderly or violent protest as a *first resort* rather than a last resort: by 19 per cent in the Czech Republic, by 11 per cent in Ukraine, and by 5 per cent in Korea.

Table 6.23. *Consequences of perception that benefits have gone to government officials*

		Public within each country				
	All four countries % yes	Czech R % yes	S Korea % yes	Ukraine % yes	Vietnam % yes
Market economy fair …					
… if feel benefits gone to ordinary people	39	39	37	12	67
… if feel benefits gone to high government officials	22	13	21	3	49
Market economy makes country more properous …					
… if feel benefits gone to ordinary people	65	57	60	49	92
… if feel benefits gone to high government officials	49	25	52	33	86
Opening up more good for country …					
… if feel benefits gone to ordinary people	85	91	74	78	94
… if feel benefits gone to high government officials	64	52	65	50	88
Opening up more advantages than disadvantages …					
… if feel benefits gone to ordinary people	78	89	64	68	92
… if feel benefits gone to high government officials	52	40	47	44	79
Rapid development good for country …					
… if feel benefits gone to ordinary people	70	69	54	71	83
… if feel benefits gone to high government officials	47	32	38	51	66
Satisfied with way things are going in our country …					
… if feel benefits gone to ordinary people	49	50	25	28	93
… if feel benefits gone to high government officials	33	23	12	14	84
Government and its policies 'good for country' ('very good' in Vietnam) …					
… if feel benefits gone to ordinary people	48	43	62	31	*56
… if feel benefits gone to high government officials	31	20	43	18	*43
Should never use disorderly or violent forms of protest …					
… if feel benefits gone to ordinary people	55	67	55	44	54
… if feel benefits gone to high government officials	46	58	51	33	43

Of course, with the exception of Vietnam, far more of the public thought the benefits of globalisation went to high government officials than to ordinary people. So perhaps we should rephrase these findings by highlighting the fact that public perceptions that the benefits of globalisation went to 'ordinary people' had a *benign* impact on attitudes towards the state – rather than emphasising that public perceptions that the benefits went to 'government officials' had a *malign* impact on attitudes towards the state. It is precisely the same finding, whichever way we express it.

6.5 Conclusions: expectations, perceptions, legitimacy

A central issue of debates about economic openness (or 'globalisation') has been the capacity of states to promote economic growth and protect their citizens from its downsides. On one side are strong arguments that increased economic integration is weakening state capacity to manage economies and sustain national systems of social protection, leading to a decline in legitimacy for the nation state. On the other side there are strong arguments that states have more room for manoeuvre, should they wish to use it, than anti-globalisation theorists have recognised. Some argue that the declining capacity of the state relative to international or supranational forces is a peculiarly 'European delusion'; that, in East Asia especially, state capacity is increasing, not declining, even as they embrace globalisation with some enthusiasm.

At street level we have found more severe criticism, especially in East Europe: that the state is a conspiracy of officials against the public; that the state is the problem not the solution; and that the state has too much autonomy (from its people), not too little (from global forces).

We found public support for a state that was able to play the roles of national entrepreneur, protector or physician, and national advocate within a global context. In its role as national *entrepreneur*, a large majority held the state responsible for the pace of economic development in their country. Though they endorsed the policy of opening up their economies to world markets, a large majority expected the state to act as *physician and protector* by taxing globalisation-winners to help globalisation-losers, by protecting farmers (as long as they were subsidised elsewhere), by protecting small businesses (until they were strong enough to compete internationally), and even by protecting obsolete businesses (while they modernised) or their national media (for cultural reasons). Overwhelmingly, they also saw a need for the state to protect their national 'way of life'. But their commitment to cultural protection reflected the importance they attached to their national culture rather than cultural fright or a wish to cut themselves off from the wider world. A large majority in

Ukraine and overwhelming majorities elsewhere felt their country could not avoid joining international and regional organisations – which few thought were 'usually fair' to countries like their own: so they would need a strong *advocate* of their national interest within them.

The public saw all these roles for government as necessary for successful participation in a globalising world, not as an alternative to it. At least for the public in our Asian countries, the global arena made an effective state more necessary than ever before.

Public demand pointed to a strong role for the state as entrepreneur, physician, protector and advocate. But public perceptions of *state performance* were far less positive. The public held the state primarily responsible for adverse economic trends in the Czech Republic, Korea and above all in Ukraine, as well as for the positive economic trends in Vietnam. Worst of all, the public feared that the state had a role as a *conspiracy against the public*. In our East European countries, few felt the benefits of economic change and opening the economy had gone primarily to those with greater skills, education or even luck, though the numbers were greater in East Asia and predominant in Vietnam. The majority felt the benefits had gone to those who were corrupt, had 'contacts', or 'already had more power' – and, except in Vietnam, much more to 'government officials' than to 'ordinary people'.

A detailed look at the officials we interviewed showed that they were far less representative of, or sympathetic to, their publics in East Europe than in East Asia. Perceptions of the state as a conspiracy against the public had measurable consequences in every country. They eroded public support for 'the government and its policies' and increased support for 'disorderly or violent' methods of protest.

Our evidence suggests that the public do *not* accept the 'decline of the state' thesis, at least in the stronger forms that we quoted at the start. The public tend to agree with Wolf that the state in a global world is neither irrelevant nor entirely ineffective, but also with Jacques that the state is getting stronger (in terms of meeting public demands) in East Asia while getting weaker, less relevant and more self-interested in East Europe.

But strong states are not seen by the public as incompatible with globalisation. Paradoxically, enthusiasm for joining regional and global organisations is greater in our East Asian countries than in our East European countries, especially in Vietnam where the public view the state as strongest. Such as it is, East European *supra*nationalism is based in part at least on public perceptions of weak, ineffective or self-serving states and the need for a stronger advocate in the global arena, while East Asian *inter*nationalism is based on public perceptions of strong states with the ability to play an effective role in the global arena.

There is an important distinction between public perceptions of the Czech and Ukrainian states as weak, however. As a consequence of EU accession, together with the very small size of the Czech state and its pre-accession integration into a wider European economic and political milieu, the Czech public had an exceptionally weak perception of their state's autonomy. Even before EU accession negotiations were complete or a referendum held, quite exceptional numbers of Czechs (around 27 per cent) volunteered the response that they had 'no choice' but to join regional or international organisations rather than expressing positive support. Only 12 per cent in Ukraine (and a mere 3 per cent in East Asia) gave that response. By contrast, the Ukrainian public's perception of a weak state owed more to perceptions of domestic incompetence or perversity than to outside forces. They wanted far more state intervention, protection, and help (especially unemployment pay) than Czechs. But Ukrainians were far more dissatisfied than Czechs with what they got: with 'the way things are going in the country', with inadequate living standards, with growing inequality, with increasing crime, corruption and pollution (all of which they were exceptionally inclined to blame on the state). Moreover, although our survey interviews suggest both East European publics were prone to view their states as a conspiracy against the public, our focus group discussions reveal far more detail, and far more bitterness about this in Ukraine than in the Czech Republic. The weakness of the Czech state was attributed somewhat more to external forces while the weakness of the Ukrainian state was attributed primarily to its own internal failings.

Given our findings on Ukrainian perceptions of their state it was not entirely surprising that they were soon followed by the challenge of the Orange Revolution. Even though that did owe much to outside forces, a basis for it already existed in the pattern of public opinion within Ukraine. In the next chapter we look at the extent to which that 'revolution' changed, as well as reflected, public opinion in Ukraine.

Since the mid 1970s, all four of our countries have had some experience of regime change. The Czech Republic emerged at the start of 1993 from the more diverse Czechoslovakia. In South Korea the increasingly democratic Sixth Republic replaced the authoritarian Fifth Republic in 1987. That change had regional implications because the authoritarian regime in Korea had reputedly favoured the 'home regions' of the authoritarian rulers (Min 2004) and the leaders of the new democratic regime came from other regions. But we focus on Vietnam and Ukraine, where the imprint of regime change might be particularly evident in regional differences in public attitudes towards marketisation and opening up – differences between public opinion in North and South Vietnam, and between public opinion in East and West Ukraine.

In Vietnam the free-market South was forcibly reunited with the communist North only in July 1976 and experienced scarcely more than a decade of classic communism between reunification and Doi Moi, in marked contrast to the much longer experience of communism in the North. If there were any legacy from the period before reunification, we might expect the public in the South to feel more competent and more comfortable with markets and an open economy and perhaps less comfortable with government from Hanoi. The historical legacy would provide a plausible explanation for polarised opinion between North and South – if that was a significant pattern. But by the time of our study almost three decades of tumultuous policy change had passed since the North and South had separate regimes, and regional differences may have faded through time, not least because the communist regime had itself embraced the concept of marketisation, openness, and individual enterprise for a decade or more prior to our study.

Ukraine has had much more recent experience of regime change. Indeed, the year after we completed our fieldwork, Ukraine was convulsed by the Orange Revolution. If anything could affect the stability of our findings, an event such as the Orange Revolution could do so. Ukraine is divided between East and West on religion (with Catholic

Uniates in the West), on religiosity (with more non-believers in the East), on language, and on ethnic identification, as well as by industry and occupation – and these different cleavages partially, if only partially, coincide. Ethnic or linguistic Russians in post-communist Ukraine might object to being Ukrainianised – as earlier generations of ethnic or linguistic Ukrainians had objected to being Russified. It would be natural in so large a country for the East to look towards greater cooperation with less market-oriented Russia, while the West looked to greater integration with the more market-oriented EU. The Orange Revolution at the end of 2004 was crudely depicted as a contest between pro-Russian and pro-western elements, equated with supporters of a controlled economy and supporters of opening up to a free-market world economy. But that might be a misleadingly overdrawn caricature of Ukrainian public opinion.

7.1   Vietnam: the legacy of reunification

North and South Vietnam had different legacies of communism, but they also differed in many other ways. There were significant socio-economic differences, different experience of economic and cultural trends, and different degrees of proximity to the national government, as well as different legacies of war and communism. All of these might have had some impact on public opinion towards an open economy.

Regionalism in Vietnam was not simply a matter of North versus South, however. Central Vietnam, especially the Central Highlands, had interests and traditions of its own – and on some questions distinctive opinions. So we have divided Vietnam into three regions: the North, comprising the North East, North West, The Red River Delta, and Hanoi, where we interviewed 549 ordinary members of the public; the South, comprising the Mekong River Delta, and the North-east South Region, including the former southern capital, Ho Chi Minh City, where we interviewed 579 people; and Central Vietnam, comprising the North Central, South Central Coast, and Central Highlands, where we interviewed 370 people. Given our total sample size, a more detailed regional division would be inappropriate. Mostly, we focus on North-South differences but, on a few issues, attitudes in Central Vietnam stand out from those in both North and South.

Socio-economic differences In some respects Northerners' experience and outlook was more parochial, less cosmopolitan, than that of Southerners. Northerners were much more likely to be self-employed farmers or work on a family farm; they were less likely to have a car or

Table 7.1. *More parochial backgrounds in the North*

	North Vietnam %	Central Vietnam %	South Vietnam %
self-employed farmers (including family-farmers)	54	28	35
car in household	1	2	3
moped/motorbike in household	62	83	76
computer	6	19	18
no personal contact with foreigners within Vietnam	62	42	52
speak English	6	26	17
most important aspect of our culture is our language	18	24	29

Note: The Vietnam data have been weighted to be representative on age, gender and education. Entries are percentages of all respondents.

a motorbike, and much less likely to have a computer at home. They were less likely to have had personal contact with foreigners within Vietnam, far less likely to speak English (6 per cent compared with 17 per cent in the South) though, despite that, they were more inclined to stress social behaviour rather than language as the key element in their culture.

Perceptions of economic and cultural trends On objective indicators such as the possession of a computer or a moped (an important means of transport in Vietnam) Northerners were clearly less affluent than Southerners. They were also more self-consciously aware that their incomes were below average; that inequality was growing (more 'very rich'; and more 'very poor'); and that the towns had done better than the villages (where so many more Northerners lived). Yet it was the Southerners that complained their – admittedly above average – incomes were only just enough to live on, and it was Northerners who, by a small margin over Southerners, were more likely to say the economy had got better; and, by a large margin of 21 per cent over Southerners, were more likely to say their family living standards had got 'much better'.

Perceived trends in corruption were much worse in the South, but Northerners were more likely to complain that pollution had got worse and their traditional way of life was 'getting lost'. Both these adverse trends were probably the consequence of Doi Moi but they had to be weighed against the perceived positive trends in living standards.

Table 7.2. *Less affluent, but feel more like winners in the North*

	North Vietnam %	Central Vietnam %	South Vietnam %
think family income below the typical income in Vietnam	26	13	17
think towns have done much better than villages	72	62	59
think more 'very rich' now	97	90	82
think more 'very poor' now	16	5	6
family income only just enough to live on	23	22	43
think economy got much better	77	84	73
family living standards got 'much' better	57	47	36
think corruption increased	24	21	42
think pollution much worse	48	38	36
think traditional way of life getting lost	42	43	34

Note: The Vietnam data have been weighted to be representative on age, gender and education. Entries are percentages of all respondents.

Legacies of war and communism The legacy of war was perhaps more evident than the legacy of the confrontation between communist and capitalist economic systems. Three decades after reunification, Northerners remained significantly more anti-American than Southerners. They were much more likely to see the US as posing a territorial threat (26 per cent in the North; 15 per cent in the South); much more inclined to exclude American culture (22 per cent in the North; 13 per cent in the South), while being four times as willing as Southerners to welcome Russian culture and twice as willing as Southerners to welcome West European culture.

Northerners were more favourable to state intervention in the economy, especially to provide help for globalisation-losers. They were 11 per cent more willing than Southerners to support greater state intervention in the economy; 19 per cent more favourable to narrowing the (visibly widening) gap between rich and poor; and a massive 28 per cent more likely to support the idea of raising taxes on winners to provide help to losers. At the same time, Northerners were no more willing to focus state help on unemployment pay, and less willing than Southerners to back state subsidies for failing businesses. Instead they were even more inclined than Southerners to focus state help on retraining the unemployed to compete better in the job market. That is more accurately described as a social-democratic formula than a classic communist formula.

Table 7.3. *The legacy of war*

	North Vietnam %	Central Vietnam %	South Vietnam %
territorial threat from US	26	12	15
exclude US culture	22	7	13
welcome US culture	2	2	5
welcome Russian culture	8	6	2
welcome West European culture (French, German, British)	7	4	3

Note: The Vietnam data have been weighted to be representative on age, gender and education. Entries are percentages of all respondents.

Table 7.4. *A social-democratic legacy of communism?*

	North Vietnam %	Central Vietnam %	South Vietnam %
want more state intervention in the economy	75	67	64
better to have smaller differences between rich and poor	80	67	61
tax winners to help losers	69	52	41
help losers primarily by unemployment pay	11	7	11
help losers primarily by subsidising companies	5	5	13
help losers primarily by retraining	66	71	57

Note: The Vietnam data have been weighted to be representative on age, gender and education. Entries are percentages of all respondents.

Far from being less favourable to opening up, Northerners were at least as favourable and, on many indicators, significantly more favourable than Southerners – despite their concern to help the casualties of globalisation.

Opening up Northerners were slightly less favourable towards foreign brands but 13 per cent more favourable towards foreign films and TV than Southerners. They were less favourable than Southerners towards unskilled immigrant workers from poorer countries but not averse to foreign experts and very slightly more favourable than Southerners towards foreign businessmen. Overall they were slightly more favourable than Southerners towards (unspecified) 'foreigners'.

Northerners were significantly more wary of supranational concepts such as an international Court of Human Rights, but though Northerners were slightly less favourable than Southerners towards joining world-wide international economic organisations 'like the WTO, IMF or World Bank', they were more favourable than Southerners towards joining regional international organisations 'like ASEAN'.

More strikingly, it was Northerners not Southerners who were by far the most favourable towards marketisation and opening up the economy. Northerners were 18 per cent more likely to say the market economy made Vietnam more prosperous, and 14 per cent more likely to say it was fair. As for opening up to world markets, three-quarters of the public in the North and South said it had more advantages than disadvantages. Northerners were 9 per cent more likely than Southerners to say opening up was good for Vietnam; and 22 per cent more likely to say it was 'the only way to go'.

If the communist legacy affected current attitudes towards marketisation and opening up, then it was a reactive legacy rather than a conformist legacy. Those areas of Vietnam with the least experience of an open market economy were the areas that were most enthusiastic about it.

Table 7.5 *More support in the North for marketisation and opening up*

	North Vietnam %	Central Vietnam %	South Vietnam %
foreigners who come are generally good for Vietnam	69	69	66
an international court of human rights is a bad idea	47	41	36
better to be a member of world organisations (WTO/IMF/WB)	61	74	65
better to be a member of regional organisations (ASEAN)	82	86	77
the market economy makes country more prosperous	95	93	77
the market economy is fair	64	42	50
the market economy is the only way to go	68	62	62
opening up the economy has more advantages	73	81	76
opening up the economy is good for Vietnam	93	90	82
opening up the economy is the only way to go	68	65	46

Note: The Vietnam data have been weighted to be representative on age, gender and education. Entries are percentages of all respondents.

Proximity to government Of course, sceptics might argue that Northerners were just so close to government, and so cowed by it, that they would cheer whatever policy it adopted, and do so without reservation or qualification. It is true that Northerners were more likely than Southerners to describe 'the government and its policies' as 'good', but we have other evidence to suggest that such scepticism is simply wrong. Northerners were not only the most enthusiastic about the Doi Moi policies of marketisation and opening up, they were also the most critical of their government in other ways.

Northerners were 13 per cent more likely than Southerners to say that the benefits of recent changes had gone to those who 'already had more power', and 12 per cent less likely to say the benefits had gone to those with 'more skill and education'. Even more strikingly, Northerners were 11 per cent more likely than Southerners to say that the benefits of opening up went mainly to government officials (and especially to 'high' government officials). They were 8 per cent less likely than Southerners to cite 'local businessmen', and 13 per cent less likely to cite 'ordinary people' as the main beneficiaries. So being nearer to the seat of government did not make Northerners less critical of it.

North and South In sum, we have found evidence in the North of a continuing war-legacy of suspicion of the US and antagonism towards American culture; and of a communist-legacy transformed into

Table 7.6. *Proximity to government*

	North Vietnam %	Central Vietnam %	South Vietnam %
the government and its policies are 'very' good	48	42	48
the government and its policies are good (incl. 'very' good)	93	88	82
main reason why some benefit more is skill, education, luck	48	60	60
main reason why some benefit more is power	24	15	11
main beneficiaries of opening up: ordinary people	10	19	23
main beneficiaries of opening up: local businessmen	15	16	23
main beneficiaries of opening up: officials	27	18	16

Note: The Vietnam data have been weighted to be representative on age, gender and education. Entries are percentages of all respondents.

social-democratic concern for state intervention to help globalisation-losers. But our evidence completely contradicts any notion of a Northern communist legacy of continuing suspicion towards the principles of competitive markets or an open economy. Rather, it suggests a degree of naïve faith in what was for them a new economic system: evidence of a reactive-legacy, the very opposite of a simple persistence-legacy.

But regional differences in attitudes towards opening up Vietnam to world markets reflected not only a North-South legacy of any kind, whether reactive or not. They also reflected a more long-term legacy, one that set the Central regions against both North and South.

Central Vietnam The Central Highlands of Vietnam were home to a distinctive minority culture. That culture included child labour in very poor rural families. Only 60 of our 370 interviews in Central Vietnam were in the Central Highlands themselves, but those who lived in adjacent areas were no doubt particularly aware of the nature and problems of the Highlands. Those who lived in the Central regions, and especially those in the Highlands, were the most likely to say their traditional 'way of life' needed protection: 94 per cent in the Highlands and 82 per cent throughout the central regions compared with an average of just 67 per cent in North and South.

Similarly, public support for a ban on the import or export of products made in unsafe conditions or by child labour was stronger in the Central regions than in either North or South. Over twice as many in Central Vietnam as in the rest of Vietnam supported a foreign ban on Vietnamese products made by children. Within the Highlands themselves, however, it

Table 7.7. *Child labour and protecting 'our way of life'*

	North Vietnam %	Central Vietnam %	South Vietnam %
completely agree, 'our way of life' needs protection	69	82 (94)	64
ban imports made in unsafe conditions	58	75 (62)	53
ban imports made by children	37	61 (43)	39
a foreign ban on our exports made in unsafe conditions would help	34	53 (42)	28
a foreign ban on our exports made by children would help	23	51 (45)	25

Note: The Vietnam data have been weighted to be representative on age, gender and education. Entries are percentages of all respondents.
Figures in brackets are based on the 60 respondents interviewed in the Central Highlands.

was somewhat less strong than in other parts of the Central regions, though still not far short of twice as much as in either the North or South. It would seem that support for banning the import and export of goods produced by child labour was greatest of all among those who were sensitised by regional proximity to the issue but who did not themselves depend upon such labour.

7.2   Ukraine: the impact of 'revolution'

The 'Orange Revolution' in Ukraine was very much about issues that were central to our study: the market economy, openness to world markets, an orientation towards the ex-Soviet East or the free-market West, and the role of the state as a conspiracy against the public. If nothing else, Ukraine provides a severe test of the stability of public attitudes as measured by our survey. Public attitudes towards broad long-term issues such as marketisation or opening up may be more stable than support for a particular party or politician. But even these may not remain completely unaffected by such great events.

Our 2002 focus groups and 2003 survey interviews revealed extreme public discontent in Ukraine and a unique level of estrangement between the public and officials. Several focus group participants explicitly looked forward to a change of regime, but without much hope: public discontent was combined with so much helplessness and resignation that a change of regime seemed unlikely without great efforts by disaffected elites and/or by outside forces to mobilise the public. If regime change did occur, however, it might mean disintegration, as in the former Czechoslovakia, rather than a mere change of policy. The 'fault-lines' of language, history and religion ran through Ukraine, and in the early 1990s it seemed Ukraine might fall apart as quickly as Czechoslovakia.

In the Presidential election at the end of 2004 rival candidates were backed by President Putin of Russia (who backed the outgoing Prime Minister Viktor Yanukovych) and a collection of western-financed organisations on the other side (who backed Viktor Yushchenko, a former Prime Minister now taking on the role of challenger). President Kwasniewski of Poland played an influential but ambiguous role as mediator.

Neither candidate won the required absolute majority in the first round of voting in October, but the electoral commission declared Yanukovych the winner by a narrow margin in the November runoff. That result was not recognised by the EU which promptly withdrew all twenty-five of its ambassadors from Kyiv. President Saakashvilli arrived to draw parallels with the revolution that had recently brought him to power in Georgia. Under extreme international pressure, backed by massive, well-funded and well-organised street protests within Ukraine, the November runoff was declared invalid and a second scheduled for December. After that December vote, Yanukovych conceded defeat and Yushchenko was declared elected.

Throughout the various rounds of voting the more eastern, ethnically-Russian and Russian-speaking areas of Ukraine, backed by Putin, voted for the candidate of the old regime. The more western, ethnically Ukrainian, and Ukrainian-speaking areas, backed by the West, by Poland, and by Saakashvilli, voted for the challenger, Yushchenko. During the long-running dispute both outgoing President Kuchma and challenger Yushchenko raised the spectre of civil war (BBC, 24 November 2004). But crude geographical analysis of winners and losers grossly over-states the sharpness of ethnic divisions within Ukraine. A New Europe Barometer poll indicates that ethnic Russians split only 3:1 in favour of Yanukovich and ethnic Ukrainians not much more than 2:1 in favour of Yushchenko (Rose 2005: p. 29). Neither regions nor ethnic groups voted exclusively for one candidate or the other.

Moreover, large public demonstrations were mounted on both sides, yet press reports indicated that the public remained surprisingly good humoured and the security forces surprisingly restrained. The long pre-dicted break-up of Ukraine once again failed to materialise – perhaps because the 'significant other' for most Ukrainians was not the other ethnic or linguistic group (Yushchenko himself was born on the eastern border with Russia, though in a rural Ukrainian-speaking community) but rather, as we have so amply documented in previous chapters, the governing class of politicians, officials and post-communist business 'oligarchs'. Indeed, as the months went by after the Orange Revolution the public were increasingly reminded that this same governing class remained in power, and the revolution was less revolutionary than the term implied.

We undertook a rerun of our 2003 survey in March 2005 (see Chapter 1 for details), after the immediate excitement of the election had died down but before there was time for disillusionment to grow. In many respects public opinion remained largely unaffected by the dra-matic events of the winter. The stability of most of our findings is impres-sive: out of 108 survey questions about perceptions and attitudes that we asked in 2003 and repeated in 2005, differences only reached as much as 10 per cent on 19 of them. Although we pay particular attention to change, all our findings about changing public attitudes have to be read against that background of broad stability. Ukrainian public opinion still remained recognisably and distinctively Ukrainian. Even a 'revolution' and regime change failed to invalidate most conclusions that could be drawn from our 2003 survey. But there were a few very dramatic changes and a considerable degree of structured but partially self-cancelling change beneath the surface stability.

The concept of a 'honeymoon' period after an election is familiar. Incoming governments are generally more popular for a few months after their election than they are even on election day. For a brief period they are given the 'benefit of the doubt' while continuing problems can still be blamed on the outgoing government. Then disillusionment sets in and the next stage in the electoral cycle is a period of mid-term blues as the public becomes aware that their over-optimistic hopes are not going to be met. After events as dramatic as those in the Orange Revolution we might expect the public to be almost irrationally euphoric for a few months after the change of regime, before the predictable disillusion set in.

The specific impacts are likely to be less predictable than this generally predictable post-election euphoria, yet more important for our study. Because the change was driven in part by street protests, it might have affected Ukrainian attitudes:

(i)   towards legitimate methods of protest.

Given that the contest was in part between ex-soviet Russia and the free-market West, it might also have affected Ukrainian attitudes:

(ii) towards Russia versus the West;

(iii) towards foreigners using Ukraine as a battle-ground for their global ambitions;

and:

(iv) towards the internal market economy, opening up to world markets, and involvement in international affairs or organisations.

The revolution was depicted as a contest between ethno-linguistically Russian regions of Ukraine and ethno-linguistically Ukrainian regions. Ukraine did not come near to breaking up, but ethno-linguistic Russians might well feel that they had been the losers, ethno-linguistic Ukrainians that they were the winners. So the revolution might also have:

(v)   polarised public perceptions and attitudes along ethno-linguistic lines.

All of these consequences of revolution are plausible. The question is whether the impact of the Orange Revolution on these perceptions and attitudes was large or small, simple or complex.

Post-revolutionary euphoria

Overall, views about the outgoing regime were almost completely unaffected by the Orange Revolution. By margins of 47 per cent in 2003 and 44 per cent in 2005, the public described the Kuchma regime and its

Table 7.8. *Public perceptions of the old and new regimes*

	Ukraine public		
On the whole the present (previous) government and its policies are (were) …	2003 Views about Kuchma government %	2005 Views about Kuchma government %	2005 Views about Yushchenko government %
very good for Ukraine	2	3	17
good for Ukraine	18	17	42
bad for Ukraine	50	38	8
very bad for Ukraine	17	26	3

Note: Per cent of all respondents. Per cents giving other/mixed/'don't know' responses not shown.

policies as 'bad' rather than 'good'. But the public were euphoric about the new regime. Although an unusually large 17 per cent were as yet unable to give an opinion, the rest, by a margin of 48 per cent, described the new Yushchenko regime as 'good' rather than 'bad' – the exact inverse of their opinion about the old regime.

When asked explicitly to compare the old and new regimes, the public, by a margin of 49 per cent, expected the new government to be 'better' than the old – though 24 per cent volunteered the response that it was still 'too early to say'. Ukrainians were therefore divided mainly between those who expected better government and those who had still to come to a view. Very few (9 per cent) actually thought the new regime would be worse than the old.

Just three or four months after the successful 'revolution' the public expected the new regime to be better than the old at handling every issue, albeit by sharply varying margins. Post-revolution Ukrainians were most optimistic about the new regime's ability to handle relations with the EU (67 per cent net 'better'). To a somewhat lesser degree they also expected it to be better than the old regime in attracting foreign investment (56 per cent net) and combating corruption (54 per cent net). But they were much less sure it would be better than the old regime at handling inter-ethnic relations within Ukraine (31 per cent net better); and still less sure (though still 11 per cent net better) that it would be better than the old regime at handling relations with Russia.

Pressed specifically on whether the new regime would 'respect', 'neglect', or even 'threaten' the status of the Russian language and the interests of Russian speakers within Ukraine, only 6 per cent saw it as a

Table 7.9. *Explicitly comparative evaluations of the old and new regimes*

	On the whole %	Relations with EU %	Attracting foreign investment to Ukraine %	Combating corruption within Ukraine %	Inter-ethnic relations within Ukraine %	Relations with Russia %
	Ukraine public 2005					
New government will handle issue:						
a lot better	26	30	24	26	15	12
a little better	32	41	37	37	35	30
a little worse	5	3	3	5	14	22
a lot worse	4	1	2	4	5	9
(VOL) too early to say	24	20	24	24	21	23

Note: Per cent of all respondents. Per cents giving other/mixed/'don't know' responses not shown. VOL indicates that a particular answer was not offered by the interviewer, but was spontaneously volunteered by some respondents.

'threat' and ten times as many (61 per cent) expected it to 'respect' the Russian language and its speakers.

Overall satisfaction with 'the way things are going for my family' improved from net dissatisfaction of 54 per cent in 2003 to net dissatisfaction of 33 per cent in 2005. That was eclipsed by improved satisfaction with 'the way things are going in our country today'. While that also remained slightly negative (9 per cent net dissatisfaction), it was a huge change from pre-revolution opinion when net dissatisfaction with the country's progress ran at 62 per cent. It reflected political change and hopes for the future more than current economic achievement, however. Over the period 2003–5, net expectations of future progress in living standards improved by 40 per cent; net perceptions of progress in family income by only 30 per cent; and net perceptions of current progress in Ukraine's economy improved still less – by only 20 per cent.

In varying degrees, however, the post-revolution surge in optimism extended to everything we asked about: to crime and corruption, to pollution, even to culture. A large majority of Ukrainians still felt that crime, corruption, and pollution were getting worse, and that their traditional ways of life were getting lost. The present still looked very bleak, but not so bleak as in 2003: the margins of pessimism over optimism declined sharply: by 27 per cent (from 74 per cent to 47 per cent) on crime and corruption; by 12 per cent (from 79 per cent to 67 per cent) on pollution; and by 19 per cent (from 31 per cent to 12 per cent) on the

Table 7.10. *Satisfaction and hope*

		Ukraine public	
		2003 %	2005 %
Overall, are you satisfied or dissatisfied with the way things are going ...			
... for your family			
	satisfied	21	30
	dissatisfied	75	63
... in our country today			
	satisfied	16	39
	dissatisfied	78	48
Over next ten years expect living standards in Ukraine to ...			
	improve steadily	41	61
	decline steadily	29	9

Note: Per cent of all respondents. Per cents giving other/mixed/'don't know' responses not shown.

erosion of their cultural traditions. Even the numbers who alleged that 'high-ranking officials' benefited most from opening up went down by 11 per cent (from 39 per cent to 28 per cent).

That had to be the *consequence* of revolution rather than a *cause*: if everything was getting so much better there was simply no basis for the Orange Revolution, no excuse, no motivation, no explanation. It is far more plausible that the Orange Revolution produced, in an unusually strong degree, the same surge in optimism that regularly follows an election victory for a former opposition, and that the revolution itself triggered a generalised euphoria that spilled over to affect perceptions of all issues and concerns. It was most visible in satisfaction with the (newly elected and as yet untested) government and in rising optimism about the future; but also visible, though significantly less so, in all perceptions of the present.

Legitimising protest?

Since street protest played such a large part, at least in the theatre of the revolution, we might expect the revolution to have some impact on Ukrainian public attitudes towards protest. Some may have felt the revolution legitimised methods of public protest that went beyond petitions and complaints: in the focus groups they had already told us that normal democratic societies experienced more public protests and were responsive to them. But others, especially those on the losing side, may have feared that it set a precedent for disorder. Different currents of opinion towards protest probably cancelled each other out to some degree. But on balance, did the success of the revolution change attitudes?

Since so many foreigners visibly participated in the Orange Revolution, Ukrainians must have reflected more than usually on the issue of whether foreign participation in domestic protest was good or bad. But whether such reflection might make them more or less favourable towards foreign involvement in Ukraine's affairs is once again not at all obvious.

Our evidence suggests that the revolution did indeed legitimise more robust methods of protest but, at the same time, de-legitimised foreign involvement. Net support for workers' demonstrations against an international company with unsafe working conditions or low pay increased by 13 per cent (from 67 per cent to 80 per cent net); for strikes by 18 per cent (from 40 per cent to 58 per cent net); and net opposition to the use of 'go slows' declined by 15 per cent (from 28 per cent to 13 per cent). However, while Ukrainians became so much more sympathetic to Ukrainian workers' demonstrations, strikes, and 'go slows' against international companies, they became 24 per cent less sympathetic towards foreigners' participation in protests (net support declined from 46 per cent to 22 per cent).

Increasing confidence?

After the revolution, Ukrainians' sense of national autonomy increased, though from a very low level. A majority of Ukrainians still felt their country's 'policies on most important matters were determined more by world markets and powerful international organisations' than by 'what Ukrainian people want'. But the margin by which they felt this lack of national autonomy declined by 17 per cent (from 49 per cent to 32 per cent net).

Despite the success of a western-backed revolution, Ukrainians as a whole showed no inclination to tilt towards East or West. Despite defeating the Kremlin's candidate for President, they felt less need to shelter behind western alliances. By a margin of 65 per cent, Ukrainians felt their former government had been wrong to commit troops to the American-dominated coalition in Iraq; and by a margin of 47 per cent they wanted to stay out of the North Atlantic Treaty Organization (NATO). No doubt that reflected the particular circumstances of the occupation of Iraq but it may also have reflected a growing sense of national autonomy. Net support for being a member of international organisations like the World Trade Organisation (WTO), World Bank (WB), or International

Monetary Fund (IMF) or regional organisations like the European Union (EU) declined by 12 per cent. All of these trends were at least consistent with a growing sense of national self-confidence. But all of them are completely inconsistent with the simple notion of the Orange Revolution as a victory for the West and a defeat for Russia.

Perhaps reflecting that growing self-confidence, the Ukrainian public warmed slightly to foreigners in general, despite their increasing opposition to foreign participation in local protests. The margin by which they thought foreigners were good rather than bad for Ukraine was always large, but it increased by 15 per cent between 2003 and 2005 – though by much less if we specified that the foreigners were either from Russia (6 per cent increase in net approval) or from the West (just 3 per cent increase). (Foreigners from Poland, whose politicians played an important role in the revolution, were viewed in very similar terms to those from the West.)

Ukrainians always took a more favourable view of Russians than westerners but the trends in attitudes towards foreigners from East and West were very similar, and both were positive. The increases were small, but at least we can dismiss any possibility that there was a substantial overall reaction against either Russians or westerners in the wake of the revolution. Similarly, when we asked specifically about whether Ukraine should now 'move closer' in terms of 'trade and international affairs' to Russia or the West, Ukrainian opinion was almost equally divided (38 per cent versus 36 per cent) though, if anything, slightly more pro-Russian despite the revolution.

Culturally, Ukrainians were equally split on liking or disliking 'foreign' films and TV. When asked specifically in 2005 about 'western – European and American' films and TV they remained equally divided. But they were overwhelmingly favourable (80 per cent net) to Russian films and TV – numbers that suggest Ukrainians did not even regard Russian films and TV as in the 'foreign' category. They may have voted against the Kremlin candidate for President but they remained very close to Russia and to Russian culture.

Growing support for the market economy

The Ukrainian public (like most outside observers) thought the new Yushchenko regime would be far better at handling relations with the EU and attracting foreign investment – better than the old regime and, in particular, better on these issues than on any other. Did the victory of the Orange Revolution imply increasing support for a market economy, open to the world?

Table 7.11. *Growing support for a market economy*

	Ukraine public	
	2003 %	2005 %
The market economy makes Ukraine ...		
more prosperous	34	45
less prosperous	25	14
(VOL) not a real market economy here	27	25
The market economy in Ukraine is ...		
fair	4	8
unfair	66	55
(VOL) not a real market economy here	19	23
For Ukraine ...		
the market economy is the only way to go	29	40
there must be a better alternative	50	37

Notes: Per cent of all respondents. Per cents giving other/mixed/'don't know' responses not shown. VOL indicates that a particular answer was not offered by the interviewer, but was spontaneously volunteered by some respondents.

Ukrainians were always convinced that the market economy increased prosperity but also that it was unfair; and in 2003 a majority thought there was a better alternative. After the Orange Revolution, the margin by which they thought the market economy increased prosperity went up from 9 to 31 per cent, while the margin by which they thought the market economy was unfair declined from 62 to 47 per cent; and the margin by which they thought there was a better alternative to the market in 2003 (21 per cent net) was eliminated altogether and replaced by a small margin (3 per cent net) in the opposite direction – a change of 24 per cent. So Ukrainians swung much more in favour of the market between 2003 and 2005. Of course that could plausibly be interpreted as a contributory cause of the Orange Revolution rather than as a consequence (unlike the post-revolution surge in optimism). What did not change between 2003 and 2005, however, was the widespread perception (held by a quarter of Ukrainians) that Ukraine 'did not have a market economy' worthy of the name.

Ukrainians were always less critical of opening up their economy to the world than they were of the internal market economy. They remained much more inclined to see the advantages than the disadvantages of opening up the economy and to regard it as good rather than bad; and

Table 7.12. *Continuing support for opening up*

	Ukraine public	
	2003 %	2005 %
Opening up the economy ...		
has more advantages	45	45
has more disadvantages	28	26
is good for Ukraine	53	52
is bad for Ukraine	18	20
is the only way to go	35	40
there must be a better alternative	41	35

Note: Per cent of all respondents. Per cents giving other/mixed/ 'don't know' responses not shown.

on this their views hardly changed. But they did swing 11 per cent more towards feeling there was no alternative to opening up.

7.3   Polarisation

Comparison of our 2003 and 2005 surveys suggests that the Orange Revolution reflected pre-existing public support for opening up, growing public support for an internal market economy and continuing public criticism of Ukraine for not yet having a 'real' market economy. Among the Ukrainian public as a whole the Orange Revolution itself produced a surge of public euphoria (about almost everything, but especially about the future), increased national self-confidence, and a more relaxed attitude towards foreigners. It increased public support for more robust methods of protest but, at the same time, it decreased public support for foreign participation in local protests. It also increased public opposition to Ukrainian participation – as a very junior partner – in western-dominated military organisations or 'coalitions-of-the-willing'. And despite rejecting the Kremlin's candidate for the Presidency, Ukrainians clearly preferred Russian rather than western media and were evenly divided over whether Ukraine should tilt more to the East or more to the West.

Perhaps this Ukrainian public as a whole never existed. Or perhaps it was destroyed by the Orange Revolution. The Orange Revolution was depicted, somewhat over-simplistically as a contest between the more eastern, ethnically-Russian and Russian-speaking regions of Ukraine, backed by Putin, and the more western, ethnically Ukrainian and Ukrainian-speaking regions, backed by the West; or even more crudely as a simple contest between Ukrainians and Russians living in Ukraine – whether defined by language, by self-assigned 'nationality' (equated with ethnicity rather than citizenship in the former Soviet Union), or by region.

Insofar as Ukraine was already divided in that way before the revolution, Ukrainian opinion must already have been polarised into two camps. But insofar as the revolution was in fact a contest between ethno-linguistic Russians and Ukrainians within Ukraine, then the degree of polarisation might have increased. Overall, Ukrainian opinion might be an artificial statistical construct – not a political reality, merely the arithmetic average of two opposing realities. The most important impact of the revolution might not be visible as a change in overall public opinion so much as in the increasing polarisation of opinion between increasingly antagonistic regional or ethno-linguistic camps. We can test that proposition.

In Ukraine as a whole, 78 per cent describe their 'nationality/ethnic background' as Ukrainian, and 20 per cent as Russian; but only 49 per cent say they 'primarily speak Ukrainian' at home, while 46 per cent say they speak Russian at home. In 2005 we identified six *oblasts* (administrative regions) where the proportion of Russian speakers was higher than elsewhere. Together these 'Russian-speaking regions' as we shall call them constitute 28 per cent of the population of Ukraine (though 43 per cent of our raw, unweighted sample, because they were oversampled by a factor of two to improve the statistical reliability of ethno-linguistic analyses: see Chapter 1).

We focus our analysis on the contrast between Russian and Ukrainian speakers because that has very practical consequences for those who are not fluent in Ukrainian. Broadly speaking, our findings are the same whether we contrast perceptions and attitudes by language, by self-assigned 'nationality', or by region – though later in this chapter we use regression to confirm the dominant role of language. The three criteria correlate of course: being a Russian speaker correlates at 0.30 with living in what we define as a 'Russian region' and at 0.48 with claiming a 'Russian nationality/ethnicity'.

There are other less obvious yet important social-background differences between Russian and Ukrainian speakers. Only 16 per cent of Russian speakers but 60 per cent of Ukrainian speakers live in villages rather than towns; and only 20 per cent of Ukrainian speakers but 31 per cent of Russian speakers claim to be university educated. Russian speakers are concentrated in the capital city, Kyiv, as well as in eastern regions. None of the Russian speakers, but around 15 per cent of Ukrainian speakers, claim to be Catholic (or Uniate). Between 2003 and 2005 Russian speakers moved from being less Orthodox than Ukrainian speakers to being slightly more so, as the numbers of Russian speakers claiming to be Orthodox rose by 13 per cent (and the numbers of non-believers declined).

Between 2003 and 2005 also, the numbers who felt 'equally or more European than Ukrainian' rose from 7 per cent to 10 per cent among Ukrainian speakers; but declined from 31 per cent to 21 per cent among Russian speakers. So while Russian speakers felt comparatively European, their European orientation was fading rapidly. Russian speakers were well over four times as likely as Ukrainian speakers to have a European identity in 2003, but only twice as likely in 2005.

By background Russian speakers were more urban, better educated, twice as likely to own a computer, increasingly Orthodox, and they still remained much more 'European' in their identities even though their identification with Europe was declining. Conversely, Ukrainian speakers were much more likely to live in villages, be less educated, and less European in their identities – despite their greater connection with the West European (Catholic) church. By social background therefore, Russian speakers should be the natural cosmopolitans and Ukrainian speakers the natural parochials in terms of attitudes towards opening up.

Polarised euphoria In 2003 Ukrainian and Russian speakers were closely agreed about the Kuchma regime. By margins of around 46 per cent they both said it was more bad than good. By 2005 both Ukrainian and Russian speakers, in retrospect, still condemned the Kuchma regime, but the margins of disapproval had risen to 68 per cent among Ukrainian speakers while dropping to just 20 per cent among Russian speakers. Conversely the margins of approval for the new Yushchenko regime

Table 7.13. *Polarising memories, polarised expectations*

	Ukraine public		
On the whole the present (previous) government and its policies are (were) ...	2003 Views about Kuchma government % good–bad	2005 Views about Kuchma government % good–bad	2005 Views about Yushchenko government % good–bad
Ukrainian speakers	−47	−68	+73
Russian speakers	−45	−20	+23

Table 7.14. *Polarised evaluations of comparative policy competence*

	Ukraine public 2005					
On the whole % better–worse	Attracting foreign investment to Ukraine % better–worse	Relations with EU % better–worse	Combating corruption within Ukraine % better–worse	Relations with Russia % better–worse	Inter-ethnic relations within Ukraine % better–worse

Expect new government under President Yushchenko to handle issue better or worse than former government under President Kuchma?

	On the whole	Attracting foreign investment	Relations with EU	Combating corruption	Relations with Russia	Inter-ethnic relations
Ukrainian speakers	+73	+63	+78	+70	+33	+59
Russian speakers	+26	+47	+57	+37	−12	+1

stood at 73 per cent among Ukrainian speakers but only 23 per cent among Russian speakers – a classic example of polarisation.

Asked explicitly to compare the old and new regimes, both Ukrainian and Russian speakers thought the new regime would be 'on the whole' better than the old, but by margins of 73 per cent among Ukrainian speakers and 26 per cent among Russian speakers. The difference between Ukrainan and Russian speakers was least on their perceptions of the new regime's ability to attract foreign investment (16 per cent) or handle relations with the EU (21 per cent); rather more on the new regime's ability to combat corruption (33 per cent); and greatest of all on perceptions of the new regime's ability to handle inter-ethnic relations within Ukraine (58 per cent) or external relations with Russia (45 per cent). Indeed the only issue on which even Russian speakers thought the new regime might be worse than the old was on handling relations with Russia.

Pressed specifically on whether the new Yushchenko regime would 'respect', 'neglect', or even 'threaten' the status of the Russian language and the interests of Russian speakers in Ukraine, 76 per cent of Ukrainian speakers but only 46 per cent of Russian speakers thought the new regime would respect the interests of Russian speakers; 10 per cent of Russian speakers thought the new regime would 'threaten' their interests and another 31 per cent that it would 'neglect' them.

Ukrainian and Russian speakers hardly differed in their dissatisfaction with the way things were going for their families – either in 2003 or 2005. Both remained dissatisfied in 2005, though less dissatisfied than in 2003. But their dissatisfaction with the way things were going for the country,

Table 7.15. *Polarising satisfaction and hope*

	Ukraine public	
	2003 %	2005 %
Overall, are you satisfied or dissatisfied with the way things are going in our country today ...		
	% satisfied–dissatisfied	
Ukrainian speakers	−63	+13
Russian speakers	−61	−32
Over next ten years expect living standards in Ukraine to ...		
	% improve–decline	
Ukrainian speakers	+9	+68
Russian speakers	+17	+35

which had been almost identical in 2003, became sharply polarised in 2005. Russian speakers remained dissatisfied though their net dissatisfaction declined by 29 per cent (from 61 per cent to 32 per cent). But 63 per cent net dissatisfaction among Ukrainian speakers in 2003 was eliminated completely and replaced by 13 per cent net satisfaction. That was also reflected in expectations of future living standards: net optimism increased by three times as much among Ukrainian speakers (by 59 per cent) as among Russian speakers (by 18 per cent).

Language, nationality and region The relative contributions of language, nationality and region towards this post-revolutionary polarisation of opinion can be assessed by using all three together in a multiple regression. On every index of attitudes towards the old and new regimes, whether on specific policy areas or not, multiple regression shows that the impact of language is around two to three times as great as that of nationality or region. Similarly, when predicting satisfaction with 'the way things are going for the country', or expectations of future trends in living standards, multiple regression again shows that the impact of language is between two and four times as great as the impact of nationality or region – if indeed nationality or region have anything at all to add to the explanatory power of language.

Swapping places on attitudes towards foreign participation in protest There is little evidence of ethno-linguistic polarisation of attitudes towards more robust methods of protest such as demonstrations and strikes. But there is evidence of polarising attitudes towards foreign participation in Ukrainian protests.

Table 7.16. *Swapping places in attitudes towards foreign participation in protest*

	Ukraine public	
	2003	2005
	% accept – reject foreign help	
	%	%
Foreigners welcome in protests against a foreign company?		
Ukrainian speakers	+35	+24
Russian speakers	+55	+18
Foreigners welcome in protests against international organisations?		
Ukrainian speakers	+40	+25
Russian speakers	+59	+26
Should we ask foreigner sympathisers to boycott products from firms that damage our environment?		
Ukrainian speakers	+54	+62
Russian speakers	+63	+56

Both Russian and Ukrainian speakers became less favourable towards foreigners joining in protests against an international company which was 'causing serious local problems'. But Russian speakers swung much more (37 per cent) against such foreign participation than did Ukrainian speakers (11 per cent). Similarly Russian speakers swung much more (33 per cent) than Ukrainian speakers (15 per cent) against such foreign participation in protests against unfair decisions by international organisations. Even on asking sympathisers in other countries to boycott firms that were polluting the local environment, there was a polarising trend – though in this case caused by increasing support among Ukrainian speakers coupled with decreasing support among Russian speakers. By all three measures, Russian speakers appeared to be much more open to foreign participation in protests than Ukrainian speakers in 2003; but *less* than Ukrainian speakers in 2005.

Swapping places on attitudes towards internationalism Membership of NATO was very unpopular among Ukrainian speakers and extremely unpopular among Russian speakers. Membership of international organisations like the WTO, WB, IMF, or the EU was popular, however, and increasingly so, among Ukrainian speakers. But Russian speakers switched from being more favourable than Ukrainian speakers in 2003 to being less favourable in 2005. Among Ukrainian speakers, net support for membership increased (from a low base) by 4 per cent; but among

Table 7.17. *Swapping places on attitudes towards internationalism*

	Ukraine public				
	International organisations WTO/WB/ IMF		EU		
	2003	2005	2003	2005	NATO 2005
Better for Ukraine to					
be a member ...	% support for membership – remain completely independent				
Ukrainian speakers	+13	+16	+7	+12	−32
Russian speakers	+27	−2	+26	−8	−63

Note: Per cent of all respondents. Per cents giving other/mixed/'don't know' responses not shown.

Russian speakers net support for membership declined (from a high base) by 32 per cent.

As we found on attitudes towards foreign participation in protests, so it was on attitudes towards Ukraine's participation in international organisations: the more urban, better educated and more naturally cosmopolitan Russian speakers – the natural globalisers – had turned against international involvement; and this time more dramatically: instead of merely coming into line with the more parochial Ukrainian speakers, on membership of international organisations Russian speakers very clearly switched sides. They differed as much or more from Ukrainian speakers in 2005 as in 2003 – but in the opposite direction.

Swapping places on attitudes towards foreigners In 2003 the more cosmopolitan Russian speakers had been far more favourable than the more parochial and nationalist Ukrainian speakers towards foreigners in general (19 per cent more), especially towards Russians (30 per cent more), but also towards westerners (13 per cent more).

After the revolution, Russian speakers just about maintained their previously favourable attitude towards foreigners in general, while Ukrainian speakers became 30 per cent more favourable; so Ukrainian speakers switched from being much less warm (than Russian speakers) towards foreigners in general, to being more. But Ukrainian speakers warmed to Russians as well as westerners, so they continued to feel warmer towards Russians than towards Poles or westerners – more evidence that rejecting the Kremlin's candidate for President was not the same as rejecting Russian people.

Table 7.18. *Swapping places on attitudes towards foreigners-as-people*

	Ukraine public						
	Foreigners (unspecified) % good–bad for Ukraine		From Russia % good–bad for Ukraine		From West % good–bad for Ukraine		From Poland % good–bad for Ukraine
	2003	2005	2003	2005	2003	2005	2005
Ukrainian speakers	38	68	50	65	43	59	61
Russian speakers	57	56	80	75	56	43	36

It was a complex picture. Attitudes were polarised before the Orange Revolution and polarisation changed more because Ukrainian speakers became much less parochial than because Russian-speakers became slightly more parochial. In terms of attitudes towards foreigners-as-people, sharply divergent trends inverted the parochialism of Ukrainian and Russian speakers, but reduced rather than increased the scale of the polarisation of attitudes between them.

Ukrainian and Russian speakers did not differ much on liking or disliking foreign films and TV, either before or after the revolution. Both were evenly split on attitudes towards 'foreign' or 'western' TV and films but overwhelmingly favourable towards 'Russian' TV and films. Even after the revolution, although net approval for 'Russian' TV and films ran at 84 per cent among Russian speakers, it was almost as high (74 per cent) among Ukrainian speakers.

Among Ukrainian speakers, perceptions of American threats to the culture and territory of Ukraine were low and declined slightly; among Russian speakers they were always higher, and they increased. After the revolution Russian speakers were over twice as likely as Ukrainian speakers to cite the US as a cultural threat (30 per cent compared with 13 per cent), and over four times as likely to cite the US as a territorial threat (25 per cent compared with 6 per cent). Conversely, perceptions of Russian threats to territory of Ukraine were very low but increased slightly more among Ukrainian speakers (by 4 per cent) than among Russian speakers (by 2 per cent) – though perceptions of Russian threats to Ukrainian culture remained exceedingly low, even among Ukrainian speakers. So perceptions of American threats became much more polarised than perceptions of Russian threats.

Table 7.19. *Polarising perceptions of threats from the US*

	Ukraine public	
	2003 %	2005 %
Is there any particular country ...		
... whose culture we should try really hard to keep out of Ukraine? US		
Ukrainian speakers	15	13
Russian speakers	22	30
... which threatens our national territory at the present time? US		
Ukrainian speakers	8	6
Russian speakers	12	25
... whose culture we should try really hard to keep out of Ukraine? Russia		
Ukrainian speakers	4	4
Russian speakers	0	0
... which threatens our national territory at the present time? Russia		
Ukrainian speakers	7	11
Russian speakers	1	3

Note: Per cent of all respondents. Per cents giving other/mixed/'don't know' responses not shown.

Swapping places on attitudes to marketisation and opening up By a margin of 23 per cent Ukrainian speakers felt Ukraine should move closer to the West in terms of 'trade and international affairs'; while by a similar margin (27 per cent) of Russian speakers felt Ukraine should move closer towards Russia.

Both Ukrainian and Russian speakers' opinion shifted in favour of the market economy: towards feeling the market economy created more prosperity, towards feeling it was less unfair, and towards feeling it was 'the only way'. But Ukrainian speakers shifted more than Russian speakers on all three indicators. In 2003 Russian speakers were generally more favourable than Ukrainian speakers towards the market; but by 2005 they were generally less favourable than Ukrainian speakers. Yet the degree of polarisation between Ukrainian speakers and Russian speakers did not change: they just swapped places on the market economy.

The same trends were evident on attitudes towards opening up the economy to world markets. Ukrainian speakers shifted towards feeling the open economy had 'more advantages', was 'good', and was indeed the 'only way to go', while Russian speakers shifted in the opposite direction. Again, opinion was not much more polarised in 2005 than 2003. Ukrainian and Russian speakers had again swapped places on all three

Table 7.20. *Swapping places on the market economy*

	Ukraine public	
	2003	2005
Market economy makes Ukraine more or less prosperous ...		
	% more – less	% more – less
Ukrainian speakers	+1	+33
Russian speakers	+18	+26
Market economy in Ukraine is fair or unfair ...		
	% fair – unfair	% fair – unfair
Ukrainian speakers	−59	−40
Russian speakers	−64	−57
For Ukraine ... **Market economy is the only way to go**		
	%	%
Ukrainian speakers	26	43
Russian speakers	32	37

Table 7.21. *Swapping places on opening up*

	Ukraine public	
	2003	2005
	% more advantages – disadvantages	% more advantages – disadvantages
Ukrainian speakers	+14	+26
Russian speakers	+21	+14
	% good – bad	% good – bad
Ukrainian speakers	+33	+37
Russian speakers	+40	+22
	% only way	% only way
Ukrainian speakers	32	46
Russian speakers	39	34

indicators: Russian speakers had been the most favourable towards an open economy in 2003, but it was the Ukrainian speakers that most favoured an open economy after the revolution.

7.4   Conclusions

Apart from significantly stronger anti-Americanism and a social-democratic concern to help globalisation-losers in the North, we could find little evidence of a simple historical persistence-legacy dividing public opinion in North and South Vietnam. Perhaps in a youthful society it was all too long ago, but there was some evidence of an inverse or reactive-legacy pattern. It was Northerners not Southerners who were more inclined to say the market economy brought prosperity and that the market economy was fair. It was Northerners, not Southerners who were more inclined to say that opening up was 'the only way to go'; and Southerners, not Northerners who were more inclined to back subsidies and protection for out-of-date businesses. Despite their enthusiasm for the Doi Moi policies of opening up, it was Northerners who were more inclined to say that the benefits of opening up had gone to officials, even 'high' officials, rather than ordinary people.

It was true that Southerners, by objective indicators, were more affluent and more cosmopolitan in terms of speaking foreign languages, meeting foreign people, accepting immigrant workers, and liking foreign brands. But Northerners had the enthusiasm of new participants in a more open market economy and more confidence in the goodwill of international economic organisations. Objectively, Northerners were not the most prosperous but they were the ones who were most likely to feel their living standards were improving as Vietnam opened up, and it was Northerners who could draw a simple contrast between privation under classic communism and rapidly rising prosperity under Doi Moi. With their more chequered past, Southerners could not draw such a simple contrast. In a complex sense, legacy did perhaps matter, but not in the simple sense of continuity. The Northern public, with the least experience of an open market regime, was the most enthusiastic about it.

In Ukraine, regime change occurred during our study rather than three decades earlier. Its impact was wide-ranging, powerful and in some respects probably short-lived. Apart from an explosion of post-revolution euphoria, much of its impact was to change the relationship between the attitudes of Russian and Ukrainian speakers, rather than to change Ukrainian public opinion as a whole. But a simple polarisation model of the impact of the Orange Revolution proves as misleading as a simple continuity-based legacy model in Vietnam.

By far the largest changes were in public approval of the government, satisfaction with the way things were going in the country, and hopes for future living standards. This was typical post-election euphoria, merely magnified in a post-revolution context. That euphoria affected both Russian and Ukrainian speakers and, to varying degrees, every aspect of policy and perception, though most of all it affected the public's as-yet-untested hopes and expectations for the future. Post-revolution euphoria, like more normal post-election euphoria, could be expected to evaporate quite quickly.

Though it may have been cause rather than consequence, public support for the market economy was much greater in 2005 than 2003, though Ukrainians still complained in large numbers that they did not have a real market economy. Perhaps more obviously a consequence of the Orange Revolution, there was a rise in the legitimacy accorded to robust methods such as demonstrations, go-slows, and especially strikes as weapons of public protest. But there was an even sharper rise in public opposition to the participation of foreigners in protests within Ukraine, which was the more remarkable because attitudes towards foreigners themselves generally improved. It was specifically foreign involvement in protest that became increasingly unpopular. Conversely, there was declining support for Ukraine itself getting into foreign entanglements with international trade organisations, the EU, NATO or even the UN.

Polarisation between Russian and Ukrainian speakers could cancel out in the aggregate. Much of the commentary on the Orange Revolution implied a simple model of polarisation in which ethnic Russians and ethnic Ukrainians moved in opposite directions and drew apart into opposing camps. We found strong evidence of polarised trends between Russian and Ukrainian speakers (though language mattered more than ethnic identity or geographic region). But we did not find much evidence for such a simple and dangerously misleading model of polarisation.

First, we frequently found that Russian and Ukrainian speakers moved in the same direction though by different amounts, indicating greater or lesser sensitivity rather than opposing perspectives. Second, and most significantly, we frequently found that Russian and Ukrainian speakers moved in opposite directions, but towards each other rather than away from each other – so that, paradoxically, they ended up closer together, or no further apart than before, though often swapping places and taking opposite positions.

In general 'swapping places' occurred because Ukrainian speakers, who had been more parochial, warmed towards the outside world; while at the same time Russian speakers, who had been more cosmopolitan, cooled towards the outside world, especially towards the West. Swapping places has very different implications from those of the simple polarisation model. It means moving in different directions without ending up very far apart, without ending up in extreme positions, and without ending up in opposing camps.

On attitudes towards the Kuchma regime, or satisfaction with the way things were going for the country, Russian and Ukrainian speakers started from a common position in 2003 but moved in different directions: the simple polarisation model applied in this case. But on attitudes towards foreign participation in local protests, Russian and Ukrainian speakers started from different positions in 2003 but converged on a common position as Russian speakers especially moved towards a less cosmopolitan position. On attitudes towards joining international organisations, Russian and Ukrainian speakers maintained much the same distance between them while swapping positions – as they also did on attitudes towards marketisation and opening up. Wherever Russian and Ukrainian speakers swapped positions, the Russian speakers had been the more cosmopolitan (and pro-market) of the two in 2003, but the less so in 2005. So even when trends were opposed, they did not necessarily polarise Russian and Ukrainian speakers into extreme camps.

Throughout earlier chapters, Ukraine stood out as the country that had experienced the most severe economic decline and where the state was so weak that many of its citizens had come to regard the state as more of a burden than a benefit. So we might ask how far the impact of the Orange Revolution altered Ukraine's place in our international comparisons. While Ukrainians had been the most critical of their government in 2003, their post-election euphoria moved them up from bottom place to be second only to the Vietnamese (of 2003) in terms of support for their (new) 'government and its policies', their more diffuse satisfaction with 'the way things are going for the country', their expectations about future living standards in their country, and even their sense that the economy was already improving.

Yet at the same time, their euphoria had much less impact on their perceptions of the trends in their own family's circumstances: it left Ukrainians in bottom place (though now joint third) in terms of perceptions of trends in family income. And despite some decline in dissatisfaction, it left Ukrainians far more dissatisfied about 'the way things are going for my family' than people in any other country.

Post-revolution euphoria was strongly focused on the newly installed government and it was likely to be as transient as post-election euphoria anywhere. Perceptions that problems of crime and corruption were on their way to a solution must have been sharply damaged when President Yushchenko sacked his new government alleging that it too was corrupt (*Kyiv Post*, 8 September 2005).

Yet there were smaller, but potentially more enduring and significant changes in Ukrainian attitudes towards the market economy, the open economy, foreigners and particularly the participation of foreigners in Ukrainian protest action. Their moderately large move towards support for a market economy pushed them up the rankings, though their smaller move towards an open economy left their ranking unchanged. In 2003, Ukrainans were the least favourable to being a member either of international organisations like the WTO, World Bank or IMF, or of regional organisations like the EU; and their support for both dropped further in 2005, leaving them very firmly in fourth place on both. In 2003, Ukrainians were already second only to the Vietnamese in their sense that their culture remained strong. They felt that even more after the Orange Revolution and came closer to the Vietnamese, but still clearly in second place. They became rather more favourable towards foreigners in general but remained firmly in third place in the rankings. They warmed enough towards foreign films and TV to push them up from fourth to third place, but the basic pattern remained one of a majority of East Asians liking foreign films and TV, while East Europeans were almost evenly split between liking and disliking them.

At the same time Ukrainians became much less favourable than before towards foreigners participating in Ukrainian protest actions. They slipped from a clear third to a very clear fourth in the international rankings. On support for strike action against an international company causing serious local problems Ukrainians had been in clear second place in 2003; but after the Orange Revolution the increase in their support for strikes raised them to first equal. Ukrainians were already, by a small margin, the most favourable to protest demonstrations even in 2003; and after the Orange Revolution their support for demonstrations increased still further to put them even more clearly in top place. Ukrainians were already by far the most favourable to 'go slows' as a method of protest even in 2003; and after the Orange Revolution they were not merely still in top place, but quite outstanding in their support for 'go slows'. (Ukrainians were already in top place on support for sabotage through 'bad work' even in 2003; and after the Orange Revolution their support for it increased still further.)

Overall, the Orange Revolution transformed the attitudes of Ukrainians as-a-whole towards their government if only because the government changed and if only for a brief post-election honeymoon period. But in most other respects, its impact on international rankings was to make Ukrainians as-a-whole even more distinctive on the issues and attitudes where they already held distinctive views. So despite its significant impact on the structure of public opinion within Ukraine, it does not alter the basic picture of Ukraine in comparison with other countries that emerged from previous chapters. In that respect, our original findings survived a severe test remarkably well.

8 The extent, nature, causes and consequences of public discontent

At the start, we posed four broad questions about globalisation and its discontents, in particular about public discontent in the developing or transitional countries of East Asia and East Europe:

- How much discontent?
- What was the nature of that discontent?
- What were the causes of discontent?
- What were the consequences of discontent?

We now return to those questions, and review the evidence.

8.1   The extent of discontent

Like United Nations Development Programme (UNDP) analysts, the public in our four countries felt that recent changes had produced sharply increasing, and unjustifiable, inequalities. They felt the beneficiaries of recent changes had been rich countries, foreigners, and local officials or businessmen, rather than ordinary local people. Except in Vietnam, they felt the local beneficiaries had been those with more power and contacts rather than those with more skill, education or even luck. They felt crime, corruption, pollution and environmental damage were increasing; and while they might claim their national culture was increasingly respected abroad they nonetheless felt their traditional way of life was threatened. Except, once again, in Vietnam, they thought the economy had declined though they expect improved living standards in the future.

The public generally blamed adverse trends on local, internal influences rather than on foreign influences, and the extent of public discontent with globalisation was limited. With respect to attitudes towards the market economy or economic openness, the public were 'critical supporters', even 'highly critical supporters', but supporters nonetheless. Despite recognising all the downsides of recent economic changes and feeling that greater benefits had gone to others, a majority overall remained in favour of rapid development. In the two richer countries, there was a small majority against rapid development, but that was outweighed by a much larger majority in the two poorer countries that favoured rapid development. Despite feeling that a market economy was unfair, the majority overall thought markets, the 'market mechanism' or 'marketisation' increased national prosperity in their country. Only the Vietnamese (by a large margin) thought the market economy was fair, but only the Czechs (by a small margin) thought it made them less prosperous. Despite recognising the injustices and the disadvantages, especially the threat to national culture, caused by opening up the economy to global trade and business, a very large majority in every country said opening up was 'good rather than bad' for their country and had 'more advantages than disadvantages'. The public were not discontent with the principle of globalisation: on the contrary, they supported it.

General public commitment to an open economy was combined with support for protecting agriculture, 'small businesses', or their national 'way of life', however. Attitudes towards protecting specific 'deserving' industries did not correlate at all well with general attitudes towards the principle of an open economy. In the public mind, protecting agriculture and small, local businesses, and even, for a short period while they modernised, 'obsolete' businesses, were exceptions to the general rule of openness. Special protection for them was regarded as an integral part of support for a generally more open economy. The public saw a role for government not only in encouraging development by implementing a domestic market and opening up to the world, but also in helping the casualties of globalisation. The methods the public proposed for helping these casualties – taxing winners to provide funds to help losers, and offering losers retraining rather than welfare payments – were in general designed to facilitate participation in a more open economy rather than to retreat from openness. Opening up might have more advantages than disadvantages but the disadvantages were significant and the public felt the state should act to offset the disadvantages while retaining the advantages.

Nonetheless it would be wrong to equate globalisation with public discontent. The public in our developing and transitional countries were strongly in favour of globalisation despite their discontents.

8.2   The nature of discontent

What was the nature of that discontent? Discontent with the principle of marketisation and opening up; or with the implementation? Discontent with the inequality and injustice of markets; or with their failure to deliver prosperity? Discontent with economic openness or with cultural openness? Discontent with the influx of consumer-culture or with the erosion of national identity? Discontent with too much economic openness or with too little? And who were the targets of public discontent: who got the blame?

In East Europe where discontent with markets was significantly greater than in East Asia, a quarter of the public responded to questions about the market economy by volunteering the (unlisted) answer that they had 'no real market here'. They accused politicians and officials of distorting the market for personal gain, even preventing foreign investment unless they stood to gain personally. From the focus group discussions it is clear that the public were sensitive to the difference between principle and practice, that they favoured the principle but were discontent with the practice. More generally, the public criticised marketisation for being 'unfair' but praised it for increasing prosperity.

The public criticised opening up most of all for its impact on their national culture rather than for any adverse economic impact. They had scant concern about the influx of foreign consumer-culture – foreign food, clothes, films and TV: the most visible aspects of foreign culture. Indeed they had mixed views about foreign brands but tended to like rather than dislike foreign media – films and TV. But they both valued and feared for their national language and for traditional patterns of social behaviour – for 'identity culture' rather than 'consumer culture'.

On the other hand, they praised opening up for its economic impact. A large majority everywhere said opening up had had a good effect on the availability of good-paying jobs. Also, except in the Czech Republic where opinion was divided (and slightly negative), a large majority said opening up had had a good effect on working conditions as well as on the pay of ordinary workers. (Czechs more than others resented the increased discipline that went with better pay.) Even on the gap between rich and poor, opening up was less criticised than internal marketisation. Indeed, in Ukraine, opening up was seen as 'good' for the gap between rich and poor while marketisation was almost unanimously regarded as 'unfair'. For Ukrainians especially, opening up presented new solutions to internal problems of crime, corruption, mismanagement and even inequality. Their criticism focused on too *little* real opening up rather than too much.

On matters like pollution, a majority felt their country should accept international standards. More generally, most felt their country had at least 'something' to learn from other countries. Almost half thought they had 'a lot' to learn from foreign countries in economic and business affairs, though somewhat less in political affairs, and a lot less in social and family affairs.

Overall, a majority of the public thought foreign companies 'helped' rather than 'exploited' their country. Czechs felt exploited and Ukrainians were divided, but a large majority of Koreans and a very large majority of Vietnamese felt foreign companies 'helped'. Ironically, public perceptions of international organisations (driven as they are by the national interests of the powerful countries within them) were less positive than public perceptions of foreign and international companies driven by profit-seeking. Nonetheless, only one-fifth of the public thought it better to be 'completely independent' rather than join either international organisations 'like the World Trade Organisation (WTO), World Bank or International Monetary Fund (IMF)' or regional organisations 'like the European Union (EU) or Association of South-East Asian Nations (ASEAN)'. They were in favour of joining these organisations even though they felt they could not rely on their country being fairly treated by them.

8.3   The causes of discontent

What were the causes of discontent? What made some publics, or some individuals within the public, more discontent than others? Did education encourage support for opening up? Or nationalism discourage it? Did contact with foreigners make the public more or less favourable towards opening up? In particular, what aspects of public criticism really translated into personal discontent? Which of the acknowledged faults of markets or openness really hurt? And which were just a price that had to be paid – recognised, acknowledged, but inconsequential? Which models of discontent provided the best explanation of public discontents: one of the many variants of a 'winners and losers' model; or some variant of a 'justice and injustice model'; a self-interested or an altruistic model? Did it matter whether the public thought the benefits of globalisation went to the deserving or the undeserving, to ordinary people, to state officials, to local businessmen, or to foreigners?

What was the legacy of history, long-term or short-term – the long-term impact of so-called 'Asian values'; the very immediate impact of the Orange Revolution in Ukraine; the more medium-term impact of varying lengths of Communist rule; or the varying experience of growth in East Asia and chaos, stagnation or decline in East Europe as both moved towards a more market economy?

We outlined a range of possible explanatory models of discontent in Chapter 1, including multiple versions of winners and losers models, justice or fairness models, ideology or nationalist models, socio-economic and cosmopolitan-contact models, governing-elite models, and regional or legacy models.

'The way things are going' Greater or lesser recognition of the downsides of recent change (growing inequality, crime and corruption, pollution, or benefits going to those with contacts and so on) did not have much impact on discontent with 'the way things are going', nor on support for rapid development. They were indeed recognised but inconsequential. Instead, our analysis shows that winners and losers models perform particularly well as explanations of public support for development or satisfaction with 'the way things are going'. But it is very much bespoke rather than off-the-peg versions that matter. No single version of a winners and losers model fits all.

In particular a personal or *family version* of a winners and losers model, based on trends in family income or living standards, explains satisfaction or discontent with 'the way things are going for my family' – but only that. The best explanation of public satisfaction or discontent with 'the way things are going for the country' is not a personal winners and losers model, but a retrospective national version, based on perceptions of recent growth in the national economy, not on changes in personal or family circumstances (nor on future expectations for the economy).

The market economy Perceptions that a market economy delivers prosperity – or is 'fair' – are also best explained by a retrospective national version of a winners and losers model, based on perceptions of recent growth in the national economy. But an international justice model, based on perceptions of whether international companies do more to 'help' or 'exploit' the country, has a secondary impact on attitudes towards whether a market economy delivers prosperity and fairness. A domestic justice model, based on perceptions of whether the benefits have gone to those with skill, education and luck or to those with more power, contacts or corruption, has a secondary impact on perceptions of market fairness, though very little impact on perceptions that the market economy delivers prosperity.

Economic openness A national version of the winners and losers model, based on trends in the national economy, is also one important explanation of support for opening up the economy – though not the most important. The most important explanation of public support for opening up is the international justice model, based on perceptions of whether international companies do more to 'help' or 'exploit' the country.

Altruistic versus selfish Altruistic versions of winners and losers models are never important. Concern for the casualties of globalisation, though often expressed, never has much impact. Altruistic versions of winners and losers models are admirable but ineffective. The public do recognise and lament the social and national injustices, as well as the pollution and corruption associated with markets, opening up and development. But although they express such concern, it has little impact on their satisfaction with 'the way things are going' either for their family or their country, or on their support for development. What matters most at any level of perspective – family, national, or international – is always being a winner rather than being concerned for the losers. The focus may switch from 'economic gains or losses for my family', to 'economic gains or losses for my country', or even to 'my country in relation to other countries' but, whatever the level, it is always a selfish model rather than the altruistic model that works best – rather than a model based on concern about general inequalities within the country or between countries.

Even the power of the international justice model is not evidence of altruism so much as evidence of public reactions to feelings of unfair and unjust treatment of 'my country' by foreign companies, powerful countries or international organisations. Justice models, like winners and losers models, can be selfish as well as altruistic. So even though the justice model echoes the arguments of western critics of globalisation, it lacks the altruistic character of much western criticism. Altruistic models must find their place in studies of anti-globalisation protestors in affluent societies.

Cultural openness Attitudes towards cultural protection, however, do not depend upon losers, even cultural losers, looking for protection. A model based on cultural fright does not work. Indeed, in some countries it is the optimists about the strength of their national culture that are the most inclined to back cultural protection. Instead support for cultural protection is best explained by a cultural nationalist model based on personal respect for national culture, on national culture being important 'to me personally', rather than on perceptions that it is in decline. Conversely, although the threat to national culture is viewed as the main disadvantage of opening up the economy, personal commitment to the national culture does not have much impact on attitudes towards opening up the economy. The public reaction is not to reject the economic benefits of opening up but to put in place special measures to protect national culture itself from the impact of opening up the economy.

Legacy/regional models Global-regional or country-specific legacy models also have an important independent impact. Satisfaction with 'the way things are going' for the family is exceptionally high in East Asia (or exceptionally low in East Europe) even after taking personal circumstances into account. Public support for rapid development is exceptionally low in more prosperous countries (though within countries it runs higher among those with higher incomes – so richer people and poorer countries are united in their tendency to support rapid development). Public support for increasing the pace of development is exceptionally high in stagnating or declining East Europe (or, equivalently, exceptionally low in faster-developing East Asia). That is completely inconsistent with a long-term Asian values model as proposed by Lee Kuan Yew (the 'sign' is wrong), but it is consistent with an East European short-term legacy of stagnation, decline and gloom.

Although statistically there is no difference between highlighting public opinion in East Europe rather than East Asia as the exception, it is easier to grasp the significance of the dismal economic record in East Europe than to not merely deny, but actually invert, Lee Kuan Yew's Asian values model (Zakaria 1994). The critical legacy here is post-communist stagnation and decline, not centuries of Asian values.

We also explored the impact of legacy models, based on the correlation between regime and region, within Vietnam and Ukraine. Surprisingly perhaps we found no evidence that the North Vietnamese were more reluctant converts to globalisation than the South Vietnamese. Northerners retained a greater suspicion of the US as both a territorial and a cultural threat, but they embraced the policies of marketisation and opening up at least as much as Southerners, indeed more so. The imprint of the longer communist legacy in the North was visible in a social-democratic concern for the casualties of globalisation – who were to be helped primarily by retraining to fit them to compete in the marketplace, however. There was also some evidence of an inverse legacy: Northerners who had the least experience of markets and openness were the most enthusiastic about the transformation it had brought to their lives.

In the aftermath of the Orange Revolution in Ukraine we found evidence of contrasting trends of opinion in East and West Ukraine, and particularly between Russian speakers and Ukrainian speakers. Surprisingly, these contrasting trends did *not* produce a polarisation of attitudes towards marketisation or opening up (though they did produce a polarisation of attitudes towards the old and new regimes). That was because the better educated, better connected, and generally more cosmopolitan Russian speakers had been more pro-market and more pro-globalisation before the Orange Revolution. After the revolution, the Ukrainian speakers became the more pro-market and pro-globalisation. By moving in different directions, the two ethno-linguistic groups moved towards the centre and even beyond the centre, thereby 'swapping places' rather than diverging to the extremes. On attitudes towards markets and openness, the Orange Revolution therefore left ethno-linguistic divisions in Ukraine no greater than before, despite the sharp change in the structure of opinion.

Governing-elite models Finally, to explain the difference between the attitudes of the public and officials towards marketisation and opening up, we considered two 'governing elite' models: a vanguard model and a conspiracy model. Both assumed that officials would be more favourable towards globalisation than their publics, but the 'vanguard' model pictured officials as public servants, more far-sighted than the public itself yet still committed to the public interest, while the conspiracy model pictured officials as simply self-serving. Empirically, the two models differed only in degree: but as public allegations against officials increased, as officials confessed to greater benefits, and as officials became more out-of-touch with their publics and less sympathetic towards the casualties of globalisation, then the 'conspiracy' model became a better description than the 'vanguard' model of the role of officials or the state.

We found an important difference between the East European countries and the East Asian: a close agreement between the attitudes of public and officials in East Asia, especially Vietnam; but a much wider difference in East Europe, especially in Ukraine. East European officials had done much better out of recent changes than their publics, and where the attitudes of East European officials differed most from their publics they always took a harder, less sympathetic line towards the casualties of globalisation. So the vanguard model fits best in East Asia, and the conspiracy model best in East Europe.

8.4   The consequences of discontent

What were the consequences of discontent? How did the public feel that discontent should be expressed? Only by those who were directly affected, or by sympathisers at home or abroad? By strictly peaceful methods or, as Monbiot reluctantly argued, by whatever had most effect? Why did some publics, or some individuals within the public, insist on strictly peaceful methods of protest while others did not? Did the public see the state as the solution to their discontents or as the problem? How did public discontent with markets, openness, and development affect public support for governments and regimes?

Support for the government Support for the government and its policies is best explained by a combination of the national winners and losers model (based on perceptions of recent growth in the national economy) and a cultural perceptions model (based on perceptions of increasing respect for the national culture). Overall both are about equally important, and while the economic model is rather more important in some countries, the cultural model is more important in others. Governments are held responsible for both the national economy and the respect accorded the national culture. Or, to put it the other way round, governments can win public favour by protecting and reinforcing the national culture, irrespective of their economic performance. The cultural dimension is therefore a potential resource for globalising governments, rather than a problem.

Even after taking into account the impact of both the national winners and losers and the cultural perceptions models, support for government policies ran much higher in East Asia than in East Europe. Judging by the focus group criticisms of officials as self-serving, that regional difference probably reflected the greater alienation between the public and officials in East Europe, especially Ukraine. That, in turn, must have helped to provide a basis for the subsequent Orange Revolution.

Acceptable forms of protest There was almost universal support for protest of some kind against international companies that caused serious local problems, or against international organisations (such as the WTO, IMF or World Bank) whose policies damaged poorer countries. For most of the public, such circumstances justified protest of some kind. The issues for most people were not therefore about protest itself, but about acceptable methods of protest, and about acceptable participation in protest.

Disorderly, disruptive or violent methods of protest were rejected by a majority. Yet a significant minority, rising to a majority within Ukraine (and increasing still further after the success of the Orange Revolution), did feel such methods were justified. Support for disorderly or violent protest varied with attitudes towards globalisation itself. It was best explained by an international justice model. Those who felt that opening up their economy had benefited other countries more than their own, and especially those that felt foreign companies exploited rather than helped their country, were more willing to back the use of relatively robust methods when some kind of protest was appropriate. Once again legacy or 'country' effects were important: Ukrainians were uniquely favourable to robust protest; and conversely, although the Vietnamese were not specially reluctant to support robust protest in principle, they were very reluctant to back any specific methods of robust protest when these were put to them explicitly.

A majority would accept the participation of sympathetic foreigners in protests, or even support calling for foreign help. In contrast to the basis of support for robust protest which correlated best with adverse perceptions of foreign companies, support for foreign participation correlated best with positive perceptions of foreigners-as-people and opposition with simple xenophobia rather than with indicators of international justice.

Everywhere we found evidence that the public wanted a strong and effective state that would encourage though not command (nor itself undertake) economic development; but a state that would minimise and offset the downsides of markets, opening up, and even development itself; and a state that would be a powerful advocate of the national interest in the international arena, especially within international organisations that could not be relied upon to treat developing or transitional countries fairly.

Globalisation has changed the role of the state but has made it no less important in the minds of the public. Unfortunately, especially in East Europe, the public judged the state had failed to meet these demands. For Czechs, that was because Europe had a range of supranational institutions and the Czech Republic was too small and too weak to stay out. For Ukrainians, the problems of the state were more home-grown: Ukrainian participants in focus groups even spoke up to defend the actions of international organisations against their own government. But in East Asia, the public looked towards greater internationalism, not supranationalism, and they had much more confidence in the competence of their state.

Overall, a clutch of egocentric winners and losers models (but *not* primarily based on personal gains and losses, however), a self-interested international justice model, a positive rather than a negative cultural model (based on the importance of national culture, not its decay), a short-term economic legacy model, and an officials-as-conspiracy model, explain most of what can be explained about the causes and consequences of attitudes towards marketisation, opening up the economy, and the role and performance of the state in an era of globalisation.

The simplicity of the 'framework for analysis' that we introduced in Chapter 1 has been somewhat obscured by the complexity of reality. But we have found a chain of causation that runs from (i) high income, to (ii) improving family living standards, to (iii) perceptions of an improving national economy, and thence to (iv) satisfaction with 'the way things are going for the country', to support for the market economy, and to support for the 'government and its policies'. The links in that chain are not so strong that the earlier elements determine the final ones, however. Irrespective of whether they were based on personal success or not, perceptions that the national economy was improving had a strong impact on satisfaction, support for the market, and support for the government. Conversely, whatever the basis for perceptions that the economy was not progressing well, such perceptions had a strong impact on discontent with 'the way things are going', with the market economy, and with government. What is more surprising is that all kinds of other specific complaints and discontent – with crime, corruption, inequality or pollution, for example – seem to have so little impact on overall discontent with 'the way things are going', with the market economy, or with government.

This chain of causation has rather less impact on public support for opening up the economy, still less on demands for cultural protection. There is another chain of causation that runs from (i) perceptions of international justice, especially perceptions that foreign companies generally help rather than exploit the country, to (ii) public support for opening up, and to public insistence that when particular circumstances justify protest (against foreign companies that are bad employers or polluting the environment), that protest should be strictly peaceful. Similarly, generally positive perceptions of foreigners lead to increased public support for welcoming foreign participation when circumstances justify protests. Xenophobia simultaneously increased support for violent protest and reduced support for welcoming the participation of foreign sympathisers.

We did not find evidence for our hypothesised chain of causation from (i) cultural fright, to (ii) demands for cultural protection, to (iii) opposition to opening up the economy. Instead we found a chain of causation that ran from (i) positive personal commitment to culture (not cultural fright), to (ii) demands for specifically cultural protection to offset the impact of opening up on culture, and thence, to (iii) support for governments whose actions had increased respect for the national culture. So national culture was not a problem for globalising governments, but a resource.

Perceptions of national economic trends directly affected government support as well as support for a market economy; what mattered most was the increasing prosperity not the means by which it was achieved. Perceptions of trends in respect for the national culture directly affected government support without at all affecting support for opening up.

Opening up was more popular than the (internal) market economy. We have argued that the public saw opening up as a Faustian bargain, sufficiently advantageous in economic terms to outweigh the acknowledged disadvantages in cultural terms. But of course they welcomed action by government to reduce those cultural disadvantages while retaining the economic advantages. So perceptions of increasing respect for the national culture increased support for the government, while perceptions of declining respect for culture did not erode support for opening up.

Explaining variations in public attitudes, or relationships between them, is not everything. We are also struck by the evidence of coherent dissonance: the way that publics (and individuals within the public) combine harsh criticism of development, of markets, and of an open economy with simultaneous support; the way they combine economic openness with the assertion of national identity and culture; the way they combine near universal support for protest against the injustices of globalisation with a fierce insistence on non-destructive, peaceful protest; the way they combine harsh criticism of international organisations with a complete refusal to withdraw from them; and the way they combine support for participating in globalisation with a strong emphasis on the role of the state. In each case, these are not regarded as alternatives, still less as contradictions, but as things that must be addressed simultaneously, taken forward together.

Thus it seems extremely unlikely that globalisation will be derailed by its discontents triggering instability in developing countries – especially if governments provide help to the losers, especially retraining to help them compete in the market, and connect with their publics by encouraging internal and external respect for national culture. The public in developing or transitional countries, such as those in our study, want globalisation despite their discontent with its downsides. The anti-globalisation protesters in the West had no option but to re-focus on international justice if they did not wish to be rejected as much by the developing world as the developed. And steps by the G8 towards providing greater international justice should be taken for positive rather than negative reasons, more as a means to reinforce and consolidate existing support for globalisation in developing countries than to ward off the imminent danger of an anti-globalisation reaction in these countries. If there is another round of truly anti-globalisation reaction and protest it is far more likely to be in the West than in developing countries, and more likely to be overtly self-interested than altruistic.

References

Alesina, A. and Perotti, R. 1996. Income distribution, political instability and investment. *European Economic Review*, 40:6: 1203–28

Appadurai, A. 1990. Disjuncture and difference in the global cultural economy. *Theory, Culture and Society*, 7: 295–310

Barnes, S. H. and Kaase, M. (eds.) 1979. *Political Action*, London: Sage

Bauman, Z. 1993. *Postmodern Ethics*, Oxford: Blackwell

Bauman, Z. 1997. *Postmodernity and its Discontents*, Cambridge: Polity

Bauman, Z. 1998. *Globalization: the Human Consequences*, Cambridge: Polity

Baxandall, P. 2003. Postcommunist unemployment politics, in Ekiert, G. and Hanson, S. E. (eds.) *Capitalism and Democracy in Central and Eastern Europe. Assessing the Legacy of Communist Rule*, pp. 248–88, Cambridge: Cambridge University Press

Beynon, J. and Dunkerley, D. (eds.) 2000. *Globalization: the Reader*, London: Athlone Press

Bhagwati, J. N. 2002. Coping with antiglobalization. *Foreign Affairs*, 81:1: 2–7 Jan/Feb

Bhagwati, J. N. 2004. *In Defense of Globalization*, Oxford: Oxford University Press

Brady, H. E. and Collier D. (eds.) 2004. *Rethinking Social Inquiry: Diverse Tools, Shared Standards*, Oxford: Rowman and Littlefield

Bursens, P. and Sinardet, D. 2003. *The Anti-globalisation Movement and International Institutions*, European Consortium for Political Research (ECPR) conference paper, Marburg, September

Centre for Economic and Policy Research (CEPR) 2001. *The Scorecard on Globalization 1980–2000: Twenty Years of Diminished Progress*, www.cepr.net or World Development Movement www.wdm.org.uk, July

Chaney, D. C. 1996. *Lifestyles*, London: Routledge

Chaney, D. C. 2000. From ways of life to lifestyle: rethinking culture as ideology and sensibility, in Lull, J. (ed.) *Culture in the Communication Age*, pp. 75–87, London: Routledge

Chang, C. 2004. How American culture correlates the process of globalization. *Asian EFL Journal*, 6:3

Chang, H. J. 2002. *Kicking Away the Ladder – Development Strategy in Historical Perspective*, London: Anthem Press

Chua, A. 2003. *How Exporting Free-Market Democracy Breeds Ethnic Hatred and Global Instability*, New York: Doubleday

Czech Statistical Office 2003. *Statistical Yearbook of the Czech Republic*, www.czso.cz, 22 November

Czech Statistical Office 2004. *Key Macroeconomic Indicators*, www.czso.cz, 30 September

Dalton, R. J., Pham Minh Hac, Pham Thanh Nghi and Nhu-Ngoc T. Ong 2002. Social relations and social capital in Vietnam: findings from the 2001 World Values Survey. *Comparative Sociology*, 1: 369–86

Dollar, D. and Kraay, A. 2000. *Growth is Good for the Poor*, World Bank Development Research Group

Dollar, D. and Kraay, A. 2002. Spreading the wealth. *Foreign Affairs* Jan/Feb, 81:1: 120–33

Ekiert, G. 2003. Patterns of postcommunist transformation in Central and Eastern Europe, in Ekiert, G. and Hanson, S. E. (eds.) *Capitalism and Democracy in Central and Eastern Europe. Assessing the Legacy of Communist Rule*, pp. 89–119, Cambridge: Cambridge University Press

Ekiert, G. and Hanson, S. E. (eds.) 2003. *Capitalism and Democracy in Central and Eastern Europe. Assessing the Legacy of Communist Rule*, Cambridge: Cambridge University Press

Evans, M. 2004. Embedding Market Reform Through Statecraft, Political Studies Association Annual Conference paper, Lincoln, March

Falk, R. 1995. *On Humane Governance: Toward a New Global Politics*, Cambridge: Polity

Featherstone, M. (ed.) 1990. *Global Culture: Nationalism, Globalization and Modernity*, London: Sage

Featherstone, M. 1991. *Consumer Culture and Postmodernism*, London: Sage

Featherstone, M. 1995. *Undoing Culture: Globalization, Postmodernism and Identity*, London: Sage

Featherstone, M., Lash, S. and Robertson, R. 1995. *Global Modernities*, London: Sage

Fraser Institute 2004. *Economic Freedom of the World: 2004 Annual Report*, www.freetheworld.com

Freedom House 2004. *Freedom in the World Comparative Rankings*, www.freedom house.org

Friedman, T. L. 1999. *The Lexus and the Olive Tree: Understanding Globalization*, New York: Ferrar, Straus and Giroux

Galbraith, J. K. 2000. Introduction, in Gills, B. (ed.) *Globalization and the Politics of Resistance*, Houndmills: Palgrave

Garrett, G. 1998. Global markets and national politics: collision course or virtuous circle? *International Organization*, 52:4: 787–824

Giddens, A. 1998. *The Third Way: the Renewal of Social Democracy*, Cambridge: Polity

Gierus, J. 2001. Globalizing the state: a comparison of three regional models. *Central European Political Science Review*, 2:5: 43–54

Gills, B. K. (ed.) 2000. *Globalisation and the Politics of Resistance*, Houndmills: Palgrave

Gold, S. J. 2000. Transnational communities: examining migration in a globally integrated world, in Aulakh, P. S. and Schechter, M. G. (eds.) *Rethinking*

Globalization(s): From Corporate Transnationalism to Local Intervention, pp. 73–90, London: Macmillan

Goodman, A., Johnson, P. and Webb, S. 1997. *Inequality in the UK*, Oxford: Oxford University Press

Gray, J. 1998. *False Dawn: The Delusions of Global Capitalism*, London: Granta

Green, D. and Griffith, M. 2002. Globalization and its discontents. *International Affairs*, 78:1: 49–68

Haass, R. N. and Litan, R. E. 1998. Globalisation and its discontents: navigating the dangers of a tangled world. *Foreign Affairs*, 77:3: 2–6

Hamilton, G. G. 1994. Civilizations and organization of economies, in Smelser, N. J. and Swedberg, R. (eds.) *Handbook of Economic Sociology*, pp. 183–205, Princeton: Princeton University Press

Harasymiw, B. 2002. *Post-Communist Ukraine*, Edmonton and Toronto: Canadian Institute of Ukrainian Studies Press

Held, D. 2004. *Global Covenant: The Social Democratic Alternative to the Washington Consensus*, Cambridge: Polity Press

Held, D. and McGrew, A. 2002. *Globalization/Anti-Globalization*, Cambridge: Polity

Held, D. and McGrew, A. 2003. *The Global Transformations Reader*, Cambridge: Polity Press

Held, D., McGrew, A., Goldblatt, D. and Perraton, J. 2000. *Gobal Transformations: Politics, Economics and Culture*, Cambridge: Polity Press

Henderson, J. and Hulme, D. 2002. Globalisation, economic governance and poverty elimination: insights from East Asia and eastern Europe. Unpubl. fina report, Manchester Business School, Department for International Development

Higgott, R. 2000. The international politics of resentment: some longer-term implications of the economic crisis in east Asia, in Robison, R., Beeson, M., Jayasuriya, K. and Kim, H. (eds.) *Politics and Markets in the Wake of the Asian Financial Crisis*, pp. 261–282, London and New York: Routledge

Hirst, P. Q. and Thompson, G. 1996. *Globalisation in Question: the International Economy and the Possibilities of Governance*, Cambridge: Polity Press

Hobsbawm, E. J. 1991. *Nations and Nationalism since 1780: Programme, Myth, Reality*, Cambridge: Cambridge University Press

Holton, R. J. 1998. *Globalization and the Nation-state*, Basingstoke: Macmillan

Holton, R. 2000. Globalization's cultural consequences. *Annals of the American Academy of Political and Social Science*, 570:1: 140–52

Horsman, M. and Marshall, A. 1994. *After the Nation State: Citizens, Tribalism and the New World Disorder*, London: HarperCollins

Hossain, N. and Moore, M. 2002. Arguing for the poor: elites and poverty in developing countries. *Institute of Development Studies*, working paper 148

Hutton, W. 2002. *The World We're In*, London: Little Brown

International Labour Organosation (ILO) 2004. *A Fair Globalization – Creating Opportunities for All*, www.ilo.org/public/english/fairglobalization

Inglehart, R. and Baker, W. E. 2000. Modernisation, cultural change and the persistence of traditional values. *American Sociological Review*, 25: 22–49

Inglehart, R. and Norris, P. 2003. *Rising Tide: Gender Equality and Cultural Change around the World*, Cambridge: Cambridge University Press

Kaldor, M. 1998. *New and Old Wars*, Cambridge: Polity

Kelly, P. F. 1997, Globalisation, power and the politics of scale in the Philippines. *Geoforum*, 28: 151–71

Kim Dae Jung 1994. Is culture destiny? The myth of Asia's anti-democratic values: a response to Lee Kuan Yew. *Foreign Affairs*, 73:6: 189–194, Nov–Dec

Klak, T. and Myers, G. 1997. The discursive tactics of neoliberal development in small third world countries. *Geoforum*, 28: 133–49

Klingemann, H. D. 1999. Mapping political support in the 1990s: a global analysis, in Norris, P. (ed.) *Critical Citizens: Global Support for Democratic Government*, pp. 31–56, Oxford: Oxford University Press

Kubik, J. 2003. Cultural legacies of state socialism: history making and cultural-political entrepreneurship in postcommunist Poland and Russia, in Ekiert, G. and Hanson, S. E. (eds.) *Capitalism and Democracy in Central and Eastern Europe. Assessing the Legacy of Communist Rule*, pp. 317–51, Cambridge: Cambridge University Press

Kudrle, R. T. 1999. Market globalization and the future policies of the industrial states, in Prakash, A. and Hart, J. A. (eds.) *Globalization and Governance*, London: Routledge

Lee, Y. H. 2000. The failure of the weak state in economic liberalization: liberalization, democratization and the financial crisis in South Korea. *Pacific Journal*, 13:1: 115–31

Legrain, P. 2004. *Open World: The Truth about Globalization*, Chicago: Ivan R Dee

Lull, J. 2000. Cultural de-territorialization, in Beynon, J. and Dunkerley, D. (eds.) *Globalization: the Reader*, pp. 114–16, London: Athlone Press

Madgwick, P. J. 1973. *The Politics of Rural Wales*, London: Hutchison

Marden, P. 1997. Geographies of dissent: globalization, identity and the nation. *Political Geography*, 16:1: 37–64

Marr, D. G. and White, C. P. (eds.) 1988. *Post-war Vietnam*, Ithaca, New York: Cornell University Press

Marsh, A. 1977. *Protest and Political Consciousness*, London: Sage

Maslow, A. H. 1970. *Motivation and Personality*, 2nd edn. London: Harper and Row

McClosky, H. and Brill, A. 1983. *Dimensions of Tolerance: What Americans Believe about Civil Liberties*, New York: Russell Sage

Michels, R. 1962 (orig. 1911, transl. E. Paul and C. Paul). *Political Parties: a Sociological Study of the Oligarchical Tendencies of Modern Democracy*, London: Collier Macmillan

Micklethwait, J. and Woodridge, A. 2000. *A Future Perfect: the Challenge and Hidden Promise of Globalisation*, London: Heinemann

Migdal, J. S. 1988. *Strong Societies and Weak States: State-society Relations and State Capabilities in the Third World*, Princeton: Princeton University Press

Miller, W. L., Brand, J., Jordan, M., Balsom, D., Madgwick P. and van Mechelen, D. 1982. *Democratic or Violent Protest? Attitudes Towards Direct Action in Scotland and Wales*, Centre for the Study of Public Policy (CSPP) paper No.107, Strathclyde University

Miller, W. L., Timpson, A. M. and Lessnoff, M. 1996. *Political Culture in Contemporary Britain: People and Politicians, Principles and Practice*, Oxford: Oxford University Press

Miller, W. L., White, S. and Heywood, P. 1998. *Values and Political Change in Postcommunist Europe*, London: Macmillan

Min, B. O. 2004. Electoral change and voting behaviour of independent voters in South Korea, 1992–2002. Unpubl. PhD thesis, University of Glasgow

Mittelman, J. H. 1998. Globalisation and environmental resistance politics. *Third World Quarterly*, 19:5: 847–72

Monbiot, G. 2000. *Captive State: the Corporate Takeover of Britain*, Basingstoke and Oxford: Pan

Moore, M. 2004. Film: *Fahrenheit 9/11*

Morton, A. D. 2004. New follies on the state of globalization debate. *Review of International Studies*, 30:1: 133–47, January

Muller, E. N. 1979. *Aggressive Political Participation*, Princeton: Princeton University Press

Muller, E. N. 1997. Economic determinants of democracy, in Midlarsky, M. I. (ed.) *Inequality, Democracy and Economic Development*, Cambridge: Cambridge University Press

Norris, P. (ed.) 1999. *Critical Citizens: Global Support for Democratic Government*, Oxford: Oxford University Press

Norris, P. 2000. Global governance and cosmopolitan citizens, in Nye, J. S. and Donahue, J. D. (eds.) *Governance in a Globalizing World*, pp. 155–77. Washington: Brookings Institution

Nye, J. S. 2003. America's soft learning curve, in *The World in 2004*, pp. 64–5. London: Economist Newspapers

Nye, J. S. and Donahue, J. D. 2000a. Introduction, in Nye, J. S. and Donahue, J. D. (eds.) *Governance in a Globalizing World*, pp. 1–41, Washington: Brookings Institution

Nye, J. S. and Donahue, J. D. (eds.) 2000b. *Governance in a Globalizing World*, Washington: Brookings Institution

Ohmae, K. 1990. *The Borderless World*, London: Collins

Ohmae, K. 1995. *The End of the Nation State: The Rise of Regional Economies*, London: HarperCollins

Orchard, P. 2004. The State as Villain, Annual Convention of the Canadian Political Science Association paper, Winnipeg, Manitoba

Parry, G., Moyser, G. and Day, N. 1992. *Political Participation and Democracy in Britain*, Cambridge: Cambridge University Press

Pasha, M. K. 2000. Globalization, Islam and resistance, in Gills, B. K. (ed.) *Globalization and the Politics of Resistance*, pp. 241–54, London: Macmillan

Pew Center 2003. *Pew Global Attitudes Project: Globalization with Few Discontents?* Pew Research Center for the People and the Press, www.yaleglobal.yale.edu, June

Pollock, A. and Price, D. 2000. Re-writing the regulations: how the WTO could accelerate privatisation in health care systems. *Lancet*, 356

Rieu, A. M. and Duprat, G. 1995. *European Democratic Culture*, London: Routledge

Robertson, D. 1985. *The Penguin Dictionary of Politics*, Harmondsworth: Penguin

Rodan, G. 1996. Theorising political opposition in East and Southeast Asia, in Rodan, G. (ed.) *Political Oppositions in Industrialising Asia*, London: Routledge

Rodrik, D. 1996. *Why do More Open Economies have Bigger Governments?* Cambridge MA: National Bureau of Economic Research (NBER)

Rodrik, D. 1997. *Has Globalization Gone Too Far?* Washington: Institute for International Economics

Rodrik, D. 1998. Globalisation, social conflict and economic growth. *The World Economy*, 21:2: 143–58

Rodrik, D. 2002. *Feasible Globalizations*, Cambridge MA: National Bureau of Economic Research (NBER) working paper W9129, August

Rose, R. 2005. Divisions within Ukraine: a post-election opinion survey. *Strathclyde University Studies in Public Policy*, 403

Rotberg, R. I. 2003. *Nation-State Failure: A Recurring Phenomenon?* Paper to the National intelligence Council (NIC) 2020 project, 6 November

Rotberg, R. I. 2004. The failure and collapse of nation-states: breakdown, prevention, and repair, in Rotberg, R. I. (ed.) *Why States Fail: Causes and Consequences*, pp. 1–45, Princeton: Princeton University Press

Rucht, D. 2001. Social movements challenging neo-liberal globalization. *Central European Political Science Review*, 2:5: 94–114

Saldivar, A. 2001. Offences of globalization and modernity. *Central European Political Science Review*, 2:5: 6–15

Scott, J. C. 1985. *Weapons of the Weak: Everyday Forms of Peasant Resistance*, London: Yale University Press

Scott, J. C. 1990. *Domination and the Arts of Resistance*, London: Yale University Press

Sen, A. 1997. Human rights and Asian values: what Lee Kuan Yew and Lee Peng don't understand about Asia. *New Republic*, 217:2–3: 33–40, 14 July

Smith, A. D. 1990. Towards a Global Culture? In Featherstone, M. (ed.) *Global Culture: Nationalism, Globalization and Modernity*, pp. 171–91, London: Sage.

Smith, A. D. 1995. *Nations and Nationalism in a Global Era*, Cambridge: Polity Press

Sniderman, P. M., Fletcher, J. F., Russell, P. H., Tetlock, P. E. and Gaines, B. J. 1991. The fallacy of democratic elitism: elite competition and commitment to civil liberties. *British Journal of Political Science*, 21: 349–70

Sniderman, P. M., Fletcher, J. F., Russell, P. H. and Tetlock, P. E. 1996. *The Clash of Rights: Liberty, Equality and Legitimacy in Pluralist Democracy*, New Haven: Yale University Press

Soros, G. 2002. *George Soros on Globalisation*, Oxford: Public Affairs Limited

Stiglitz, J. E. 2002. *Globalization and its Discontents*, London: Penguin

Strange, S. 1996. *The Retreat of the State: the Diffusion of Power in the World Economy*, Cambridge: Cambridge University Press

Sumner, A. 2003. *From Lewis to Dollar and Kraay and beyond*, Development Studies Association (DSA) conference paper, London: Overseas Development Institute

Sweeney, S. 2005. *Europe, the State and Globalisation*, Harlow: Pearson Longman

Teunissen, J. J. and Akkerman, A. (eds.) 2004. *Diversity in Development: Reconsidering the Washington Consensus*, The Hague: Forum on Debt and Development (Fondad), www.fondad.org

Thurow, L. C. 2000. Globalization: the product of a knowledge-based economy. *Annals of the American Academy of Political and Social Science*, 570:1: 19–31

United Nations Conference on Trade and Development (UNCTAD) 2004. *World Investment Report 2004: The Shift Toward Services*, New York and Geneva: United Nations

United Nations Development Programme (UNDP) 1999. Globalisation with a human face. *Human Development Report 1999*

United Nations Development Programme (UNDP) 2002. The state and progress of human development. *Human Development Report 2002*

Walgrave, S. and Verhulst, J. 2003. Worldwide Anti-war-in-Iraq Protest. A Preliminary Test of the Transnational Movements Thesis, European Consortium for Political Research (ECPR) conference paper, Marburg, September

Wallerstein, I. 1990. Culture as the ideological battleground of the modern world system, in Featherstone, M. (ed.) *Global Culture: Nationalism, Globalization and Modernity*, pp. 31–56, London: Sage

Way, L. A. 2002. The dilemmas of reform in weak states: the case of post-Soviet fiscal decentralization (in Ukraine). *Politics and Society*, 30:4: 579–98

Weiss, L. 1998. *The Myth of the Powerless State*, Cambridge: Polity

Weiss, L. 2003. Introduction: bringing domestic institutions back in, in Weiss, L. (ed.) *States in the Global Economy: Bringing Domestic Institutions Back In*, Cambridge: Cambridge University Press

Wolf, M. 2001. Will the nation-state survive globalization? *Foreign Affairs*, 80:1: 178–90

Wolf, M. 2004. *Why Globalization Works*, Yale: Yale University Press

World Bank 1993. *The East Asian Miracle: Economic Growth and Public Policy*, Washington DC: World Bank

World Bank 2003a. *World Development Report 2003*, Washington DC: International Bank for Reconstruction and Development (IBRD)

World Bank 2003b. *World Development Indicators 2003*, Washington DC: International Bank for Reconstruction and Development (IBRD)

World Bank 2004. *Development Indicators*, http://devdata.worldbank.org/data-query/

World Economic Forum/Environics International 2002. *World Economic Forum Poll: Global Public Opinion on Globalization*, www.environicsinternational.com

World Trade Organisation (WTO) Secretariat 2001. *Trade Policy Review: Czech Republic*, 19 September, www.wto.org, accessed 26 November 2004

Zakaria, F. 1994. Culture is destiny: a conversation with Lee Kuan Yew. *Foreign Affairs*, 73:2: 109(18) March–April

Media sources and websites

Media sources

BBC, 24 November 2004. 'Ukraine on brink of civil war', accessible at www.news.bbc.co.uk

Guardian, 24 August 2000. Sally James Gregory 'A world of protest against the global economy' p. 3

Guardian, 19 September 2000. Paul Whiteley 'Rich picketings' p. 11

Guardian, 6 April 2001. Naomi Klein 'World poor in sale of the 21st century' p. 20

Guardian, 20 April 2001. Charlotte Denny 'Free trade free-for-all' p. 19

Guardian, 2 May 2001. David Walker 'Global's good side' p. 15

Guardian, 2 May 2001. Jonathan Freedland 'In place of violence' p. 15

Guardian, 18 June 2001. Ian Black and Michael White 'Travel ban to block anarchist leaders' p. 1

Guardian, 29 June 2001. Philip Willan 'Italy invites third world leaders to G8 to deter mobs' p. 12

Guardian, 12 July 2001. Philippe Legrain 'The left must learn to love the World Trade Organisation' p. 17

Guardian, 20 July 2001. Larry Elliott 'Genoa summit: let battle begin, in and outside the talks' p. 18

Guardian, 21 July 2001. Ewen MacAskill and Larry Elliot 'Protester killed in summit chaos' p. 1

Guardian, 23 July 2001. Larry Elliott 'Protests may breed leaner, meaner summits' p. 5

Guardian, 23 July 2001. Peter Preston 'We gave them the oxygen' p. 17

Guardian, 23 July 2001. John Vidal, Rory Carroll and Ewen MacAskill 'The weekend war' G2 p. 2

Guardian, 24 July 2001. David Walker 'The aid game' p. 17

Guardian, 24 July 2001. George Monbiot 'Raising the temperature' p. 17

Guardian, 12 November 2001. Larry Elliot 'Time for the West to put up or shut up' p. 22

Guardian, 8 May 2002. Mark Milner and Charlotte Denny 'It's penalty time for Argentina' p. 22

Guardian, 24 June 2002. Ha-Joon Chang 'History debunks the free trade myth' p. 23

Guardian, 24 June 2002. Larry Elliott and Charlotte Denny 'Resistance is futile as G8 meets in remote Canadian hideaway' p. 15

Guardian, 9 October 2002. Philippe Legrain 'Business doesn't rule' p. 17

Guardian, 19 May 2003. Stephen Byers 'I was wrong. Free market trade policies hurt the poor' p. 18

Guardian, 31 May 2003. Sophie Arie 'Protesters flood in for alternative summit' p. 5

Guardian, 24 June 2003. George Monbiot 'I was wrong about trade' p. 21

Guardian, 27 June 2003. David Teather 'Nike loses case over freedom of speech' p. 19

Guardian, 12 September 2003. John Vidal and David Munk 'Farmer who got a hearing by paying the ultimate price' p. 19

Guardian, 23 January 2004. Larry Elliott 'Mumbai activists engaging with the real problems of globalisation' p. 27

Guardian, 16 February 2004. Gordon Brown and Jim Wolfensohn 'A new deal for the world's poor' p. 15

Guardian, 12 March 2004. Joseph Stiglitz 'A world consensus is emerging on the destructive effects of globalisation' p. 25

Guardian, 13 May 2004. David Teather 'Gap admits to child labour violations in outsource factories' p. 18

Guardian, 15 May 2004. Martin Jacques 'The claims of western values are mocked by Iraq and the rise of Asia' p. 23

Guardian, 29 July 2004. Martin Jacques 'Face it: no one cares' p. 25

Guardian, 7 November 2005. Larry Elliott 'There are too many losers in globalisation' p. 28

Herald, 2 May 2001. James McKillop and Keith Sinclair 'Police defeat protestors in battle of Mayhem day' p. 1

Independent, 13 September 2000. Justin Huggler 'Prague's police aim to tolerate protests' p. 14

Independent, 12 August 2004. Askold Krushelnycky 'Official spying on election candidate exposed' p. 22

Kyiv Post, 8 September 2005. 'Yushchenko dismisses his government amid corruption allegations'

Observer, 24 September 2000. Mary Riddell 'Do we really want collective bargaining by riot or should we be fighting instead to keep democracy?' p. 28

Scotsman, 15 April 2000. Tim Cornwell 'Battle in Seattle's veterans target capital' p. 11

Scotsman, 16 June 2001. Jon Hibbs 'Anarchists riots bring terror to EU summit (at Gothenburg)' p. 1

Scotsman, 2 May 2002. Karen McVeigh '4000 police stifle May Day demo' p. 3

Scotsman, 26 June 2002. Jason Beattie 'World summits; violent demonstrations' p. 3

Websites

Asian Development Bank: www.adb.org/VRM

Asian EFL Journal: www.asian-efl-journal.com

Bank of Korea Economic Statistics System: www.ecos.bok.or.kr

BBC: www.news.bbc.co.uk

BBC Wales: www.news.bbc.co.uk/1/hi/wales/3544851.stm

Centre for Economic and Policy Research: www.cepr.net

CIA *World Factbook 2004*: www.cia.gov/cia/publications/factbook/index.html

Election results for Ukraine or any other country can be found on: www.electionguide.org

Forum on Debt and Development (Fondad): www.fondad.org

Guardian: all *Guardian* articles can be accessed without restriction at *Guardian Unlimited*, www.guardian.co.uk

Kyiv Post: www.kyivpost.com

United Nations: www.un.org, See in particular www.un.org/Depts/dpko/dpko/contributors/index.htm.

United Nations Development Programme (UNDP), *Human Development Report (HDR)*: www.hdr.undp.org; Human Development Index (HDI) for any year since 1990: hdr.undp.org/reports/

World Bank: www.worldbank.org

World Development Movement: www.wdm.org.uk

World Trade Organisation: www.wto.org

Index